The Burden of Religion In Haiti

A CALL FOR REVOLUTION

Wilson Maceno

Choublak Publishing

The Burden of Religion in Haiti: A call for Revolution
Copyright© 2025 by Wilson Maceno
All rights reserved

Published by Choublak Publishing
Minneapolis, Minnesota 55428
In association with Wilson Maceno
www.wilsonmaceno.com

Cover design: Wilson Maceno,
Cover images: Nathan Ziemanski / New York Public Library

Printed in the United States of America

Dedication

This book is dedicated to a good cup of organic dark roast coffee. God took a sip on the sixth day of creation, and He saw that it was very good.

To my brothers and sisters:

Yes, I did.

To my parents, Pastor and mommy Pré:

People are more important to you than their religious beliefs.

Contents

Acknowledgements

This book has been a long time coming. I have many people to thank for supporting me throughout this process. I'm deeply grateful to my wife and my kids for their love and unwavering support. Their feedback and encouragement were very valuable. I love you more than I can express.

A special thank you to my gorgeous daughter, Kariyah, who read the manuscript and shared her insights. Thank you to my sister Madeleine and her husband Nick Avignon. I value our special bond. To the memory of my father, Pastor Pré, who taught me the value of hard work and resilience.

A big thank you to my friends and family for their support, including Rose-Michelle, Nardine, Deb, Ginette, Lorna, and Rose Marie. I'm honored to be your friend.

This book would have been very different if not for the valuable input of my editor Amma Twum-Baah. I'm also grateful to my former seminary professor Dr. Clifton Clarke for stimulating my interest to embark on this journey.

I wish to express my gratitude to my Woodland Hills Church community and the scores of individuals—knowingly or unknowingly— who have influenced and supported me throughout this journey.

I'm indebted to those of you in Haiti who had patiently dialogued with me during my research, especially the staff and people at Cofhed in Camp-Perrin, including Kessaire, Menès, Franthiel, Flostie, and Marie Josée.

Abbreviations

AIC	African Indigenous Churches
ATR	African Traditional Religion
CEEH	Concile des Eglises Evangéliques d'Haïti
CIA	Central Intelligence Agency
CRS	Catholic Relief Services
IBL	Institut Biblique Lumière
MEBSH	Mission Evangélique Baptiste du Sud d'Haïti
NASB	New American Standard Bible
NGO	Non-governmental organization
NLT	New Living Translation
NT	New Testament
OT	Old Testament
PK	Pastor's Kid
STM	Short-Term Mission
WIM	West Indies Mission
WT	World Team

Introduction

It is well-known that Haitians are deeply religious. Throughout Haitian history, religion has served many purposes and still plays a significant role in the social, cultural, and spiritual life of its people, among others, enslavement, fearmongering, healing, politics, power consolidation, and force of change.

Religion has also, historically, provided a source of comfort, community, and guidance in times of difficulty, and has been intertwined with various aspects of Haitian identity and culture.

While Roman Catholicism is the default religion in Haiti, Vodou is widely practiced by the majority of Haitians. It has been said, with reason, that "Haiti is 60% Catholics, 40% Protestants, and 100% Vodouisants."[1]

Once called the "Pearl of the Caribbean," Haiti is more currently known for its long economic struggle. For years, Haiti has been labeled as the "poorest country in the Western hemisphere," a reductionist characterization used by Western powers and non-profit organizations.

Scholars and economists have argued for decades on the causes of the nation's lingering poverty, while religious people have theorized and shared their opinions. The proposed solution among

---

[1] There is a variation of this common saying by scholars such as Desmangles (2010) and Karen McCarthy Brown (1991). The numbers have changed over the years as people moved from one religion to another.

Haitian evangelicals and Spiritual Mappers[2] is for the country to renounce Vodou and come to Christ. Consequently, there is a strong belief among Haitian Christians[3] that for Haiti to be saved, prosperous, and developed, Vodou must be eradicated.[4] This formula has been tried without success since colonial times. The Catholic Priest Micial Nérestant, in his book *Religion et Politique en Haiti*, agrees, *"La disparition complète du Vaudou dans la société haïtienne est une pure illusion."*[5] (The total disappearance of Vodou in Haitian society is a pure illusion.)

Eighty-five percent of Haitians say religion is important in their daily lives, this is according to a 2009 Gallup survey of 114 countries. The same survey found that the poorer a country is, the higher its religiosity.[6] But while religion is a key factor in the lives of Haitians, there has been no proven link between religion in Haiti (especially Vodou) and its poverty. In fact, the prosperity of a nation does not depend on it being a Christian nation.

---

[2] Spiritual Mappers are a group of right-wing Christians who map out territories so that they can wage war against demons.

[3] Since most Haitians identify themselves as either Catholics or Protestants, Haiti is by default a Christian nation. However, the Protestants do not consider the Catholics Christians. For them, they are one and the same with the Vodouists, and they are all going to hell. But for the lack of a better term and to avoid confusion, I will use Protestant for the evangelicals and "Christians" to denote both Haitian Catholics and Protestants where it's appropriated. Note that in Haiti, a Christian could simply mean a human being, as in *"kretyen vivan"*.

[4] This assumption is based on the false belief that God is a Christian, and Vodou is satanic.

[5] Micial, Nerestant J., *Religions et Politique en Haïti* (Paris: Éditions Karthala, 1994), 147

[6] For more, see Gallup survey on *"Religiosity Highest in World's Poorest Nations,"* accessed 4/5/2020, https://news.gallup.com/poll/142727/religiosity-highest-world-poorest-nations.aspx

Haitian evangelicals and missionaries fail to understand that Vodou is what makes a Haitian a Haitian. Therefore, to leave Vodou is to stop being Haitian. Furthermore, Haitian evangelicals and missionaries need to stop the deculturalization of the Haitians. Haitians are first of all Vodouisants, and most of them happen to be Christians. While Western missionaries may have brought Christianity to Haiti with the slave trade, they did not bring God. He was already active in every area of the life of every Haitian.

The constant demonization of Vodou has caused many Haitian Christians to live a double life – Christian during the day and Haitian at night. This *faire-semblant* phenomenon has resulted in a dual allegiance where Haitians convert to Christianity for various reasons while still practicing the core beliefs of Vodou. This is what is known as "riding two horses" in Tanzania. Leslie Desmangles refers to it as a "symbiosis." The Jesuit priest, Jaime Bulatao, calls it a "split-level Christianity," or better yet what Tony La Viña describes as "natural religiosity" in the Philippines.

Having dual allegiance is nothing new. In the Old Testament, the people of Israel had this pattern throughout their history (Exod 32:1-9, I Sam 28:24, I Kings 14:24, II Kings 17:33-41). In the New Testament, many Jewish believers embraced both the gospel and their Jewish customs (Acts 15, Gal 2). In Europe, notably in France, many Protestant leaders have also been lodge members for centuries. Some African Christians blend Christianity with different forms of their African Traditional Religions to form the African Indigenous Churches. In the United States, allegiance can be to the American dream, political party, country, money, fame, and power.

Since the beauty of the cross and the resurrection of Christ have not been contextualized by the Haitians, religion then becomes a trap. Haitian evangelicals are afraid to dance to the beautiful rhythm of *konpa*,[7] wear certain pieces of clothing and jewelry, or eat certain foods, for fear of being associated with Vodou and being labeled *lemond* (of this world). But they still do all of that in secret in various settings.

In their book, *Encountering Theology of Mission: Biblical Foundations, Historical Developments, and Contemporary Issues*, Craig Ott, Stephen Strauss, and Timothy Tennent argue, "When missionaries and church leaders focus on changing the outward behavior of converts, it is likely the gospel will never change their core beliefs, values, and emotions."[8] Consequently, the Vodouists are freer to fully express themselves than the Haitian evangelicals who are supposed to be free in Christ.

Maybe you are a pragmatist, and you want the next step now. The short answer is to drop your religion and follow Christ. For the rest of us, I want to flush out the burden of religion in the Haitian experience and propose a way out of its shackles. I realize that religious beliefs are hard to change. It took me years to rethink, change, and finally be free from religion. Therefore, I urge you to keep an open mind while reading this book.

To my Haitian brothers and sisters of the diaspora who insist, "*Se an Ayiti ki gen levanjil*," meaning literally "the real gospel is in Haiti," don't be so quick on your conclusion. As Bonhoeffer argues, "To be a Christian does not mean to be religious in a particular way." Participating in religious activities is not the same as following

---

[7] Konpa is the rhythm associated with the widely popular Haitian music.
[8] Craig Ott, Stephen J. Strauss and Timothy C. Tennent, Encountering Theology of Mission: Biblical Foundations, Historical Developments, and Contemporary Issues (Grand Rapids: Baker Academic, 2010), 276

Christ, and being an imitator of Christ is not a mere change of religion. To say yes to Jesus is to let him transform you from the inside out. One can be a Christian without being a Christ-follower. This is the essence of religion: man searching for God, while God is being replaced with rules, rituals, and good works.

In other words, religion is mainly about what you do, but I'm inviting you to what Jesus has done. As Edwards Tyler in his book, *Zombie Churches* says, "Good works— prayer, reading the Bible, going to church, tithing, even serving—can be done without any love for God in our hearts."[9] To follow Christ is to become like him. You do that by ceasing to be self-centered and becoming Christ-centered.

For this reason, it is wrong for you to judge others for not being as religious as you are. Stop. Judgment reduces your ability to love. As a matter of fact, the more you judge others, the less likely you are to love them. The gospel cannot be reduced to your judgment of "who is in, and who is out". As my pastor always says, "Our one job is to ascribe unsurpassable worth to all people." As this Haitian proverb says, *"Avan w ri moun bwate, gade jan w mache."* [Before you laugh at those who limp, check how you walk.]

Religion, including Christianity, is not God's revelation. Jesus is. Participating in religious activities and having a community of shared values and moral codes is all good. But I believe there must be more. If you want to stick to religion, this is the only one you should have: "Pure and genuine religion in the sight of God the Father means caring for orphans and widows in their distress and

---

[9] Edwards Tyler, *Zombie Church* (p. 47). Kregel Publications. Kindle Edition.

refusing to let the world corrupt you (James 1:27 NLT)." But I'm inviting you to do more.

I admit the content of this book will challenge the views of many readers, and some of you might find it offensive to your religious practices. It's not my intention to attack your spirituality, but if you are agitated by some of the statements I made, and if you find the need to be defensive, it may be because you're getting life from your religion and the rightness of your beliefs rather than from Christ. Keep calm. You and I may have different opinions, but hear me out. My intent is to stir up some conversation by sharing with you some uncomfortable truths.

In the early 90s, while I was visiting a Haitian couple in Florida, the husband and I went out to run some errands. We stopped at Publix to get some groceries, including toilet paper for their master bathroom. While we were unloading the groceries, his wife saw the toilet paper and said to him, "What is this? Why did you buy white toilet paper? Don't you know they have to match the bathroom's color?" The bathroom's color was pink. She had him return them because she wanted pink toilet paper. Yeah! Back in the day, they used to make toilet paper in different colors. Unfortunately, some people use religion in much the same way. They want it to match their worldview and their status. But like toilet paper, your religion has only one role: to search for a god that you can mold to your image. Jesus's call to us is to follow Him, but it's hard to do when you cling to religion. To follow Jesus, your religion is as irrelevant as a pink toilet paper.

If I come across as being against the institutional church and any form of organized religion, please know that this is not the case. I have four brothers who are all active pastors of the church. I applaud them for their contribution to advancing the kingdom of God. I was raised in the conservative Baptist tradition of MEBSH (Mission Evangélique Baptiste du Sud d'Haiti) where my dad served as a pastor for over sixty years. Growing up, I witnessed how various religious denominations treated people of other faiths.[10] I also witnessed many Sunday morning sermons of pastors who criticized and condemned Catholics to hell, while these same pastors happily received the big trucks of CRS (Catholic Relief Services) bringing food for their schools, on Monday morning.

I witnessed many pastors who entrusted their kids' education to Catholic priests and nuns instead of putting them in their low-standard and poor-quality schools. So my aim here is not to criticize a particular denomination or religious group, but to expose the burden of religion on the Haitian people.

Some of you might even think that I am a Vodou apologist. I'm not. However, while I'm not a Vodouist, as a Haitian, I'm a Vodouisant.[11] Contrary to Christianity, Vodou is not something the Haitian joins or converts to, it's our way of life.

Therefore, I'm advocating for the valorization of Vodou by validating its social norms, values, art and music, folklore, and healing power. By taking back from the West the Vodou narrative, the Haitian, then, can be freely Haitian (Vodouisant) and a follower of Christ. In other words, can the Haitian keep his cultural heritage

---

[10] It used to be the case, as recently as the early 90s, Haitian church leaders would not let their congregants marry someone from a different denomination. A Baptist would not be allowed to marry a Pentecostal.

[11] There is a subtle difference between a Vodouisant and a Vodouist. While a Vodouist is an adherent to the practices of Vodou, a Vodouisant is what every Haitian is. It's the bulk of the Haitian culture.

while loving God, serving the poor, loving his enemy sacrificially, feeding the hungry, loving the outcasts, caring for the widows, welcoming the strangers, and healing the sick? Religion will tell you no, but isn't it the essence of the gospel?

So, does your religion keep you from the life that God desires for you? Are religious rituals taking a toll on your resources? Are you addicted to religious activities? Are you living in fear of making the *Iwa* (spirit/spirits) angry? Do you feel coerced to do *manje Iwa*, tithe, and make offerings? Are you tired of religious traditions, rituals, and taboos? Does your religious leader control your life? Do you want to substitute all that for a cross-centered experience in Christ? Keep on reading.

Have you ever scrolled straight down to the comments section of an article or a piece of interesting news event online without reading it? I have. Some people put it bluntly: "I'm only here for the comments." Some people use religion the same way. They are in as spectators and for the benefits. For some, it is heaven with its 'jeweled walls', 'pearly gates', 'crystal palace', 'crowns', and 'golden chair'; for others, it is protection, security, blessings, fame, and money. In contrast, the follower of Christ is not primarily concerned with the benefits, but with how to bear witness to Jesus Christ by loving sacrificially. Throughout this book, I'll be appealing to you to reevaluate your belief system and let it be challenged. In 1791 our ancestors officially revolted against slavery, consequently, the premise of this book is a call for a religious deprogramming of the mind and a revolution against religious oppression. Be free from religion since you have been set free in Christ.

This book is concerned with the three major religious traditions in Haiti. However, it will focus specifically on Protestantism. This is where I will take a more critical approach. This book is divided into four parts.

Part I is a short history of Haiti and a brief understanding of Haitian culture.

Part II focuses on a brief survey of Vodou, Catholicism, and Protestantism in Haiti.

Part III takes a look at the role of missions and missionaries and the burden of religion in the Haitian experience.

And lastly, part IV concludes with a way out of religion and some closing thoughts.

CHAPTER 1

Haiti: A Short History from Columbus to Duvalier

Frères, nous avons tous brisé le joug infâme
Qui, trop longtemps, courba nos fronts;
Jaunes et noirs, brûlant d'une héroïque flamme,
Nous avons vengé nos affronts;
Et le Dieu juste et fort couronnant notre audace,
Noir ou jaune, à l'égal du blanc,
A pu se dire enfin: « J'ai créé pour ma race
Une patrie avec mon sang. »

Pierre Faubert

Haiti was always like a dream; everything seemed so unreal. Was it possible that such a beautiful country, possessing so many natural advantages, a country at one time settled and built up by the industrious French, could have become the abode of such horrors, such cruelty, and such degradation?

Jordan William

En dépit de tout, Haïti est un adorable petit pays, même pour nous Haïtiens quand nous sommes obligés de le fuir.

Frédéric Marcelin

Pre-Colonial Haiti

When Christopher Columbus and his companions stumbled upon what is now Haiti in 1492, the Tainos, Arawaks, and Ciboneys were living peacefully in their land, enjoying life and creation in their tropical paradise.

When one of Columbus' vessels, the famous *Santa María*, ran aground in shallow waters near the coast of Cap-Haitien, the Tainos came to rescue the men and their cargo. Out of the goodness of their heart, they welcomed the strangers into their modest homes, fed them, and showered them with gifts. Unlike their "Christian" visitors, they displayed a Christ-like character to the strangers. Columbus, himself, testifies: *"Ce sont des gens tout amour, sans convoitise. Ils aiment leur prochain comme eux-mêmes. Ils ont un parler très doux, et toujours ils sourient...Ils sont dépourvus d'envie pour ce qui appartient à autrui."*[12] (They are all loving people, without lust. They love their neighbors as themselves. They are very soft-spoken, and they always smile ... They are not envious of what belongs to others.) After glimpsing at the beauty of Hispaniola, he thought the shipwreck of Santa Maria was divinely ordained. He later wrote, "I recognize that our Lord has caused me to run aground at this place."[13]

Instead of enjoying the hospitality shown toward them, Columbus and his companions let greed, avarice, and ambition fill their hearts. Armed with a cross in one hand and a sword in the other, they saw the naivety of the Indians as an opportunity for riches

---

[12] Marianne Mahn-Lot, *Christophe Colomb* (Paris: Editions du Seuil, 1960), 83

[13] Zvi Dor-Ner, Columbus and the Age of Discovery (New York: William Morrow and Company, Inc., 1991), 185.

and glory. As Columbus gestured that he came in the name of the Spanish Crown and the Church, the locals thought the visitors came from heaven. However, according to Bartolomé De Las Casas, Columbus knew it was not about sharing the gospel. He had very different intentions:

> The Spaniards first set Sail to America, not for the Honour of God, or as Persons moved and merited thereunto by servent Zeal to the True Faith, nor to promote the Salvation of their Neighbours, nor to serve the King, as they falsely boast and pretend to do, but in truth, only stimulated and goaded on by insatiable Avarice and Ambition, that they might forever Domineer, Command, and Tyrannize over the West- Indians, whose Kingdoms they hoped to divide and distribute among themselves.[14]

Consequently, avarice and ambition led them to abuse, as the settlers conquered the land, overworked the inhabitants, and forced them to work in gold mines, eventually exterminating them. Most historians estimate there were more than a million Tainos and Arawaks in Haiti in 1492. By 1515, there were only about sixty thousand of them left, and by 1535 they had been wiped out completely. On this, De Las Casas later notes:

> The Indians did not, nor was it in their power to give any greater occasion for the Commission of them, than Pious Religioso's Living in a well-regulated Monastic Life did afford for any

---

[14] Casas, Bartolomé de las. A Brief Account of the Destruction of the Indies Or, a faithful NARRATIVE OF THE Horrid and Unexampled Massacres, Butcheries, and all manner of Cruelties, ... the time of its first Discovery by them. (Kindle Locations 1273-1276). Kindle Edition.

Sacrilegeous Villains to deprive them of their Goods and Life at the same time, or why they who by flight avoided death should be detain'd in perpetual, not to be ransom'd Captivity and Slavery... the Indians were not so much guilty of one single mortal sin of Commission against the Spaniards, that might deserve from any Man revenge or require satisfaction.[15]

Colonial Haiti

With the extinction of the Indigenous people and the introduction of sugar cane on the island, the colonialists needed a robust workforce. De Las Casas, a Catholic priest, suggested to Nicolas Ovando, the new governor of the island, to get slaves from Africa.[16] The fusion of the sword and the cross created the most despicable slave trade in history. According to Elizabeth Abbot, "In one hundred years, Haitian slavery killed nearly one million Africans often after the briefest sojourn there. Thousands more escaped intolerable life by suicide, spiting their owners and guaranteeing a joyous return to Africa, where, they believed, their spirits would return."[17]

The first slaves who arrived as early as 1506 were forced to be baptized into the Catholic faith. Catholic missionaries were brought in, not only to provide baptism but also to teach the slaves submission to colonial rules. The Jesuits and the Franciscans, as

---

[15] Ibid.

[16] Bartolome de las Casas was a controversial figure. As a priest and a colonist, he may have been hailed as the "Protector of the Indians", but ironically he was also the "Destructor of the Black Africans". Although he later realized he made a mistake and repented, the damage was already done.

[17] Elizabeth Abbott, *Haiti: The Duvaliers and their Legacy* (New York: Touchstone, 1988),11

religious orders within the Catholic Church, ended up being huge slaveholders.

The Spanish controlled Haiti and its riches for nearly 200 years, and then they moved on to greener pastures such as Peru and Mexico.

During that time, French buccaneers and *flibustiers,* turned pirates, had settled on a smaller island named Tortuga, raiding ships of their cargo. With the Treaty of Ryswick in 1697, Spain ceded Haiti to France, and they retained the eastern portion of Hispaniola now known as the Dominican Republic. Within a few years, Haiti had become France's wealthiest colony. However, by the mid-1700s, small pockets of resistance and conflict had begun to emerge as the slaves revolted against the brutality and cruelty of their French masters. As the resistance grew, new leaders from the maroons' community emerged. One of them was a well-known runaway slave named François Makandal. He was known to have extensive knowledge of leaf medicine and poisonous plants and, with a group of sympathizers, he coordinated a plan to poison plantation owners. Thousands were killed on both sides, but in 1758, Makandal was eventually captured and burned at the stake.

Makandal's death was a setback, but it did not stop the insurgence because the seeds of freedom had already been sewn into the hearts of the slaves. According to most historians, things came to a head when Boukman and other runaway slaves organized a religious ceremony at Bois Caïman, near Morne-Rouge, during a tropical storm in August 1791. At the ceremony, Boukman, Cécile Fatiman, Jean-François, Halaou, Romaine Rivière, and others pledged to fight for freedom and avenge the wrongs against them. Within a few weeks after the ceremony, the slaves rose and started burning plantations. That was the beginning of the war for freedom. As it was with Makandal, Boukman was trapped and killed. His head was cut off and stuck on a pike.

By 1801, Toussaint Louverture, a prominent leader of the revolution, drafted a new constitution, freed the slaves, and declared himself president for life. Still fresh from a power grab, Napoléon Bonaparte, leader of the French Republic, could not bear losing the colony, so he sent his brother-in-law, Charles Leclerc, with 25,000 troops and about 70 warships to crush the revolution and reinsert slavery. As new waves of rebellion emerged, Leclerc was losing troops at a high rate due to yellow fever and the tropical heat, which eventually killed Leclerc in 1802.

Toussaint was tricked into a meeting with the French where he was captured and sent to France, but the revolution carried on. After hard-fought battles carried out by the slaves, notably, Dessalines, Christophe, Biassou, Capois, Magny, Gérin, Vernet, Clervaux, Jean-Louis François, Cangé, Férou, Yayou, Bazelais, Charlotin Marcadieu, Toussaint-Brave, Jeannot, Goman, Geffrard, Jean-Baptiste Sans Souci, Petion, and others, the bloody twelve-year war was over.

On January 1, 1804, Dessalines declared Haiti an independent country.

Post-Colonial Haiti

Although Haiti was free, the country had numerous difficulties to tackle from the start. Dessalines' call to *"koupe tèt, boule kay "* after the independence led the newly freed slaves to burn down plantations and kill the remaining French whom Dessalines promised to protect. As former slaves, not only the quasi totality of the population could not read nor write, but also, as military men, the leaders of the revolution did not have any past governing experience other than the colonial system. Governing a free country was something new. Marred by power struggles and factionalism, the founding fathers had a hard time setting forth a democratic structure of government.

Dessalines became the first Haitian president and was assassinated after being in power for just two years.

In 1806, The United States, in collaboration with other world powers, put a trade embargo and cut all diplomatic connections with Haiti. Consequently, the country was isolated by the international community and the Vatican for over sixty years. Although France had recognized Haiti as a sovereign country after Haiti agreed to pay to secure its independence, The United States had not done the same until Abraham Lincoln recognized Haiti's independence in 1862.

Still, Haiti's problems were just getting started. Powerful nations such as the United States, France, Spain, Germany, and England had crippled the young nation's economy by their constant meddling in the country's affairs. Some of these countries didn't have an official diplomatic presence in Haiti, so they used missionaries and businessmen as their main points of contact with the Haitian government. Consequently, these missionaries enjoyed dual roles, as ambassadors of the kingdom of God and as de facto diplomats of their respective countries, a role they continued to play after the U.S. invasion in 1915. For example, L. Ton Evans and Parkinson Turnbull were missionaries who, at one point, appealed to the American government to invade Haiti. For almost two centuries, even after normal diplomatic relations were restored, the missionary movement continued as an unofficial ambassador of their respective countries.

U.S. Occupation

Before the U.S. intervention, some American bankers, such as Roger Leslie Farnham and John H. Allen, who were in Haiti with the National City Bank of New York were already trying to destabilize the government of Sudre Dartiguenave.[18] By 1908, German merchants already controlled 80% of Haiti's trade. Hence, in 1915, under the guise of national security and to keep away the Germans from their back door, but mainly for economic interests, the U.S. Marines invaded Haiti. They occupied the country until 1934.

The Marines were mostly Protestants from the Bible Belt (southern region) of the United States. With a Bible in one hand and a rifle in the other, the Marines did not waste any time to show their disdain for Catholicism and Vodou. Moreover, they were actively engaged in racial capitalism by demonizing Haitian culture, rekindling class and color conflict, and committing a long list of human rights abuses. After they shredded Haiti's constitution, they proceeded to ban Vodou practices by destroying Vodou temples, smashing sacred objects, and taking away their sacred drums.

Then, soon afterward, they established a brutal system of oppression, including forced labor, known as corvée.

---

[18] For more, see Peter James Hudson's article "*The National City Bank of New York and Haiti, 1909–1922*" in https://read.dukeupress.edu/radical-history-review/article-abstract/2013/115/91/22215/The-National-City-Bank-of-New-York-and-Haiti-1909?redirectedFrom=fulltext

In one of the biggest bank robberies organized by the U.S. government, the Marines transferred the Haitian gold reserve (equivalent to $25 million in 2024) to New York and replaced the National Bank of Haiti with the City Bank of New York. During the first few years of the occupation, more than fifteen thousand Haitians were murdered as the Marines hunted down the opposition (Cacos) and the peasants through hills and valleys. Ultimately, they nailed the most famous leader of the opposition, Charlemagne Peralte, to a door and paraded his body in the streets.

With the Marines in firm control, Protestant missionaries from the U.S. came in droves. Once again, the fusion of the cross and the sword was on full display. As is often the case, U.S. military conquests go hand in hand with "Christian missions". While the former is looking for gold, the latter is conquering "lost souls". It didn't take long for small pockets of open conflicts to erupt between various sectors of foreign missions: from Catholic Bretons who claimed to have absolute control of religion in Haiti with the Concordat to American Catholic priests, such as John Burke, who wanted to use the Marines to implement the American way of doing things.

If the missionaries stationed in Haiti were supposedly tasked with uplifting the Haitians spiritually, then they failed miserably. Not only were they engaged in political activism but they also acted as government agents up to the end of the Duvalier regime.[19] In his book *A Violent Evangelism: The Political and Religious Conquest*

---

[19] During the U.S. occupation and up to the end of the Jean Bertrand Aristide presidency, Haitians were highly suspicious of some US nationals having a dual role in Haiti as missionaries and as operatives for the American government, mainly the CIA.

of the Americas, Luis Rivera put it aptly, "He who carried the cross becomes the legitimizing agent of the one who uses the sword."[20] There are several examples of these very instances of missionaries with crosses and bibles invading foreign spaces. For example, in the early days of the fifteenth century, the Portuguese brought priests with them to Africa. Their intent was not to convert the Africans to become followers of Christ but to make them slaves so that, socially, they could be more controllable. And when the U.S. invaded Nicaragua in 1912, and the Dominican Republic in 1916, there was a huge surge of missionary activities in those countries.

While Catholicism was still the state religion, Protestantism was seen as the religion of the occupying force. At one point, Bishop François-Marie Kersuzan was so alarmed by the injunction of the Protestants that he complained: "Does the U.S. want to impose Protestantism, by force, à la Mohammed?"

For more than 25 years, the United States had controlled Haiti's politics and finances by sponsoring puppet presidencies and then taking hold of customs, tax collection, and governmental institutions. Knowing that the Marines would intervene if the Haitian government faltered and turned against their interests, foreign banks such as the National City Bank of New York took over the Haitian financial system. The bank arranged for high-interest loans so that billions of dollars could be siphoned out of the country. According to James Weldon Johnson, who was sent to Haiti by the NAACP to check on Haiti during the occupation, the real and only

---

[20] Luis N. Rivera, A Violent Evangelism: The Political and Religious Conquest of the Americas (Louisville: Westminster/John Knox Press, 1999)209

reason the US invaded Haiti was to create financial havoc on the island. In his report, Johnson notes,

> To understand why the United States landed and has for five years maintained military forces in that country, why some three thousand Haitian men, women, and children have been shot down by American rifles and machine guns, it is necessary, among other things, to know that the National City Bank of New York is very much interested in Haiti. It is necessary to know that the National City Bank controls the National Bank of Haiti and is the depository for all of the Haitian national funds that are being collected by American officials, and that Mr. R. L. Farnham, vice-president of the National City Bank, is virtually the representative of the State Department in matters relating to the island republic.[21]

Farnham later testifies,

The Occupation was always drifting in the absence of any policy in Washington. As far as I know, nothing was ever done for the economic rehabilitation of the country, the establishment of schools generally, the development of agriculture, or the development of the capacity of the Haitian people for self-government. The Occupation was a failure and, when I say a failure, I mean the failure of the United States Government. Washington, not Port au Prince, was to blame.[22]

By the time the Marines left Haiti in 1934, the treasury was empty, and Haiti was still indebted to France and now the United States. What is worse, democracy was nowhere to be found. Johnson later argues that "The Occupation has not only failed to achieve

---

[21] James Weldon Johnson, "Self-Determining Haiti." for more see The Nation https://www.thenation.com/article/archive/self-determining-haiti/

[22] Helena Hill Weed, "Hearing the Truth About Haiti" The Nation (Nov. 1921), accessed 5/12/2021 in https://www.windowsonhaiti.com/windowsonhaiti/index-news.html

anything worthwhile but has made it impossible to do so because of the distrust and bitterness that it has engendered in the Haitian people."[23] As film scholar Jennifer Fay rightly contends, the US occupation was "an attempt to secure Haiti for the sake of geopolitical power and to discipline its economy for the sake of American investment."[24]

General Smedley Butler of the U.S. Army who led a contingent Marines force against the Cacos at Fort Rivière knew the agenda very well. He later admitted, "I helped make Mexico, especially Tampico, safe for American oil interests in 1914. I helped make Haiti and Cuba a decent place for the National City Bank boys to collect revenues in."[25]

As it is with most U.S. interventions in a foreign land, money was the ultimate motif of the U.S. Occupation of Haiti. Its widely known "dollar and gunboat" diplomacy is still in place in Haiti, more than a hundred years later. Although the U.S. occupation did not produce the desired outcome, it has nevertheless produced a zombie nation marred in a vicious circle of violence. Zombies are by nature incapable of any thoughts, and without conscious experience, they take commands to do tasks. Consequently, as a great imperialist *bòkò*,[26] The U.S. has turned Haiti into the ultimate

---

[23] Johnson, "What the United States Has Accomplished" see
https://www.gutenberg.org/files/35025/35025-h/35025-h.htm
[24] Fay Jennifer. "Dead Subjectivity: "White Zombie," Black Baghdad." CR: The New Centennial Review 8, no. 1 (2008): 81-101. Accessed July 31, 2020. www.jstor.org/stable/41949582.
[25] For more see Smedley Butler's quotes in
https://www.brainyquote.com/authors/smedley-butler-quotes
[26] In Haitian folklore, a *bòkò* is a sorcerer or an evil version of the *ougan*. A *bòkò* uses his skills, power, and knowledge for evil.

zombie republic which eventually keeps breeding zombie churches.

The Duvalier Era

After the U.S. Marines left in 1934, Haitian leaders tried to restore national pride. They were unsuccessful because military coups and U.S. policies that undermined Haiti's democracy and economy persisted. Then in 1957, François Duvalier was elected president. To save his skin and his government and to bully his opponent, Duvalier created a parallel force known as *Volontaires Sécurité Nationale*, best known as *Tonton Makout*. The bulk of the Haitian army's elite were mulattos who had a penchant for fermenting numerous coups to retain power. As a student of history, Duvalier vowed that what had happened to Sudre Dartiguenave and Dumarsais Estimé would not happen to him. To make sure of this, he preemptively exiled the mulatto leaders of the army. For fourteen years, Duvalier, known also as Papa Doc, terrorized his political and religious opponents by jailing, killing, and exiling them. As Anne Greene points out, "The only positive thing that can be said about his presidency is that Francois Duvalier provided some new opportunities for the black urban middle class...and he offered unprecedented chances for blacks to enter the civil service."[27]

Religion was another secret weapon of terror used by Duvalier. Under the influence of Jean Price-Mars, François Duvalier and Lorimer Denis founded the noirisme movement to valorize Vodou and black leadership. As the Catholic Church sided with the minority mulatto elite in their disdain for Vodou, Duvalier

---

[27] Anne Greene, *The Catholic Church in Haiti: Political and Social Change* (East Lansing: Michigan State University Press, 1993), 34

masterfully used the traditional religion to instill fear in his enemies and to score points with the masses. And in 1971, before he died, he named his 19-year-old son Jean-Claude as his successor. Surrounded by his Makouts, the young Duvalier continued his father's reign of terror and corruption until his downfall in 1986. However, the younger Duvalier failed to maintain the balance of power that his dad cleverly used.

Consequently, nearly all sectors of Haitian society, including the Catholic church, revolted against him, and he was eventually toppled and exiled to France.

Through the sword and the cross, Haiti is still paying a historic price for her freedom. While the sword is used to manipulate the country through gunboats and dollar diplomacy, the cross is used to subjugate the souls of Haitians with the shackles of religion. But as Jacques Nicolas Léger points out,

> For more than a century it has been the usual thing to ridicule Haiti; none of the means which might bring discredit on her has been neglected. Nevertheless, she still exists and has proudly maintained her independence. This fact may seem to be unimportant to many; but it is the best evidence that a country placed in so disadvantageous a position as was Haiti, and has nevertheless shown such a vitality, cannot be a mere collection of ignorant, corrupt, and abjectly superstitious men. Such a nation must unquestionably possess a certain amount of sterling qualities.[28]

---

[28] Léger, Jacques Nicolas, 1859-. Haiti, her history and her detractors (Kindle Locations 6102-6106). New York, Neale.

CHAPTER 2

Being Haitian: Nuances in Haitian Culture

———— ❧ ————

Haiti is more African than many countries in Africa.
Herbert Ekwe-Ekwe

Nous sommes des enfants d'Afrique autant par nos corps et nos peaux, que par nos croyances et notre culture."
Louis Maximilien

Although it is most certainly true that America has an infinitely more thorough knowledge and is more capable of government than is Haiti, yet the Haitians have what many Americans of even the upper classes often lack, a knowledge of culture and excellent manners.

J. Dryden Kuser

Haitian Culture Then and Now

Haitian culture is a rich and diverse blend of African, European, and some indigenous Taino influences that have been lost and evolved over time. It has been shaped by its tumultuous political instability and Western influences including the legacy of slavery and colonialism. Despite the challenges faced by the country, Haitians take pride in their cultural heritage and work hard to preserve it for future generations.

Years ago, before mobile phones and other forms of technology were available to the general public, Haitians lived their life as a series of unrelated and unexpected events. It appeared that people were living one day at a time. No one was exempt from unannounced visits, and there were no such things as privacy and personal time. A man once walked eight hours to consult with my father, only to find out when he got to our house that my dad was out of town, and would not be back for a few days.

When I was living in Haiti, our family had planned a weekend getaway for weeks, then unexpected guests showed up, and we were obliged to host them for the weekend. How many in Haiti would ride the bus to town to take care of a personal matter or business, but once they got there, they found out the person they were hoping to see was not available? Or how many others would plan social activities without a reliable weather forecast, only to have the event rained out? And yet, most people did not seem to be bothered by these interruptions.

Haitians were also known for their hospitality and care towards strangers. Homes were open to all, and food and drink were shared with as many as possible. As my dad used to say, "*Manje kwit pa gen mèt'* (Cooked food has no owner). Family ties used to be highly valued in Haitian society, and it is not uncommon for several generations of family members to live together in the same household. Belonging to a community was essential since Haitians often rely on their neighbors and friends for support and assistance. That was then.

This is now. Haitian culture has evolved, and some of the previous characteristics have gradually changed. A sense of community is being replaced by individualism. Traditional family values are gone, and kids are emulating the cultural influences of the West. Gone are the popular children's games of the past. Social, friendship, and camaraderie games such as *ronde*, dominoes, *osselets*, *rome*, and *besigue* have been replaced with individual games played on tablets and cellphones. Courtesy, politeness, (*bonjou*), and civility are no longer the pillars of Haitian culture. In their place, we now have fear, mistrust, and self-preservation. These are now the underlying characteristics of the culture.

Harold Courlander was an American novelist, folklorist, and anthropologist who studied Haitian life. In his book *The Drum and the Hoe*, Courlander writes the Haitian is "outwardly simple and poor, but inwardly he is a complicated and rich man. He is rich in music, the capacity for spiritual expression, tradition, folklore, and memories."[29]

When I was a kid, nightfall storytelling, riddles, and jokes were a popular and exciting time for kids and grown-ups alike. Under the moonlight and sitting on the *glasi* (cement porch), we would listen

---

[29]Harold Courlander, The Drum and the Hoe (Berkeley: University of California Press, 1960), 2-3

to a narrator's funny stories of the legendary Bouki and his antagonist Malis, the beloved fairytale of the Magic Orange Tree, scary stories of mermaids, stilt-clad giants, and one of my favorites, Tezen, the Magic Fish. The renowned Haitian scholar and statesman Dantès Bellegarde, in his book *Haiti et ses Problèmes*, explains how to understand Haitian culture. He writes:

> One of the surest ways to understand the psychology of the Haitian people is to study their beliefs and feelings of his thoughts, which are expressed in their proverbs. In his games, in his arts, in his tales. Fables and legends. In his songs and dances, which together constitute folklore. There is a popular Haitian literature. It is oral. Since it has no other means of expression than the Creole. It consists of proverbs, enigmas, fables, spoken tales, sung tales, song*s*.[30]

Mastering the Language

Language is one of the most important elements of any culture. Dr. William Hodges, a former Haiti missionary, knew the importance of language when he said, "Language is the expression of culture, the means of transmitting it to future generations, and therefore it must convey the world-view, the mood, the psychodynamics of behavior, and the reason of life."[31] On paper, French and Creole are Haiti's official languages, but Creole is the true and only language spoken by all Haitians.

---

[30] Dantes Bellegarde, *Haïti et ses Problèmes* (Montréal: Éditions B. Valiquette [1941?])

[31] William Hodges, *A Philosophy of Christian Mission*, see Selected Essays by William Hodges, 59

However, as in any other country, there are a lot of notable differences in the words used in various regions of Haiti.[32] In southern Haiti, it's normal to say *"Mwen kwoke rob la"* (I hang the dress), but if I go to northern Haiti and I say the same thing, the people there would think that I had sex with a dress. For them, *"kwoke"* means to have sex with.

Whether it is said out of ignorance or sheer prejudice, some people say Haitian Creole is broken French or patois, but to fully understand Haitian culture, one must master the people's language. Haitian Creole is not what Walter Rosaldo called a "dirty hybrid form of French"[33] when he heard Creole/Kreyòl or *Ayisyen* being spoken for the first time. Is English a dirty form of German? Is Spanish a water-down version of Italian? Is Portuguese corrupted Spanish? French and Haitian Creole are two distinct languages.

After the devastating earthquake of 2010, many foreigners have written books and articles about Haiti and the Haitian people without a clue about the language or the customs of the people. Some have only spent a few days there, while others have traveled as short-term missionaries in a particular village for as little as five days. There are some cases where those "experts on Haiti" have never set foot there. How much can you learn and understand about a people's culture on a five-day trip? How do you write about a people's customs without living and interacting with them for several years?

---

[32] For example, the use of *"ap"* and *"pe"* as in *"m ap vini"* versus *"m pe vini"*. Also the verb to find as in *mwen jwenn li* in the south or *mwen trouve l* in the north. The word *mamit* (can) in the South means *kanistè* in the North; or *balèn/bouji* is used instead of *chandèl* (candle) in different areas of Haiti.

[33] Walter Rosaldo, *Without Hope* (Pittsburg: KDP, 2019) 137

The following stories illustrate why it's important to have a good understanding of a language before making assumptions about what is being said. In his book *Mots Créoles du Nord d'Haïti,* Max Manigat tells the story of a French-Canadian priest who visited Haiti and wanted to impress his hosts by demonstrating the similarities between Quebecan and Haitian proverbs. In telling the proverb, he fumbled the translation. The Haitian proverb *"Babye malfini an, babye poul la tou"* in Creole means, "Blame the eagle, blame also the hen." The French-Canadian translated it as "The barber of the eagle is also the barber of the hen." Ouch! But "babye" in this particular proverb means to reproach or to blame; it's not the French word *"barbier".*[34]

Another case of language blunder happened when an American visited the countryside of Cavaillon. While looking for the bathroom, he asked the host, *"Mwen se twalèt la?"*, meaning "I'm the toilet", instead of *"Kote twalèt la ye?"* "Where is the bathroom?"

Social Stigmas and Stereotypes

A bishop from the Order of Monford was visiting Haiti for the second time. During his conversation with an old bishop who had been there for decades, he said: "Monsignor, this is my second trip to Haiti. I didn't understand very much the first time. But this time I have the feeling that I've really understood the Haitian way of thinking."

---

[34] Note that *"babye"* can also mean complaining, as in "ase babye" (stop complaining or you talk too much).
Manigat Max, *Mots Créoles du Nord d'Haïti* (Coconut Creek: Educa Vision Inc, 2007), 231.

"You're lucky," said the bishop. "I've been here sixty years and still don't understand anything."[35]

Short-term travelers and most missionaries in Haiti have a habit of painting Haitians with a broad brush. They usually portray character traits of an individual they encounter to the whole country. Because of a lack of understanding of the history, the language, the manners, and the customs of the people, they use phrases like "Haiti is..." or "Haitians are..." to lump everything in one lot as if their experience with a few Haitians in a city or a village characterizes all Haitians.[36] Paul Orjala, who was a missionary with the Church of the Nazarene, agrees, "We can't quite understand why writers who come to Haiti for a few days to a month or two think this is such an exciting mysterious place—wild and dangerous!"[37] The reason they think like that, Mr. Orjala, is because they always see Haitians not as human beings but as subjects to be studied.

In *A place called Haiti*, Amy Wilentz explains it this way,

"Perhaps it is exactly that mystery, that strangeness, that holds foreigners in Haiti's sway long after they have abandoned other places. Unfortunately, that Haitian mystery—if it is a mystery, this darkness, this seeming otherness, the heat and vibrancy, the refusal to cave to hemispheric pressures—has too frequently been

---

[35] Roger Riou, The Island of my Life (New York: Delacorte Press, 1975), 150-151

[36] Some writers deliberately used "the Haitian" to attract a larger audience and to sell books. Without proper context, a reader would not know if the stories are confined to a particular period and a particular village. For example, to raise funds, a short-term missionary nurse visited a remote village and saw an infant without diapers, but she reported back to supporters that all Haitians kids wear no diapers. See, April Perry, *They Suffer in Faith* (Maitland: Xulon Press, 2005), See also Walter Rosaldo, *Without Hope* (Pittsburg: KDP, 2019), 138-144, and Doug Fritts, The White Haitian (North Fort Myers: Faithful Life Publishers, 2012).

[37] W. F. Jordan, *Crusading in The West Indies* (New York, Fleming H. Revell company [c1922], 90-91

manipulated for ulterior motives. The savage cannot govern himself: we must take over. The unknowable heathen is cruel: we must convert him."[38]

Jordan William was with the American Bible Society when he visited Haiti in 1909. In his book *Crusading in The West Indies*, he did not even try to hide his interest: "It would be well worthwhile for someone to master the native Patois and in the interests of literature, psychology, and folklore, record these creations of the African mind before they disappear from the face of the earth with advancing civilization."[39]

Denigrating an entire nation because you interact with a few people who appear to be ignorant shows more about who you are than who they are. As Louis-Joseph Janvier argues,

> *"Pour bien juger des usages et des coutumes d'un peuple, il faut avoir égard au milieu social, intellectuel et moral de ce peuple ; il faut surtout ne pas émettre de fausses appréciations, en oubliant les conditions physiques de milieu, d'habitat dans lesquelles ce peuple s'est développé".[40]*

(To judge the manners and customs of a people, we must take into account their social, intellectual, and moral environment; it is

---

[38] Amy Wilentz, "A Place Called Haiti", Aperture, Winter 1992, No. 126, HAITI: FEEDING THE SPIRIT (WINTER 1992), pp. 4-21, Accessed 12/8/2020, http://www.jstor.com/stable/24472308

[39] W. F. Jordan, *Crusading in The West Indies* (New York, Fleming H. Revell company [c1922], 90-91

[40] Louis-Joseph Janvier, La Republique d'Haiti et ses Visiteurs (1840-1882): Un Peuple Noir Devant les Peuples Blancs (Paris: Marpon et Flammarion, Libraires et Editeurs, 1883), p. 67-68

important not to make false assessments, forgetting the physical conditions of the environment and the habitat in which they have lived.)

From my experience, there seems to be a deliberate use of a blatant generalization of the Haitian people by outsiders. In his book, *The Island of My Life*, the Catholic priest Roger Riou writes, "The Haitian doesn't like beds-he says they make him dizzy."[41] Mildred Anderson, in *Beyond All This*, describes Haitians as a "backward but simple-hearted people."[42] Former missionary Doug Fritts, who arrogantly called himself "The White Haitian," says, "Haitians have almost nothing to read, they are pleased to get a gospel track."[43] The longtime missionary to northern Haiti William Hodges says, "The Haitian, for instance, does not usually repent from sin... he seeks deliverance from the evil of this world".[44] James E. McDonald, a friend of Riou, who was on his way to Port-de-Paix to work at an eye clinic project, says, "Children run naked in Haiti until about the age of three. It is much simpler that way. We saw lots of them, and they were all skinny."[45] I was not running naked as a toddler, and I don't remember any other kids in the neighborhood who were either. So who is "the Haitian" they are talking about?

---

[41] Riou, "The Island of my Life", 207

[42] Mildred Anderson, *Beyond All This: Thirty years with the mountain people of Haiti* (Light Messages, 2010),

[43] Doug Fritts, *The White Haitian* (North Fort Myers: Faithful Life Publishers, 2012),76

[44] Hodges, "A Philosophy of Christian Mission", 55

[45] James E McDonald, FOCUS eye care in Haiti and Nigeria 1961-1996+, Produced from: 2015 01 06 Focus in Haiti W Jay and Lyn McDonald- PDF version.docx, 74

How a Haitian acts in the northern region of Haiti does not necessarily reflect the customs and manners of the south.

There are also stereotypes and stigmas associated with different areas of the country. For example, Camp-Perrin is known as one of the most beautiful small towns in Haiti. When I meet people from other parts of the country, and I tell them I'm from Les Cayes, they immediately say, "*E! nèg Okay pa bay fanm lajan*" (Men from Les Cayes don't give money to their women). In contrast, men from Cap-Haitien are believed to be very jealous, but they give lavishly to their women.

People from Baradères and Plaisance du Sud are known for their association with the Petro rite of Vodou. They are usually accused of being *dyab* (evil). Men are warned to avoid women from Jérémie and Desdunes because they talk too much, and they are not easy to live with. People from Petit Bourg de Borgne in the Northern department don't like mixing up with outsiders. They marry each other. Men from Desdunes are also known to have high tempers, but people from Les Cayes are moderate and have good manners. While Leogane is known for its Rara, ougans, and Vodou temples, in Port-au-Prince, you have to be careful because people are not always who they say they are. Although all those examples could be isolated cases, nevertheless these social stigmas and stereotypes are known throughout the country. If you're not a Haitian (being) and if you have not lived (doing) with the people, you would not necessarily know these differences in certain regions of the country. Patti Marxsen put it brilliantly:

> Not only is Haiti foreign to western manners, mores, language, religion, and culture, it is peculiarly beyond our scope of perception. Whether we come as neighbors, helpers, friends, or

missionaries, we can only begin to hear the call of Haiti when we begin to acknowledge our role in the silences of its historical past. In the end, we are outsiders."[46]

Out of Africa

African culture has played a significant role in shaping the country's customs, traditions, and way of life. Haiti was a major destination for enslaved Africans during the transatlantic slave trade, and it is estimated that around 90% of the population today is of African descent. Indeed, the essence of the Haitian personality is deeply rooted in its African origin.

When Hebert Ekwe-Ekwe was arguing for the inclusion of Haiti in the Council of African Nations, he titled his article in Pambazuka News, "Haiti is More African Than Many Countries in Africa."[47]

Some of the key ways that African culture, particularly those of West and Central Africa, has influenced Haitian culture include:

1. Religion: The most well-known African influence on Haitian culture is Vodou. This popular religion incorporates elements of African spirituality and those acquired from plantation Catholicism.

2. Music and dance: Haitian music and dance have been heavily influenced by African rhythms and styles, particularly in using drums and other percussion

---

[46] Patti M. Marxsen, *"Haiti's Heavenly Waters"*, Journal of Haitian Studies, Fall 2005, Vol. 11, No. 2 (Fall 2005), pp. 14-29, Published by: Center for Black Studies Research. http://www.jstor.com/stable/41715310

[47] See Hebert Ekwe-Ekwe, *"Haiti is more African than many countries in Africa"* "http://www.pambazuka.org/pan-africanism/haiti-more-african-many-countries-africa

instruments. African rhythms and melodies can be heard in many Haitian music genres, including *konpa*, *rara*, and *mizik rasin*. Many dances such as Yanvalou, Banda, and Ibo originated from traditional African dances.

3. Cuisine: Haitian cuisine is heavily influenced by African cuisine, with many dishes featuring ingredients and cooking techniques that are common in West and Central Africa. Some examples include cassava, *bouyon* (a stew made with meat and vegetables), rice dishes, fried plantains, and *griyo* (deep-fried pork).

4. Art: Haitian art often features imagery and themes that are rooted in African culture and traditions, such as depictions of deities from Vodou, wild animals from the African jungle, or scenes from everyday life in Haiti that are reminiscent of African village life.

5. Language: Haitian Creole, which is the primary language spoken in Haiti, has roots in West African languages, including Fon, Ewe, and Kikongo.

Haitian Culture and the West

The majority of Haitian Protestants who have been Westernized tend to describe the way of life of unbelievers as *lemond* (of this world), basically satanic. These Protestants have been brainwashed by missionaries to believe that their God-given gifts are actually from the devil. Is Haitian culture God's gift? Can a non-Protestant Haitian glorify God's creative work in a song, a painting, or a sculpture? Could Protestantism be a handicap in the creative minds of Haitians? Other than Amos Coulanges, do you know any famous Haitian, born into a Protestant family, who is a sculptor, painter, or musician? The handful of Protestant artists and writers had either rejected or dismissed their pre-conversion works. They labeled their previous accomplishments as worshiping the *dyab*.

Most Protestants don't know who Hector Hyppolite was. The famous Haitian painter is more widely known abroad than he is known in Haiti. The names of Okel Ultimo and Wilfred Azemar mean nothing for some Haitians, although Ultimo was the top tap-tap (colorful buses) maker and Azemar was a sought-after mural and tap-tap artist in Port-au-Prince.

It has been said that Haiti is a land of contrasts. This label is mostly from foreigners who frequently compare and contrast Western values vs African values, rich vs poor, urban dwellers vs rural masses, and Vodou vs Christianity. It's people like Linda Crow, a former Wesleyan missionary, who insist on contrasting Haiti's cultural heritage with the West. In the introduction to her book *Victory Over Voodoo*, she reasons,

> I ponder sometimes the contrast between our Haitian people, both rich and poor, and our Christians at home. We who have had so much and they who for the most part have had little of these earthly goods. We who have had such great opportunities and they who have had so few. We who have had a Christian heritage and they who have known nothing of Christian principles.[48]

Haiti shares the island of Hispaniola with the Dominican Republic (DR). People here in the U.S. often ask why Haiti is so poor and the DR is not, even though they have never traveled to

---

[48] Linda Crow, *Victory over Voodoo* (Kansas City: Nazarene Publishing House, 1975), 10

either country. These armchair travelers know that it's the same island and the same level of corruption. This question has a racial undertone which implies that the DR embraces a Eurocentric (superior/God) culture while the Haitians keep their Afrocentric (inferior/devil) culture. It's not a question, but a statement based on religious and cultural biases contrasting Spanish Catholicism and Vodou. Sure, the DR economy is in a much better shape than Haiti, and the DR is politically stable for investment. But the private resorts of La Romana and Punta Cana don't tell the whole story. Have you been to Santo Domingo where the U.S. travel advisory is at its highest level? Have you ever been to the DR's slums and shanty towns such as the Ozama Riverbank, La Barquita, Gualey, Domingo Savio, or Los Guandules? The poverty in those places is as bad as the slums of Port-Au-Prince.

We live in a fallen world. Inevitably, every country on earth has its own set of contrasts, even the richest countries. In the U.S., while we're pushing to ban gas stoves and fossil fuels, we're making nuclear bombs and warheads that can destroy the entire planet. While we claim to be a nation of the cross, we pick up the sword daily at home and around the globe. While we call embryos babies, we support the death penalty. While we worry about a failing education system, we're banning books. While we are the richest country on earth, over half a million people live on the streets.

French and American Cultural War in Haiti

Following the U.S. occupation of Haiti in 1915, William Jennings Bryan, Secretary of State to U.S. President Woodrow Wilson said, "Dear me, think of it, niggers speaking French!". That was the beginning of the demise of French influence in Haiti and the rise of the Americanization of Haitian culture. Although French has been the official language since the country's birth, for the past fifty years, it has been in decline due to ways and means of U.S. policies towards Haiti, the official status of Creole, and the emergence of English usage.

Mastering French is no longer an advantage for the middle class. While some Haitian authors have been members of the French Academy, young Haitians finally realize that it's not enough to know about Hugo, Voltaire, Balzac, Baudelaire, Molière, and other great French writers. They recognize that flaunting their Sorbonne University degree is more prestigious than economics. The old slogan of the Haitian aristocrats was to "See Paris and die." That fantasy died a long time ago in Miami.

Paris is no longer the dream destination for a young Haitian student seeking higher education. They prefer admittance into U.S. universities. In a country dominated by American NGOs, showing off your French is no longer the advantage it was for prospective job candidates. I predict by 2050; Haiti will be completely a multilingual country where French will be relegated to the least spoken language[49].

U.S. Occupation in Haiti has influenced Haitian culture in different ways. English words were introduced and creolized. Words such as black-out, muffler, tank, sit-in, love, show off, feeling, buzz, beep, voice, check, and backup are used daily in Creole. Both sexes wear pieces of used clothes known as *pèpè* or "Kennedy" because they originated during the Kennedy presidency. Ironically, some of

---

[49] A lot of Haitians also speak Spanish notably in the towns neighboring the Dominican Republic.

these pieces of clothes were originally made in Haitian sweatshops, shipped to U.S. stores, worn out, and sent back to Haiti as second-hand clothes. Some *pèpè* come with vulgar, funny, and dehumanized language that Haitians wear without knowing what they mean.

I was once in downtown Port-au-Prince when I saw a man wearing a t-shirt that said: "I'm pregnant". Paolo Woods photographed some of the slogans worn by unaware Haitians: "Kiss me I'm a blonde", "This is my tailgating shirt", "Kiss me under the mistletoe", "I pee in pools - Key West, FL"[50]

The Internet and the rise of social media usage in Haiti are some of the greatest contributing factors influencing the dominance of American culture in Haiti. Haitians have been exposed to American music genres like jazz, blues, rap, hip-hop, and rock and roll. The games I used to play when I was a kid, such as marble, *kap grandou* (kite), and *besigue* (a popular card game in Les Cayes), are now all gone.

Instead, young people are glued to Facebook, Instagram, TikTok, YouTube, and other media available to them. They've copied and acted out everything American. As Adam Serwer argues, "Like so many post-colonial nations once dominated by white supremacy, Haiti's culture reflects the brutality and inhumanity of the powers that once ruled it. Disassociating its cultural dysfunction from the "West" is revisionism."[51]

---

[50] Paolo Woods, "Pèpè", https://www.paolowoods.com/pepe

[51] Adam Serwer, *"On Haiti's "Culture."*", accessed 12/28/2020, https://prospect.org/article/haiti-s-culture./

Intermediaries in the Haitian Culture

In my teenage years, I used a friend to gauge interest and to declare my love to a girl that I liked. Our mutual friend was my intermediary. He was supposed to help me share my feelings for this girl. He was in essence my private mailman, as I often wrote love notes and letters to my anticipated girlfriend. Ironically, my intermediary ended up with the girl for himself (*Li pran l nan menm*).

The use of intermediaries is deeply woven into Haitian culture. Haitian people, in general, will not ask a favor directly from a person in authority or from someone whose social class is perceived to be higher than theirs. Thus, they use a go-between person or an intermediary.

Growing up, I witnessed my dad being used as an intermediary, countless times, in his work as the local pastor in various villages in Haiti. In some instances, my dad would be the second or the third person in a multiple-layered intermediary scheme. In Haiti, intermediaries are most useful at government agencies and some private institutions such as banks, hospitals, and schools. Getting things done faster will depend on who you know.

For example, there can be hundreds of people lining up to see a teller at the bank. But you can skip the line if you know the teller, or you know somebody who is a friend of the teller. When I used to go to the DGI (Department of Revenue) to renew tags and motor vehicle insurance, I was in and out because one of the clerks used to be my neighbor.

I will argue in various parts of the book that the use of intermediaries in Haitian society has given Haitians a distorted picture of God. It's no wonder God is often seen as being so far away and so holy that they can't approach him, except through the *lwa* (spirits) and other religious leaders as intermediaries. It's the same idea as using intercessors when Haitian Catholics pray in front of the icon of a saint or when they go to the confessional as if God is only accessible to them through the priest. For the Haitians, God is always seen as the Supreme authority. Out of respect and reverence, Vodouists make use of the lesser spirits as intermediaries, while Haitian Christians use priests and spiritual leaders as God's representatives on earth.

Saying Yes Without Meaning It

Any serious researcher in Haiti will tell you that reliable statistical data is hard to obtain. Surveys in Haiti, especially the ones taken by government agencies, are in general skewed, and they are plagued with methodological problems. Not only will the survey takers sometimes fill out the questionnaire themselves, but respondents will respond "yes" to some questions, even if it's not the logical answer. Consequently, it creates a major problem for the researcher, especially in healthcare, language, and religious studies.

A few years after he was sent back as a MEBSH pastor in a rural area church, my dad did two surveys: the first one was six months after he arrived, and the other one was a few years later. He wanted to know how the church was doing in the community and how he could improve his pastoral skills and relationship with community members. Three of the questions were: "How do you rate the pastor? "Are you okay with the work he is doing?" and "What do you blame him for?" Ninety-nine percent of the respondents said he was doing a good job, and they had nothing to reproach him for. The remaining 1% declined to answer. I'm sure more people did not agree with my dad and had some ideas about where he could improve his skills, but because the survey participants were also elders and leaders of the church. It could be that the respondents were afraid to say something that could put them in a negative light with the leaders. If the survey takers were outsiders, some people would have answered differently.

The short-term travelers and some missionaries will sometimes accuse Haitians of being deceptive when what's really happening is a lack of understanding of Haitians. Haitians have often been taken advantage of. Because of this, some Haitians have learned to ask, "What's in it for you?" and "Why are you being so nice?" Amy Wilenz points this out, as she writes:

> It is not the fault of Haitians if, for two centuries, right up into our own enlightened day, Haiti has been obscured by mystification, prostituted by foreign adventurers milking it for the exotic, and slandered by foreign politicians, missionaries, and businessmen, all out to denigrate the black man and help themselves to his island's natural riches.[52]

A Country of Faux-Semblants

Posturing is also a big part of Haitian culture. In Haiti, what you see is not necessarily what it is. When I was in high school in Port-au-Prince, a man in my neighborhood used to wake up every day, put on a suit, get his briefcase, and put on the appearance of going to work. But he had no job. In Haiti, putting up a pretense is woven

---

[52] Amy Wilentz, "A Place Called Haiti", Aperture, Winter 1992, No. 126, HAITI: FEEDING THE SPIRIT (WINTER 1992), pp. 4-21, Accessed 12/8/2020, http://www.jstor.com/stable/24472308

into the fabric of society. Maximilien Laroche, in his book *Portrait de l'Haitien,* argues,

> *L'âme tiraillée par deux cultures, l'Haïtien est ainsi amené fort souvent, dans ses attitudes, ses sentiments, ses prises de position et ses opinions par un besoin de compensation et de valorisation à jouer à Paraître plutôt qu'à Être tout simplement ce qu'il est au fond.*[53]

(The soul torn by two cultures, the Haitian is thus often brought, in his attitudes, his feelings, his positions, and his opinions by a need for compensation and valorization to play to appear rather than simply to be which is what he is deep down.)

In *Culture haïtienne: Abrégé de cours,* Yves Blot agrees, *"L'apparence a une grande importance pour l'haïtien, car le paraître prime sur l'être. La bonne image de soi est une préoccupation fondamentale."*[54] (Appearance is of great importance to the Haitian, because appearance takes precedence over being. Good self-image is a fundamental concern.)

In Haiti, you can fool most people by putting on a suit. A man was visiting a small village in southern Haiti, and when Sunday came, he put on his suit and attended the local Protestant church. Upon seeing the well-dressed visitor in the assembly, the pastor

---

[53] Maximilien Laroche, *Portrait de l'Haïtien* (Montréal: Les Éditions de Sainte-Marie, 1968), 100

[54] Yves Blot, *Culture Haïtienne, Abrégé de Cours* (Montréal: Université de Montréal, 2018), 16.

called on him to bless the church with a prayer.[55] The man stood up and said: "I'm an *ougan* (Vodou priest). Do you still want me to pray?" The *ougan* was not pretending to be a Protestant, but it was the pastor who fell for the suit.

In a country of clowns, titles are also essential. Young men and women want to be called doctors on their first day in medical school, engineers by taking a seminar on water treatment, agronomists by learning soil protection from an NGO, pastors by holding a Bible on Sundays, and lawyers (Mèt) by dressing nicely. You know Haiti is a big joke when parents call their kids by their titles (Doktè, Agwo, Enjenyè) instead of their first names.

From the government to the clergy, to the peasantry, it's a country made up of stand-up comedians in the club of faux-semblants. Everybody is having their 15 minutes of fame. Haiti is probably the only country where a small corner store owner, a street vendor, and a one-man photocopy service would call themselves PDG (Président/Directeur Général) or CEO.

---

[55] *Anpil pasté gen vye defo sa a.* (Some Haitians pastors have this bad habit of calling on strangers and visitors to do the final prayer or blessing during church service.)

CHAPTER 3

Vodou: The Misunderstood Religion

———— ❧ ————

"Voodoo is part of the air that Haitians breathe"

(Leslie Griffiths)

Voodoo is the backbone of the emotional and cultural life of the Haitian

(Lilas Desquiron)

"At its core, Vodou is a celebration of love and life."

(Saint-Juste, a Ougan)

Debunking the Myth

Haitian Vodou is probably one of the most misunderstood and the most despised religions in the world. So, what is it about Vodou that makes it intriguing to some people? Is it because people tend to associate the Haitian religion with black magic, human sacrifices, evil spirits, superstitions, curses, dolls, and zombies, or is it because of the thrill depicted in Hollywood shows and movies?

Not to be confused with New Orleans and the Hollywood version of Voodoo, many factors contributed to the misconceived ideas of Vodou. First, the Haitians themselves are in part responsible for the negative publicity of Vodou.

Second, there have been fictitious travel accounts and articles written by sensationalist travel writers and foreign press representatives such as Charles Texier, William Seabrooke, Hesketh Prichard, Sir St. John Spencer, Lawrence Harrison, and David Brooks, that falsely depict Haitians as backward and savage.

Third, Hollywood's obsession with magic, zombies, and the occult has produced movies such as *Voodoo Queen, White Zombie, The Serpent and the Rainbow, The Believer,* and many more.

Fourth, Christian missions and the Catholic church's relentless war on Vodou pushed Protestant missionaries, motivated by their own interests, to use Vodou as a scapegoat for their failure in evangelism, as they labeled Vodou a satanic religion.

Last, some detractors from the U.S. Marines published sensationalized stories from their time spent in Haiti. Faustin Wirkus wrote *The White King of La Gonave*, and John Houston Craige wrote two books *Black Bagdad* and *Cannibal Cousins.* All of these books aimed to portray Vodou and the Haitians as primitive, devilish, superstitious, violent, and erotic.

Although there is a growing body of literature on Vodou that is available to the general public in multiple languages, detractors of Vodou and Western critics choose to distort the truth by using voodoo instead of Vodou to fit their agenda. In the last fifty years, there have been considerable scholarly articles and books written extensively and published by Vodou apologists, ethnologists, anthropologists, and religious scholars who have written extensively to shed light on and debunk the myths associated with Vodou.

Chapo ba (reverence) for the work of such writers as Milo Rigaud, Laennec Hurbon, Lilas Desquiron, Claude Planson, Odette Mennesson-Rigaud, Patrick Bellegarde-Smith, Elizabeth McAlister, Mimerose Beaubrun, Claudine Michel, LeGrace Benson, Kate Ramsey, Michel Laguerre, Leslie Desmangles, Guérin Montilus, Jean Fils-Aimé, Harold Courlander, Gasner Joint, Joseph Augustin, Marie Vieux-Chauvet, Karen McCarthy Brown, Celucien Joseph, Benjamin Hebblethwaite, Katherine Dunham, and many more.

Vodou: A Definition

Is Vodou a devil-worshiping religion as some people tend to believe? You would think it is if you read most of the missionary literature about Haiti. The dominant theme in these books and articles is "the Vodou drums of the devil worshipers" or "these people worship and make sacrifices to the devil". Contrary to the Western narrative, Vodou is not a cult of devil worshipers. It's a religion like any other religion in the world. It's a lack of cultural intelligence that causes missionaries to think the sounds of Vodou drums are devil worship.

The truth is that the Vodouist is like a Protestant who pays no attention to the Father and the Son but worships only the Holy Spirit. In other words, the Vodouists are a people of the spirits.

So then, what is Haitian Vodou? In her book, Serving the Spirits, Patricia Scheu, aka Mambo Vye Zo Komande LaMenfo, writes, "If you compare the theology of religions, such as Hinduism… Greek, and Roman, you will find incredible similarities between them. They all espouse one supreme creator who created a multitude of pantheons of otherworldly spirits who act as servants to both man and God."[56] For Scheu, "It'a a religious practice, a faith that points toward intimate knowledge of God."[57] Georges Mc Donald Mulrain expresses the same idea in his book *Theology of Folk Culture.* He writes, "Vodou, like Christianity, is a system of beliefs and practices involving the worship of a Supreme Being."[58]

For Leslie Desmangles,

Vodou in Haiti is a system of beliefs and practices that gives meaning to life; it uplifts the spirits of the downtrodden who experience life's misfortunes, instills in its devotee a need for solace and self-examination, and relates the profane world of humans world to that

---

[56] Patricia Scheu, *Serving the Spirits* (Lexington: n.p., 2011), 16

[57] Scheu, "Serving the Spirits", 12

[58] Mulrain, Georges MacDonald. Theology in Folk Culture: The Theological Significance of Haitian Folk Religion. Frankfurt amMain: Verlag Peter Lang, 1984, 11

of incommensurable mythological divine entities, called lwas, who govern the cosmos.[59]

For Nathanael Murell,

"The aim of Vodou is not to cause hexes, inflict pain on helpless victims, and propagate evil in the world, as portrayed in horror movies and the media, but to counteract evil actions and forces with ashes, or spiritual power."[60]

For Jean Price-Mars,

Vodou is a religion because all its followers believe in the existence of spiritual beings that live somewhere in the universe in close association with human beings over whose activities they exercise control.[61]

For Maya Deren,

"It proposes that man has a material body, animated by an esprit or gros-bon-ange - the soul, spirit, psyche or self--which, being non-material. Vodou is a dance of the spirit: a system of movements, gestures, prayers, and songs in veneration of the invisible forces of life."[62]

For Karen McCarthy Brown,

---

[59] Leslie G. Desmangles, The Faces of the Gods: Vodou and Roman Catholicism in Haiti (Chapel Hill: University of North Carolina Press, 1992), p2

[60] Nathanael Samuel Murell, Afro-Caribbean Religions: An Introduction to their historical, Cultural, and Sacred Traditions (Philadelphia: Temple University Press, 2010), 60

[61] Price-Mars, Jean. Ainsi Parla l'Oncle: Essais d'ethnographie (New York: Parapsychology Foundation Inc., 1928. Nouvelle édition, 1954), 45

[62] Deren Maya, *Divine Horsemen:* The Living Gods of Haiti (Kingston: McPherson &Company, 2004), 15-16

Vodou, the new religion that emerged from the social chaos and agony of Haiti's Eighteenth-century slave plantations… is the system they have devised to deal with the suffering that is life, a system whose purpose is to minimize pain, avoid disaster, cushion loss, and strengthen survivors and survival instincts.[63]

Unfortunately, Haitian Vodou still has its detractors. I thought the days when Western missionaries associated Vodou with satanism were long gone. But recently in 2018, Jacklyn Vanderpool with the Christian non-profit organization *LiveBeyond* in Thomazeau had this to write about Vodou: "Vodou, an openly Satanic religion, is the national religion in Haiti. The practitioners invite demons to possess them; they make sacrifices; they curse, poison, and kill their enemies."[64]

This statement shows that Vanderpool has never been to a Vodou ceremony nor taken a crash course on religion in Haiti. A quick read of her story shows that it is more likely that she is looking for pity and attention, and trying to raise funds for her non-profit organization.

The Catholic priest Claude Etienne, in an interview with *Radio Nationale,* had this to say about Vodou:

Le Vodou n'est qu'une activité profane, qu'une sorte de sorcellerie satanique qui ne comprend que des danses orgiastiques qui n'ont rien de religieux. Sans dogme, sans doctrine, sans moralité, sans moyens

[63] Brown Karen McCarthy, *Mama Lola: A Vodou Priestess in Brooklyn.* Berkeley: University of California Press, 1991, 10

[64] Jacklyn Vanderpool, *"How One Ordinary Woman Overcame the Murderous Threats of Vodou Priests"* https://www.charismanews.com/world/70155-how-one-ordinary-woman-overcame-the-murderous-threats-of-demonized-vodou-priests

de sanctification, en un mot sans système de valeurs, le Vodou ne présente qu'un culte voué à des créatures spirituelles autres que Dieu et ne cultive que la haine chez ses adeptes. Maléfique donc, le Vodou doit être détruit.[65]

[Vodou is only a profane activity, a kind of satanic witchcraft which includes only orgiastic dances which have nothing religious. Without dogma, without doctrine, without morality, without means of sanctification, in other words without a value system, Vodou is only a cult dedicated to spiritual creatures other than God and only cultivates hatred among its followers. Since it is evil, Vodou must be destroyed.]

And then there are people like renowned Haitian scholar Carl Brouard, a fervent defender of Vodou, who converted to Catholicism and argued that "Vodou is not a religion because it has neither inspired a prophet nor a book. It is a sect inspired by low-profile demons. Encouraging it is unpatriotic."[66] Later in his life, Brouard said, "Before God and before men. I renounce all my voodoo writings."[67]

Fredo Saint Charles affirms that Vodou is a satanic religion because adherents of Vodou worship spirits that are submissive to Satan.[68]

---

[65] Cited in Claude Etienne, Radio Nationale interview 1986, in Max Beauvoir, Vodou et Paix

[66] Carl Brouard, *Pages Retrouvées* (Port-au-Prince: Editions Panorama, 1963), 152

[67] Ibid, 156

[68] Fredo Saint Charles, *Sauvé par la Grâce* (self-pub., XulonElite, 2017), 17

A former missionary to Haiti Doug Fritts says, "In Haiti, Satan comes out into the open, revealing his nature through his mediums - the hougans, mambos, and Voodooisants."[69]

While Stephen Bonsal of the New York Times calls Vodou "the degrading superstitions and the disgusting rites"[70]

The African Connection

Like the Haitian Creole, Haitian Vodou is unique in its characteristics. It finds its origin among the Fon, the Ewe, the Yoruba, and in various places from Ghana to Togo, but mainly in the ancient kingdom of Dahomey, now called Benin, in West Africa.[71] According to historical records, there were numerous African tribes from various countries in Africa.[72] Alfred Metraux mentions some of these tribes in his book *Voodoo in Haiti.* These tribes made up the majority of the slaves who were brought over from Africa: the "Senegalese, Wolofs, Foulbe, Bambara, Quiambas, Arada, Minas, Caplaus, Fons, Mahi, Nago, Mayombe, Mondongues, Ankole, etc."[73]

In West Africa, the term Vodou refers to a genre of ritual music and dance performed in honor of a particular category of spirit. The

---

[69] Doug Fritts, *The White Haitian: A poignant story of a missionary's immersion into the Haitian culture* (North Fort Myers: Faithful Life Publishers, 2012), 16.

[70] Stephen Bonsal, "The Passing of Nord Alexis of Haiti: A Typical Turn in the Wheel of Popular Fortune by Which Presidents Are Made and Lost in the Black Republic. https://www.nytimes.com/1909/02/21/archives/the-passing-of-nord-alexis-of-haiti-a-typical-turn-in-the-wheel-of.html   Feb 21, 1909

[71] Laennec, Hurbon. *Voodoo: Search for the Spirit* (New York: Harry N. Abrams, Inc, 1995), 14

[72] Mimerose Beaubrun, Nan Domi: An Initiate's Journey into Haitian Voodoo (San Francisco: City Lights Books, 2010), 13.

[73] Alfred Metraux, *Voodoo in Haiti* (New York: Schocken Books Inc, 1959), 25

term derives from the Fongbe word for spirit; many slaves who came to Saint-Domingue from Dahomey spoke this language."[74]

In his essay, *Role of Black Religion in Political Change: The Haitian Revolution and Voodoo*, Robert Hood notes that "Voodoo is the New World heir of African Old World religion which resisted its conversion to the Christian God. Instead, it converted the Christian God and all His saints to itself."[75] The African influence is so deep into the Haitian Vodou that Hood later argues that "Haiti is possibly the most Africanized country outside the continent of Africa."[76] Today, It is estimated that Vodou reached about 50 million followers worldwide, including in the United States, Brazil, and the Caribbean. Haitian Vodou has neither written scriptures nor hierarchical clergy. It is ritual and not dogmatic.

Concept of God

Haitian Vodouists traditionally believed in a single Supreme Being, the creator of all life, whom they called *Bondye*, literally meaning Good God, who is above all. Although there is little interaction with God in their religious ceremonies, the Vodouists would agree that they worship the same God that the Christians worship, the creator of all things and the sustainer of the universe.

---

[74] Richman, Karen. "Who Owns the Religion of Haiti?" In Who Owns Haiti?: People, Power, and Sovereignty, edited by Maguire Robert and Freeman Scott, by Wilentz Amy, 106-24. Gainesville, Tallahassee, Tampa, Boca Raton, Pensacola, Orlando, Miami, Jacksonville, Ft. Myers, Sarasota: University Press of Florida, 2017. Accessed July 31, 2020. doi: 10.2307/j.ctvx06xcf.13

[75] Hood, Robert E. "Role of black religion in political change: the Haitian revolution and Voodoo." Journal Of The Interdenominational Theological Center 9, no. 1 (September 1, 1981): 45-69. ATLA Religion Database with ATLASerials, EBSCOhost (accessed November 23, 2014).

[76] Ibid

However, there is no attempt by the Vodouists to define God by his attributes. For the adherent of Vodou, God is who God is. Consequently, not only is God too great to be approached by humans, but He is also too distant and has limited contact with their daily lives.

Since *Bondye* is too busy and too powerful, He lets lesser spirits or *lwa* in charge of day-to-day events, and they serve as mediators between God and the *sèvitè*.

However, given the specific circumstances of the encounter between Christianity and the religious beliefs of slaves arriving in Haiti, it is impossible to distinguish radically between the Grand Master of Vodou and the Christian God on one hand, and between the Catholic saints and lwa on the other. Slaves were forcefully baptized and obliged to show outward signs of allegiance to the Catholic faith, so they developed a tactic to preserve their religious beliefs. This assimilation is even easier for the Vodouist since Haitian Vodou is not a missionary religion.

In an opinion piece for the Christian Research Institute, J. A. Alexandre claims that "The Gran Mèt of Voodoo is not the God of the Bible. The god of Voodoo is Satan, who through various schemes has infiltrated the culture and religion to create distortions in terminologies and practices to cause humanity to worship him and his demons in the place of the only true God."[77] Alexandre, a Haitian Baptist pastor in Boston and a graduate of DTS (Dallas Theological Seminary), deliberately used the derogatory Western spelling "Voodoo" instead of the commonly accepted form

---

[77] "VOODOO AND CHRISTIANITY: Compatibility or Irreconcilable Differences?", J. A. Alexandre in Christian Research Journal, volume 36, number 01 (2013)

"Vodou" to make his point. Voodoo is not practiced in Haiti. But everyone has a right to their own opinion, even a Baptist.

Laennec Hurbon in his book, *Dieu dans le Vaudou Haïtien*, argues that in the spirit world of Haitian Vodou,

> God appears as the keystone that underlies the whole system of spirits and all Voodoo practices. He is the creator and minds, and the corresponding Catholic saints, and in this regard, it may be difficult to distinguish the God of Catholicism, in so far as it has always been present in preaching, catechism, hymns, and prayers as the creator of the universe, the creator of angels and saints.[78]

Since the *Iwa* can be capricious and can have a direct influence on their daily life, one must seek to understand them and seek their favor by offering prayers and sacrifices. For most Vodouists, *Bondye* is a God who rewards the just, punishes the wicked, and blesses those who uphold moral values. He may cause sickness, death, and curses. Therefore, one should be careful in life. Do good, and fear God. Detractors and critics of Vodou wrongly claim that Vodou practitioners worship the devil, but Haitian Vodouists are a classic example of unbelieving believers.

Statement of Faith

Here is an excerpt of the Vodou statement of faith as described by Leslie Desmangles:

---

[78] Hurbon Laennec, *Dieu dans le Vaudou Haïtien* (Paris: Maisonneuve et Larose, 2002), 121

I believe in Bondye, the Almighty Father of the sky, who manifests his spiritual nature in me; in a large number of spirits; and all things visible and invisible.

I believe in the lwas, the gods of Africa, and all the saints of the Catholic Church. Masters of the universe, they are manifestations of Bondye, who see all things and direct the course of all things; that some have made themselves known to us through our ancestors in Africa, and that others we have come to know, emulate, and serve in our new home in Haiti; that these lwas are potent enough to mount us, their children, in spirit possession; and that through their mounting, they can inspire us as to the needs of our community; that our moral duty is to faithfully serve them; that the lwas are capable, like us, of gentleness and mercy, but also of anger and revenge.

I believe in the power of ancestors who watch over us and serve us before the lwas; that they must be remembered and served faithfully.

I believe in the right granted to us by the lwas to interfere through magic in the normal flow of events as established by Bondye's will; in the efficacy of the medicines derived from the local fauna endowed to us by the lwas. I believe in the Holy Roman Catholic Church, in the communion of saints, and in life everlasting.[79]

Role of the Spirits or Lwa

In Haitian Vodou lwa are not gods. They are not believed to have powers to control air, land, or water; the powers of lwa are far more circumscribed and are limited to involvement and interference in discrete humans' personal affairs."[80] In his book,

---

[79] Leslie G. Desmangles, *The Faces of the Gods* (Chapel Hill: The University of North Carolina Press, 1992), 63

[80] Richman Karen, "*Who Owns the Religion of Haiti?*" In Who Owns Haiti? People, Power, and Sovereignty, edited by Maguire Robert and Freeman Scott, by Wilentz Amy, 106-24. Gainesville, Tallahassee, Tampa, Boca Raton, Pensacola,

Afro-Caribbean Religions, Nathaniel Murrell notes, "The aim of Vodou is not to cause hexes, inflict pain on helpless victims and propagate evil in the world, as portrayed in horror movies and the media, but to counteract evil actions and forces with ashe, or spiritual power."[81]

In *Voodoo: Search for the Spirit*, Haitian sociologist Laennec Hurbon explains that the spirits mediate between the Vodouist and the world. He notes that "they are thought to be present in all realms of nature: in the trees, the streams and the mountains, in the air, the water, and fire."[82] These personifications or representatives of the supreme God, called spirits or lwa are numerous throughout the Haitian Vodou religion.

In his essay, *Caribbean Religion: the Voodoo Case*, Pierre Roland claims, "The major divinities in the Voodoo pantheon are found among the Fons and the Yorubas: Legba, Dambala-Ouedo, Aida-Ouedo, Héviéso, Agassou, Ezili, Agou'e-Taroyo, Zaka, Ogoun, Chango still have their temples in the towns and villages of Togoland, Dahomey and Nigeria."[83]

Haitian Vodou recognizes two main hierarchies or three families of lwa:

Orlando, Miami, Jacksonville, Ft. Myers, Sarasota: University Press of Florida, 2017. Accessed July 31, 2020. doi: 10.2307/j.ctvx06xcf.13.

[81] Murrell, Nathaniel S. *Afro-Caribbean religions: An Introduction to their Historical, Cultural, and Sacred Traditions* (Philadelphia: Temple University Press, 2010). p 60

[82] Hurbon, "Voodoo: Search for the Spirit", 66

[83] Pierre, Roland, "Caribbean religion: the voodoo case." SA. Sociological Analysis 38, no. 1 (March 1, 1977): 25-36. ATLA Religion Database with ATLASerials, EBSCOhost (accessed November 23, 2014).

Rada Lwa

According to Anthropologist Melville Herskovits, the group of Rada lwa are said to be rather benevolent spirits, who are offered a "service" to conciliate their good grace or to avoid their anger or their pettiness.[84]

The most important among the Rada lwa is probably Legba or Papa Legba. He must be the first lwa honored and invoked at the beginning of every service because it is he who holds the key that can communicate with the spirit world. In other words, without prior permission, no other spirit can manifest as part of a ceremony.

Hurbon explains that "Legba serves to open the gate that separates humans from the supernatural world."[85] Legba is often depicted as an old man, with a satchel on his back, and a pipe in his mouth. A key is another of these symbols, which is why it is also sometimes depicted as Saint Peter. Another rada lwa, very popular and particularly benevolent, is Danbala, a source of peace and tranquility, often depicted as a snake, and whose symbol is white. He has two wives: Aida-Ouèdo represented by the rainbow sky, and Erzulie, the spirit that symbolizes beauty, glamor, art, and sensuality.

Probably the second most popular voodoo spirit, Aida Ouèdo is often depicted as the Virgin Mary. Her favorite colors are pink and blue. We should also mention, among the important spirits of the Rada family, Ogun Feray, blacksmith and warrior lwa, the equivalent of the Greek Zeus. It is believed to have inspired the idea

---

[84] Melville Herskovits, life in a Haitian Valley (Princeton: Markus Wiener Publishers, 2012), 149-150

[85] Hurbon, "Voodoo: Search for the Spirit", 72

of independence for slaves. He is depicted as Saint-Jacques-le-Majeur, or that of St. Patrick driving the snakes from Ireland. His symbols are the sword and the color red.[86]

Petro Lwa

Unlike Rada *lwa* of African origin, some spirits (*lwa*) are native spirits, born in Haiti in the context of slavery and resistance to oppression. This contextualization is important to understand the violent and dangerous character usually attributed to Petro *lwa*. The main rite Rada spirits have their alter ego in the petro rite, but the latter, instead of being caring and reliable, are often evil, uncontrollable, and involve black magic. According to Scheu, these *lwas* "are easily agitated, quicker to actions, and in some cases, are more dangerous to deal with regarding magical work and outcomes."[87]

The Vodouist would take a huge risk to invoke them or to use them to obtain favor. This is why 95% of Vodou rituals are Rada and only 5% are likely to flirt with the Petro *lwa*. Nevertheless, it is often through imagery and practices under the Petro rite that the Haitian Vodou is portrayed to the outside world by its detractors.[88]

The most well-known spirit of Petro *lwa* is Baron Samedi, the spirit of death, the master of cemeteries. His symbols are the top hat shape and the black and purple colors. He is the leader of the Gede, gruesome and salacious minds as symbols with a black cross, a

---

[86] Hurbon, "Voodoo: Search for the Spirit", 75-77

[87] Scheu, *"Serving the Spirits"*, 159

[88] Bartkowski, John P. "Claims-Making and Typifications of Voodoo as a Deviant Religion : Hex, Lies, and Videotape." Journal For The Scientific Study Of Religion 37, no. 4 (December 1, 1998): 559-579. ATLA Religion Database with ATLASerials, EBSCOhost (accessed November 23, 2014).

corpse, and the same colors as their master Baron Samedi. Kalfou, in Petro lwa, is the counterpart of Legba. It controls the cross-roads, to signify symbolically it controls the forces of evil, black magic, and witchcraft.[89]

The Jesus Question

One of the main points of contention in Haitian Christianity and Vodou is the Jesus question. How does the Vodouist see Jesus? Is He God, or is He only a good man who was unjustly condemned and nailed on the cross? In his book *Must God Remain Greek?*, Robert Hood argues, "It is not the Christian God who causes problems for Afro cultures, it is the Christian Christ."[90]

While in some ATRs Jesus is seen as nganga (ganga, medicine man), a Great Ancestor, or a big brother. In Haiti, Jesus has lost the elder brother title. Although in some Vodou families, Jesus is called upon before a ceremony, for some Vodouists, Jesus is seen as the Great Ancestor instead of the Messiah figure. For others, He is the mediator between Gran Mèt la and the lwa. Since most Vodouists are also Catholics or Protestants, it's impossible that on the one hand, they don't know who Jesus is, but on the other hand, they don't know how to fit Him into their theology. The iconic *rasin* group Boukman Eksperyans prays to Jesus for deliverance in their song *Pèpèyè,*

Jezu, o Jezu o, Jezu, o Jezu o,
Wa ban mwen fòs

---

[89] Hurbon, *Voodoo: Search for the Spirits"*, 78-80
[90] Hood, Robert. *Must God Remain Greek?: Afro Cultures and God-Talk* (Minneapolis: Fortress Press, 1990),
p. 145.

Retire ponya nan do mwen

Jesus, oh Jesus oh, oh Jesus oh
Give me strength
Take this spell off my back

The Catholic church in Haiti believes that Jesus Christ is truly God and the Second Person of the Trinity, but its teaching is not always clear. Jesus is mostly known to the Haitians as the Son of Mary. In some Haitian Vodou circles, the cross is a sign of weakness. Jesus cannot be like God because He let Himself be crucified. A god can't be that weak. So for some Vodou adherents, Jesus can't be compared to God.

Spirit Possession

Being possessed by spirits in Haitian Vodou is no different from what happens in other cultures and religions. Dr. Lamarque Douyon took a psychiatric approach to spirit possession in Vodou when he wrote in his essay *Vodou en Haiti: La crise de possession,*

> La crise de possession est un Syndrome clinique caractérisé par une hyper excitation psychomotrice, précédée généralement par une phase d'hyperventilation et suivie par un état d'abattement ou même de coma passager, avec parfois révulsion des globes oculaires et affectant un individu considéré comme normal par son groupe culturel.[91]

> Possession crisis is a clinical syndrome characterized by psychomotor hyperexcitation, generally preceded by a phase of

---

[91] Lamarque Douyon, *Vodou en Haiti: La crise de possession,* in Etudes, Tome 365, no.6, Décembre 1986, 631

hyperventilation and followed by a state of dejection or even temporary coma, sometimes with revulsion of the eyeballs and affecting an individual considered normal by his cultural group.

As Alfred Metraux rightly points out, "The number of people subject to possession is too large for all of them to be labeled hysterics unless the whole population of Haiti is to be regarded as prone to mental disorders."[92]

For the practitioners of Vodou, possession or being mounted by the *lwa* is the ultimate experience. While Vodou detractors tend to associate it with hysteria, mental disorder, or demons, it is nevertheless the main line of communication between the Vodouist and the spirits.

Animist and Syncretic Religion?

Is Vodou an animist and syncretic religion as some people, including some Vodouists, have claimed? Who borrowed from whom? And aren't all religions syncretic? The juxtaposition of Catholic saints and ritual calendar in Vodou is only a smokescreen, a façade. In analyzing this claim, one needs to remember that Vodou is not a uniform religion. It is as different in various parts of the country as two mangos from the same tree. It's not surprising if a family focuses on honoring its ancestors.

In Haitian Vodou, there is a subtle difference between honor and worship. While worshiping ancestors may be true for some versions of African traditional religion, Haitian Vodou is not in that

---

[92] Metraux, "*Voodoo in Haiti*", 135

sense ancestor worship. It's similar to what some people do in the West.

Americans have a habit of visiting their dead at the cemetery, they bring fresh flowers, and they spend hours talking to them. When a loved one dies, it's common to hear Christians in the United States say, "he/she is looking down on us" or his/her spirit is with us. For some, the dead are their guardian angels. Others are pretty sure the spirit of their loved ones is nearby. Should we conclude that Americans worship their dead and ancestors?

For a Few Dollars More

One of the main points of interest of travelers to Haiti is to see with their own eyes the "exotic Vodou dances and ceremonies". For a few dollars more, charlatans and tourist guides looking to make a quick buck can produce various staged ceremonies with all the bells and whistles, leading the unaware foreigner to be easily duped into believing that he/she is assisting a genuine Vodou ceremony. This uninformed traveler then goes home to write books and articles about the "mysterious" religion of the Haitians.

As with anything relating to Haitian culture, a word of caution is in order here. Those haphazard ceremonies are for the most part tourist attractions which started back in 1949[93], a practice that has profaned the core Vodou practices for a few U.S. dollars.

---

[93] According to Bernard Dietrich, in 1949, a campaign to attract tourists to Haiti turned Vodou into a show. Dietrich, *"The Asson and the Cross"*, 262-263

Is Vodou Satanic?

Detractors and critics of Vodou always point to some ceremonial aspects of Vodou to insist that it's evil and satanic. For instance, in his book *Caractère, Culture, Vodou,* Rodolphe Derose claims, "Vodou...is the cult of the dreaded *Iwa,* particularly those of the Pethro rites... These *Iwa* are satanic."[94] While religion can provide comfort and healing to those in need, it can also be exploitative, controlling, and dangerous in the wrong hands.

As with any belief system, some Vodou adherents can manipulate a religious system and use it for evil. It's more a human problem than a religious one.

The Southern Baptist Convention in the U.S. has a major issue with sexual abuse in their churches. Known cases of abuse by church leaders total more than 700 and counting. Isn't it evil when priests and pastors are constantly sexually abusing young boys and girls who trust them as their spiritual fathers? Isn't it evil when church leaders steal church funds for drugs and sexually immoral activities?

For centuries Catholic nuns and priests all over Haiti have engaged in the sexual assault and abuse of young girls and boys who are in their care. So, like Christianity has her evil priests and pastors, so does Vodou.

Crimes and sacrifices allegedly committed during Vodou ceremonies are, for the most part, narratives of Western critics. When white people commit outrageous crimes, it is brushed off by

[94] Rodolphe Dérose, *Caractère, culture, vodou: formation et interprétation de l'individualité Haitienne* (Port-au-Prince, 1955), https://ufdc.ufl.edu/UF00078462/00001/4x, 125.

other white people as mental illness. Jason Alan Thornburg of Texas did not need a Vodou ceremony to kill three people because he believed he had "an in-depth knowledge of the bible and believed he was being called [by God] to commit sacrifices."[95] James David Russell of Idaho was not doing a Vodou ceremony when he killed David Flagett, mutilated his body, and ate, among others, parts of his testicles.[96] Was Matthew Taylor Coleman of California considered primitive when he killed his two kids because his interpretation of visions, signs, and Bible numerology pointed to the kids growing into monsters?[97]

If the same crimes were committed in Haiti, the headline all over the Western world would be, "Savage and barbaric people of Haiti make human sacrifices to their voodoo god". It was the same accusation Dessalines got when he ordered the killing of the remaining whites after independence. Western critics say that it was barbaric. But aren't atrocities done by Western militaries always portrayed as collateral damage and costs of war?

While one can question the morality of the killings after Haiti's independence, how was it any different from when the U.S. Marines killed more than 15,000 Haitians during the occupation?

---

[95] Jerry Lambe, "*Texas Man Already Accused of Killing Three Is Indicted for Allegedly 'Slicing' Roommate's Throat, Blowing Up House*", https://lawandcrime.com/crime/texas-man-already-accused-of-killing-three-is-indicted-for-allegedly-slicing-roommates-throat-blowing-up-house/

[96] Gina Tron, "Accused Cannibal Who Allegedly Microwaved Elderly Man's Body Parts Fit To Stand Trial", https://www.yahoo.com/entertainment/accused-cannibal-allegedly-microwaved-elderly-214913846.html

[97] Steve Helling, "*Matthew Coleman's Wife Says He Got 'Significantly More Paranoid' While Researching QAnon Before Child Murders*", https://people.com/crime/matthew-colemans-wife-said-he-got-significantly-more-paranoid-while-researching-qanon-before-child-murders/

Are Haitians more brutal than the French Colons who used gallows, furnaces, and other forms of torture on the slaves? Are Haitian Vodouists more cruel than Western Christians who burnt Makandal at the stake, cut Boukman's head and put it on a stick, and nailed Charlemagne Peralte to a door and left his body rotten in 90° temperature for three days?

The Myth of a Satanic Pact

After the 2010 earthquake in Haiti, religious zealots jumped at the opportunity to renew their attack on Haiti and Vodou.

Joseph Conley, former director of the West Indies Mission agency (WIM), said: "In 1791 Haiti had been dedicated to Satan, while in 1991, President Aristide rededicated the country to voodooism –a fact that may help explain modern Haiti's anguish as the most impoverished nation in the Western Hemisphere."[98]

Marc Mailloux, an American evangelist of French descent who teaches at the Institut Biblique et Théologique de la Floride, had this to say:

> Haiti traces the origin of its very independence from France to a gathering of voodoo priests— the infamous Cérémonie du Bois Caiman of August 1791 when the country was consecrated to the "enemy of the French God," i.e. Satan! Lest the reader think that this is merely a quaint historical anecdote, know that this diabolical ceremony is repeated regularly by voodoo practitioners in Haiti who

---

[98] Conley Joseph L., *Drumbeats that Changed the World* (Pasadena: William Carey Library, 2000),197

remain legion. One does not thumb his nose at the Almighty with impunity.[99]

Chavannes Jeune, a prominent pastor and former president of one of the largest Baptist denominations in Haiti (MEBSH), as well as a former presidential candidate, clearly believes that Haiti's social, political, and economic problems are tied to the pact of a Vodou priest made with the devil. Jeune argues that the only way out is to retake the country back from the devil and dedicate her to Christ.[100]

Stacey Ayars tells how students and staff prayed to prevent a "renewal with the demon of Bois Caiman" in a fundraising piece written on behalf of Emmaus University in Haiti. In her article, *Even The Pig Did Not Die*, she writes, "Last year's pact with Satan had been totally ruined, and so many politicians and witch doctors were motivated to renew the pact and start again...When the 14th came and we were all praying and fasting, the days arrived for their ceremonies and it was complete and utter chaos."[101]

Conley, Mailloux, Jeune, and Ayars point to the ceremony that Boukman, a Jamaican-born runaway slave, organized in the middle of a forest near the plantation of Lenormand de Mezy at Bois

---

[99] See, Marc Mailloux, "*Haiti vs. Israel*" in *Haiti and Israel: A Study in Contrasts,* accessed 10/5//2020, http://darrowmillerandfriends.com/2014/07/21/haiti-israel-study-in-contrasts/

[100] Barrick, Michael. 2005. Evangelical Leader to Seek Haitian Presidency: Chavannes Jeune looking to reverse 200 years of corruption and poverty. Lincoln Tribune. August 6. Available online:
http://chavannesjeune.blogspot.com/2005_09_13_archive.html

[101] Stacey Ayars "*even the pig did not die*", December 8, 2020
https://emmaus.edu.ht/even-the-pig-did-not-die/

Caïman in 1791. Boukman, they argue, was a Vodou priest (ougan) who presided over a sort of orgy and sacrifices to Satan. Who was the "French God" that Mailloux points out? If there is one God and He is white and French as Mailloux argues, then is God a white racist?

Since the slaves were successfully free, is he saying that Satan won? Can anything good come from the devil? Are these pundits saying that slavery was a gift from God while freedom is from the devil? Could it be that their belief is tainted by racism, religious fanaticism, and a distorted picture of God? It's hard to believe that, as of this writing, some Haitians are still students of Mailloux in Florida.

When the Indian Ocean Tsunami killed over a quarter of a million people back in December 2004, what was their deal with the devil? Are natural disasters, such as the Bangladesh floods of 1991, Hurricane Katrina in 2005, or the Ethiopian drought of 1984, part of God's judgment on the people and countries affected?

Luke 13:1 is an obvious rebuttal to this picture of God, yet, some influential religious leaders would have us believe that natural disasters and misfortunes are a result of God's judgment.

Scapegoating Vodou to explain Haiti's woes is a Western tactic to undermine one of the most remarkable stories of liberation in the history of mankind. In his essay, *Haiti's Pact With The Devil (Some Haitians Believe This Too)*, cultural anthropologist Bertin M. Louis Jr. explains the problem with scapegoating Vodou:

> This radical, revisionist view of Haitian history reveals more about Haitian Protestant views NL with regard to Vodou than it does about why Haiti is so poor, or why Haiti was devastated by an earthquake.

The enduring practice of Vodou, in the view of some Haitian Protestants, is the reason why Haiti is so poor, why its economy is in shambles, and why God chose to "punish" the island and its people with an earthquake. In other words, Vodou is the same as worshiping *dyab* (the Devil). Some Haitian Protestants who hold this view choose to scapegoat Vodou instead of looking at other parts of Haitian history to explain Haiti's current misery.[102]

Boukman's secret gathering was nothing new. Throughout the Americas, secret prayer meetings were always part of the weapons slaves used in their fight for freedom. Let's take a look at the prayer that Boukman allegedly prayed during the ceremony. In his book, *The Black Jacobins*, C.L.R. James quotes the words of Boukman at Bois Caïman:

The god who created the sun which gives us light, who rouses the waves and rules the storm, though hidden in the clouds, he watches us. He sees all that the white man does. The god of the white man inspires us with crime, but our god calls upon us to do good works. Our god who is good to us orders us to revenge our wrongs. He will direct our arms and aid us. Throw away the symbol of the god of the whites who has caused us to weep, and listen to the voices of liberty, which speaks in the hearts of us all.[103]

Is there anything satanic in this particular prayer? Boukman, like the colonizers, may have had a polluted picture of God, but I have a hard time believing that his prayers were addressed to Satan. Was

---

[102] Bertin M. Louis, Jr., "*Haiti's pact with the devil? (Some Haitians Believe this too)*", accessed 1/15/2020. https://tif.ssrc.org/2010/02/18/haitis-pact-with-the-devil-some-haitians-believe-this-too/

[103] C.L.R. James, *The Black Jacobins* (New York: Random House, Inc, 1963) p. 87.

Boukman's longing for freedom worse than the founding fathers of the United States whose claims of manifest destiny led them to annihilate the indigenous people?

Some people point to the slaughtering of the pig and the drinking of its blood to argue that the ceremony was satanic. I beg to differ. I believe that the ceremony was much more a swearing-in and a bond-building ritual. Regardless of the elements of the ritual, wouldn't you say that the God of Boukman is the same as the One in the Bible? Don't you think Boukman sounds more like Moses in Exodus 15 and David in his writings in Psalms 37, 54, 69, and 109?

For example, in Psalm 10, David writes,

> But you see the trouble and grief they [the wicked] cause.
> You take note of it and punish them.
> The helpless put their trust in you.
> You defend the orphans.
> Break the arms of these wicked, evil people!
> Go after them until the last one is destroyed.
> The Lord is king forever and ever!
> The godless nations will vanish from the land.
> Lord, you know the hopes of the helpless.
> Surely you will hear their cries and comfort them.
> You will bring justice to the orphans and the oppressed,
> so mere people can no longer terrify them.

Did you find any similarities with those prayers? Both David and Boukman wanted their God to go after their oppressors. Their prayers were a cry for justice and freedom. Consequently, their picture of God was tainted with their worldview and the situation at hand. Again in Psalm 137, David writes:

> O Babylon, you will be destroyed.

Happy is the one who pays you back
for what you have done to us.
Happy is the one who takes your babies
and smashes them against the rocks

It's clear that David's theology, in these verses, does not reflect nor paint an accurate picture of God's character. But this is where he was. With limited knowledge and limited revelation, this is what he understood. He was just being honest, and God was okay with that. When we call on God to destroy the wicked and our enemies, our prayers are no different than Boukman's. Like Moses and David, Boukman's theology was a hermeneutics of liberation and freedom that is more aligned with the heart of God. Boukman understood that the heart of God is lined up with the oppressed and the captives, and he was asking God to liberate them from their oppressors as he did for Israel from the Egyptians. Judging from Boukman's prayer, isn't it safe to say that he was probably the first liberation theologian of the so-called New World?

So, by blaming Haiti's natural disasters, and social and economic problems on a pact with the devil, some critics are suggesting that Haiti was better off under slavery and colonial rule. Sad!

In an opinion piece for the New York Times, Mark Danner argues, "Haiti's harms have been caused by men, not demons."[104] As the National Catholic Reporter puts it, "There was no "pact with the devil"...The only devilish element in the Haitian mix might be the domination and manipulation of the nation and its populations

---

[104] Mark Danner, "*To Heal Haiti, Look to History, Not Nature*", accessed 2/2/2020. https://www.nytimes.com/2010/01/22/opinion/22danner.html?ref=opinion&pagewanted=all

over centuries by world powers serving their own needs."[105] If there ever was a pact with the devil, it was Christianity who made the deal. When Constantine, with the Edict of Milan in 313 AD, offered the church protection, power, and wealth, they took the bait, and this fusion of the sword and the cross was the beginning of a pact with the devil.

In the case of Haiti, it was Christopher Columbus who made the pact when he planted the Spanish flag and a cross at Mole St Nicholas side by side in 1492.

Vodou: Progress-Resistant Religion?

Some people believe that Vodou is a progress-resistant religion, but, is it really? Is Vodou the cause of suffering among Haitians?

In his book, *Haiti: The Tumultuous History - From Pearl of the Caribbean to Broken Nation*, Philippe Girard argues that it might be when he wrote, "Voodoo hinders Haitian's entrepreneurial spirit by portraying godly intercession, not human activism, as the most important efficient method of human betterment."[106]

In a piece he wrote for the New York Times, David Brooks contended that Haiti suffered from "a complex web of progress-resistant cultural influences," including "the voodoo religion, which spreads the message that life is capricious and planning futile."[107]

---

[105] *"The history that created Haiti"*, NCR Editorial Staff, accessed 11/18/2020, National Catholic Reporter, https://www.ncronline.org/news/history-created-haiti

[106] Philippe Girard. *Haiti: The Tumultuous History - From Pearl of the caribbean to Broken Nation* (New York: Palgrave macmillan, 2010), 33

[107] Cited in Ramsey Kate, *The Spirits and the Law: Vodou and Power in Haiti* (University of Chicago Press. Kindle Edition.), 21

Lawrence Harrison, in an article he wrote for the Wall Street Journal, argues that Haiti had "defied all development prescriptions" because its "culture is powerfully influenced by its religion, voodoo," which he described as devoid of "ethical content."[108]

I am always concerned about foreigners who claim to be experts on Haiti. Those who, when given the opportunity, don't hesitate to share their expertise on the root causes of Haiti's woes. They set up shop online through their blogs, and they pen books and articles based on the writings of other bloggers like them.

Take, for instance, Ghanaian blogger Chris Ampadu, a self-acclaimed expert who probably speaks neither French nor Haitian Creole, and has neither set foot in Haiti nor has a direct relationship with local Haitians or even with those abroad, but who in a post suggests, "The roots of the poverty and suffering in Haiti go much deeper than economic and political causes. Haiti's people suffer the harvest sown from Voodoo and its lies."[109] As if he was so sure of himself, Ampadu continues, "Ignorance, illiteracy, a defeatist self-image, and the largely untapped state of human resources are also the fruit of Voodoo's lies. Few people are highly skilled, and those with skills are often unwilling to work hard."[110] In other words, Ampadu assumes that Haitians are poor because they are uneducated, lazy, and Vodouisants.

---

[108] Ibid

[109] Chris Ampadu, "Voodoo: An African Perspective on Haiti's Poverty", accessed 12/20/20, http://darrowmillerandfriends.com/2010/09/23/voodoo-an-african-perspective-on-haitis-poverty/

[110] Ibid.

I have to disagree. Ampadu probably believes the big lie of the popular "wealth gospel" in some Protestant circles, the gospel that suggests that one's material prosperity goes hand in hand with his/her spiritual maturity. There are a lot of countries that are considered Christians but poor, and there are other non-Christian countries that are doing well. The Democratic Republic of Congo, Liberia, and the Central African Republic are among the poorest in Africa although 95% of the population are Christians.

Ampadu failed to see that ignorance is when the well-to-do and evangelical Christians, play god in the lives of the poor. The thought that it's the poor who need to change is a point that people who have a religious superiority complex want to always emphasize.

Scapegoating Vodou is embedded in racism and cultural superiority. While religion can be an obstacle to progress, some very successful Haitian entrepreneurs and scholars are Vodouists. Haitians, in general, are very entrepreneurial. They don't wait for the *Iwa* to tell them to plow their fields and to put their seeds in the ground. Given the opportunity, they would start a business, go to school, and be their best. The fact that the bulk of the Haitian economy is made up of individual businesses in the informal sector is proof that Vodou has nothing to do with the state of Haiti.

Benjamin Hebblethwaite, a scholar who has done extensive research on Vodou, agrees, "In reality, Vodou practitioners enhance progress in their attention to the planning and giving of ceremonies, in the hierarchical organization they establish in communities, in their ritual and language, and in the education imparted through inheritance, teaching, and initiation."[111]

While I agree that religion can influence Haitian thought, opportunity matters. It's well-known that the Haitians carry their religion abroad, but they make the most of the opportunities they are given in their adopted countries. There are a lot of Haitian Vodouists who are highly educated, and there are many successful Haitian entrepreneurs in the diaspora. Haitians would fare much better at home if the U.S. and other powers stopped crushing her for the last 150 years. After all, it is outside influences and policies, especially U. S. policies toward Haiti, that are, in my view, the biggest progress-resistant in Haiti.

If a religion is progress-resistant in Haiti, it's Protestantism. The Protestants sit around waiting for God to do something, like Estragon and Vladimir in Samuel Beckett's *Waiting for Godot,* or, like Pozzo, they are too blind to see that God has been here a while, and He is actively doing.

---

[111] Hebblethwaite, Benjamin. "The Scapegoating of Haitian Vodou Religion: David Brooks's (2010) Claim That "Voodoo" Is a "Progress-Resistant" Cultural Influence." Journal of Black Studies 46, no. 1 (2015): 3-22. Accessed January 1, 2021. http://www.jstor.org/stable/24572926.

CHAPTER 4

Protestantism in Haiti

"Ou pa ka sèvi Bondye yon pye anndan, yon pye deyò."

(You cannot serve God one foot in one foot out.)
(Popular saying in Haitian churches)

It is true that the Protestant faithful are self-important and their egos are enormous. This stems from training that inculcates the idea that to know Scripture is to possess True knowledge, which leads to their use of the intellect to learn Biblical verses by heart only to prove their superiority.

(Aunt Tansia) in Mimerose Beaubrun's "Nan Dòmi"

Many Christians have been imagining the wrong story concerning God and His people...that story very rarely produces actual follower

Todd Hunter

God in the Protestant Churches

On the wall behind the altar of a Baptist church where my dad served, he inscribed in big red letters: "The Lord is in his holy temple; let all the earth be silent before him (Hab 2:20)." And on a side wall, the verse was "Prepare to meet your God (Am 4:12)". The Church of God down the street had "It is a dreadful thing to fall into the hands of the living God (Heb 10:31)." Another local church in the area had on their wall, "Our God is a consuming fire (Heb 12:29)."

The walls of many Haitian evangelical churches are filled with similar Bible slogans that are aligned with their fear-based theology. The songs they sing, *"Kè mwen boulvèse anba kolè Bondye"*[112] (My heart is tormented under God's wrath), *"Tous les flots de ta colère, sur moi, Seigneur, ont passé."*[113] (All the waves of your anger have passed over me, O Lord.), and the sermons they preach *"Si w mete Bondye an kolè, ou pa gen anyen k ap mache"*[114] (If you make God angry, nothing will work for you); all express their mental image of a dreadful God.

Although *"Bondye bon"* (God is good) is the most expressed attribute of God by Haitians, their mental picture of God is a God of terror, rage, destruction, anger, and vengefulness. No wonder Haitian Protestants are torn when it comes to reconciling a warrior God and a peace-making Jesus or reconciling a vengeful God with a turn-the-other-cheek Jesus.

---

[112] See Révéillons-Nous, No. 21

[113] See Les Chants d'Espérance, No. 172

[114] From a sermon during IPN (Intercessory Prayer Network) daily prayer network meeting on 09/10/2013

If our mental picture of God determines our relationship with him, then the popular view of God as a stern judge is drowning Haitian Protestants in fear. The consequence of this is the Protestants, so afraid of punishment, that they are constantly begging God for forgiveness. It also produces a Protestant so terrified by irrational fears that they call *Bondye bon* to appease his wrath. They believe that God is love but they also know that *kolè Bondye se dife* (God's anger is fire). As such, they are terrified of his tongue-spitting fire. If Jesus is the image of who God is (Col 1:15) and the total revelation of God to us (Heb 1:1-3), why is it so hard for Haitian Protestants to believe?

Unbelieving Believers

Haitian Protestants have a hard time believing that God can love them for free. They wrestle to trust God's love for them in their struggle to reconcile what they hear during Sunday morning sermons and their day-to-day lives. Haitian Protestants can recite all the Psalms in the Bible and sing all the songs in their *Chants d'Espérances* by heart, but their daily life does not mirror their beliefs.

One of my cousins was about 14 years old when he recited a verse in all of the 66 books of the Bible during Vacation Bible School. While memorizing verses and songs is a great accomplishment, it is simply a religious exercise if you don't believe what you're memorizing. Being free from condemnation (Rom 8:1) and knowing they are righteous, holy, and blameless in Christ becomes simple intellectual knowledge for the one who does not believe what they know. The problem with unbelieving believers is not a lack of belief but a lack of trust.

Protestant *Wangatè* (Witchdoctors)

The majority of Haitian Protestants, especially the Pentecostal stream, seem to view God as some great witch doctor. They accuse Catholics and Vodouists of practicing witchcraft and magic while they're doing the same thing in Jesus' name.

In some churches in Haiti and the diaspora, being at a gathering of Haitian Protestants feels like being at the *bòkò's* temple. Spiritual leaders use formula-based prayers, words, and verses as if they were magical potions. They believe if they repeat a verse three times, say "Jesus, Jesus, Jesus", constantly clap their hands, stomp the ground, and pray lying on sackcloth, then God will give them the desire of their hearts. If they do the right supernatural ritual like walking around their house seven times, then they will certainly crush the enemy.

In their quest for deliverance from their circumstances, the Protestants look to God as if He were their *bòkò*. Unfortunately, when their requests are denied, they blame their lack of faith, and they accuse God of being unfair.

The popular Haitian Prosperity Gospel pastor, Gregory Toussaint, preached several sermons on miraculous prayers. An example is *"Priyè Pou Demantibile Miray Jeriko"* [Prayer for Crushing Jericho's Wall]. For Toussaint and other preachers like him, God is so hard to reach that the only way He will hear you is if you buy their a la carte books of formulaic prayers. In his book *365 Spiritual Warfare Prayers,* Toussaint has a pre-packaged prayer for every foreseen circumstance in the believer's life. Here is a sample:

Prayer against instability: "I condemn every hellish power trying to manipulate my destiny in Jesus' name."[115]

Prayer for children: "May every object that represents my child in the invisible realm catch fire in the name of Jesus!"[116]

When we talk to our earthly fathers, we don't use fancy words and formulaic sentences. Yet, we call God our Father, but we need somebody else to tell us how and when we should talk to our Daddy. Is prayer a magical formula to get what you want from God or a conversation with Him?

I believe in the influential power of prayer, but I deny that God can be manipulated by some rituals, words, and human techniques.

Taking a page from the Prosperity Gospel, Health-and-Wealth, Word-Faith, and the Name it and Claim it gospel, some Haitian preachers and religious charlatans take advantage of the desperate state of their adherents to rob them of their money and to take total control over their thoughts and actions.

In his article *Les prophètes s'enrichissent, les fidèles deviennent plus pauvres « au nom de Jésus »,* Georges Harry Rouzier paints a fascinating picture of some evangelical leaders who prey on their unsuspecting flock. One such predator told Rouzier that he was mounted by a spirit named Cherubin. "This spirit manifests itself during Sunday services to miraculously describe sick people whose presence he feels in the assembly,"[117] according to this pastor.

---

[115] Gregory Toussaint, *365 Spiritual Warfare Prayer* (Kindle Edition, 2023) p 349

[116] Ibid, 128

[117] Georges Harry Rouzier, *"Les prophètes s'enrichissent, les fidèles deviennent plus pauvres « au nom de Jésus »"*, accessed 10/3/2020.

The Bible warns us against diviners (Mat 7:15, Mat 24:24, 2 Tim 4:3-4), but you would not know this with the way they are so popular in Haiti and abroad.

God Told Me

Modern-day "prophets" have a major influence in some Protestant churches in Haiti and the diaspora. They are the ones who use the magical phrase "God told me" to convince their followers of their divine authority. You will find these so-called prophets on YouTube, Facebook, and other online resources, insisting that *Bondye di m di w* (God tells me to tell you) and *Bondye ban m yon komisyon pou ou* (God gives me a word for you). While these imposters accuse others of using God's name in vain, they intentionally use the "God told me" card to manipulate their followers into believing that they hear directly from God and that they are more spiritual than other people in their congregations.

One of many self-appointed prophets of the "God told me" movement, Bishop Joel Jeune claims in a book he wrote called, *I Sneezed in My Casket*, that most of the time, God talks to him in the shower. He is sure that he was taking a bath when God showed him "a revelation about overthrowing the kingdom of Satan by breaking the Voodoo curse over Haiti."[118]

These preachers use verse-lifting techniques by cherry-picking the Bible to deceive their followers. This is one of the reasons the Pentecostal church is the fastest-growing denomination in Haiti.

---

https://ayibopost.com/photos-les-prophetes-senrichissent-les-fideles-deviennent-plus-pauvres-au-nom-de-jesus/

[118] Joel R. Jeune, *I Sneezed in My Casket!: For God Cannot Lie* (Xlibris, 2012), 101.

Unfortunately, these religious psychics have a crowd of followers who blindly trust these vipers instead of Christ. The poorer the Pentecostal, the more likely he/she will fall victim to these religious imposters.

Real prophets such as Micah and Jeremiah have warned against these fortune-tellers in their money-making ministry. Like the *bòkò*, they lie for money because there is a market for it. There can never be any hope for the betterment of the Haitian people with these religious leeches inside the church. Carter Woodson understood this phenomenon well when he argued,

In the church where we have much freedom and independence, we must get rid of preachers who are not prepared to help the people whom they exploit. The public must refuse to support men of this type. Ministers who are the creations of the old educational system must be awakened, and if this is impossible they must be dethroned. Those who keep the people in ignorance and play upon their emotions must be exiled. The people have never been taught what religion is, for most of the preachers find it easier to stimulate the superstition which develops in the unenlightened mind. Religion in such hands, then, becomes something with which you take advantage of weak people. Why try to enlighten the people in such matters when superstition serves just as well for exploitation?[119]

---

[119] Woodson, "*The Mis-Education of the Negro*", 68

Finger-Searching Verses

Finger-searching verses is another magical trick used by some Haitian pastors. The formula goes like this: close your eyes, open the Bible, and put a finger on a page. The verse where the tip of your finger lands, that's what God is telling you. The following stories illustrate how ridiculous this practice is.

A Haitian pastor in Canada was celebrating a wedding. When it was time for him to say a word of encouragement to the couple, he closed his eyes, opened his Bible, and placed his fingers on a page. His fingers landed on Luke 23:34 (Father, forgive them; for they do not know what they are doing). Upon hearing the pastor, the groom took his bride and walked out of the church.

Bishop Joel Jeune tells another story of a pastor from his church who had a habit of doing the same thing when seeking God's directive for his life. The pastor was contemplating suicide and decided to ask God for advice. Going to the motions, his finger landed on Mat. 27:5 (So Judas threw the money into the temple and left. Then he went away and hanged himself). The pastor panicked (Haitians don't kill themselves), and then he repeated the magic formula. This time he landed on John 13:27 ("What you are about to do, do quickly."). He concluded that God really wanted him to kill himself. Still, he wouldn't do it. He explained his dilemma to another pastor who convinced him of his irrational divination technique.[120]

---

[120] Jeune, "I Sneezed in My Casket!: For God Cannot Lie", 154-155

Sin and Sin

Judging others by pointing out their sins is one of the greatest attributions of Haitian Protestants. Some of them think they are doing God a favor by pointing out the sins of others. So, phrases, such as, *"intel tonbe nan peche*[121] (fall from grace), *"w ap neye nan peche"* (deep in sin), or *"w ap viv nan peche"* (living a sinful life), are used to describe someone who committed some type of sexual sin. I, once, heard a pastor say that every time we sin we nail Jesus on the cross again. Ouch! Later in his sermon, he claimed, "Any sin you fail to acknowledge and confess before God after you became a believer will automatically be recorded against you."[122] In other words, God only forgives pre-conversion sin. This teaching reminds me of this Haitian saying *"Kreyon Bondye pa gen efaswa"*. [God's pencil has no eraser].

One of the dominant beliefs in Haitian Protestantism is that God deals with us according to the nature of our sins. For some Christians, the more reprehensible a sin is, the harsher the punishment. Although in Psalm 103:10 the psalmist says that God "does not treat us as our sin deserves", the tainted image of a vindictive God still persists in the minds of some Christians. This is why when something bad happens in someone's life, they say *"Se Bondye k ap kale l, ou byen se Bondye ka p fè l peye sa l fè"* (God is punishing him/her).

---

[121] Used most of the time for a Protestant woman who got pregnant out of wedlock. The "guilty" man usually gets a pass, but will be forced, in most cases, to marry the woman.

[122] Sermon preached during an IPN (Intercessory Prayer Network) meeting on 11/10/2014.

Of course, there are consequences for our bad decisions and actions, but we must not blame God for giving out the punishment. I often hear in Christian circles things like, *"Jistis Bondye se kabwèt bèf"* (God's justice is like a cart being pulled by an ox), meaning God's justice may be slow, but it will come sooner or later. It's no wonder that Haitian Protestants are obsessed with a vengeful God. And this obsession keeps them from loving and serving their neighbor.

Haitian Protestants tend to judge sin on a sliding scale. Some are socially more acceptable, and others are morally wrong. They regard other people's sins as worse than theirs, therefore it is easier for them to rank and condemn others to hell. For most Protestants, sin is what other people do.

For Previlus, one of the main characters in Edris St Amand's novel *Bon Dieu Rit*, it's either you're a Protestant or a child of the devil. He learned from Pastor Henry that, *"Le péché ça c'est pour ceux qui sont dans la religion catholique...Tous les catholiques ne sont-ils pas d'avance des damnés? Ils ont le droit d'offrir des services, de faire des ouangas, en même temps qu'ils vont à l'église et communient."*[123] (Sin is for those who are in the Catholic religion...Aren't all Catholics already damned? They have the right to offer services, do witchcraft, and at the same time, go to church and receive communion.)

Most Haitian evangelicals suffer from what Dr. Samuel Perry called "sexual exceptionalism" which is ranking sexual sin as worse than others. People who commit sexual sins such as fornication, masturbation, adultery, divorce, and remarriage, are certainly hell-

---

[123] Edris Saint-Amand, Bon Dieu Rit (Paris: Hatier, 1989), 24-25

bounded. Greed, gossip, and lying are not sins at all. In their Haitian Creole translation of the Westminster Shorter Catechism, the Reformed Presbyterian Church of Haiti asks:

K. *Èske tout vyolasyon lalwa yo abominab nan menm degre?*

R. *"Kèk peche nan yo menm menm, paske yo vin grav pou plizyè rezon, yo pi abominab devan je Bondye pase kèk lòt peche"*.[124] (Q. Are all transgressions of the law equally heinous? A. Some sins in themselves, and because of several aggravations, are more heinous in the sight of God than others.)

When we rank sin, we're hiding our sins by contrasting them to others. We're judging who is more righteous than others (James 4:12). As Jeremy Myers points out, "By classifying some sins as less forgivable than others, or some people as less worthy of our love and acceptance, we have forsaken the gospel and abandoned the message of life in Jesus Christ, and have replaced it with our unloving, judgmental condemnation of others."[125] Although the apostle Paul in Romans 2:1 warns about playing God, we still want to be the judge.

The *Tèt Mare* (Headscarves Cult)

Over the last twenty years, there has been an emergence of a special type of cult in Haitian Protestantism in the diaspora and Haiti. Not to be confused with the *Lame Selès* (Celestial Army) cult, the *Tèt Mare* are a growing number of women spiritual leaders who

---

[124] For more, see TI KATECHIS WESTMINSTER Avèk Pasaj Biblik, https://www.rpc-haiti.org/haitian-creole-reformed-resources

[125] Jeremy Myers, *Dying to Religion and Empire: Giving up Our Religious Rites and Legal Rights* (Close Your Church for Good Book 3) (Redeeming Press. Kindle Edition: 2018), 124.

choose to stay single, usually after a failed marriage, to dedicate the rest of their life to "serve God" (yo *ba Jezi ti rès la*). The *Tèt Mare* wear headscarves all the time and everywhere. They usually demand total obedience from their followers and twist some verses in scripture to keep their followers in line.

If you are part of this cult, you are defined by the mistakes of your past. The Tèt Mare will monitor the behavior of their followers so that there are no contradictions with their own lifestyle. Some have a network of daily intercessory prayers over the phone; a few have prophesied, but about past events; while others are dreamers whose dreams are, most of the time, "revelations" for other people.

Additionally, they have an exclusivist view: it's either you're serving God as they do or you're serving the devil. They not only deprive their followers of their free will, but in certain cases, the Tèt Mare are also the ones who decide for them, where they should live, what they should eat, and what they should wear.

Talking to the *Tèt Mare* doesn't feel like talking to a real human. As "super Christians", they always have some spiritual ending in their answers. A greeting conversation over the phone with a *Tèt Mare* would go like this:

- *Alo, bonjou* (Hello, good morning)
- *Bondye beni w, alo* (God bless you, hello)
- *Kouman w ye?* (How are you?)
- *Mwen byen ak Jezi* (I'm well with Jesus)
- *Kouman tout bagay ye pou ou?* (How is everything?)
- *M ap beni ak Jezi* ou byen *M ap benyen nan gras la.* (I'm blessed with Jesus or I'm swimming in the grace)

- *Enben, m ale. N a pale* (Well, I got to go, talk to you later)
- *Ke le san de Jezi kouvri w.* (Be covered by the blood of Jesus)

Other than their headscarves, these cult leaders are also known for their asceticism. They avoid any type of sexual relationship, and they do not wear pants because doing so attracts the devil. They don't wear makeup and jewelry because makeup and jewelry are satanic accessories.

For them, the design or drawing on a piece of furniture, the flowers on a dress, or the logo on a can of vegetables can be related to the devil.

A *Tèt Mare* does not watch TV shows such as The Mask Singers and Disney's animated movies because they are part of the devil's empire. If they could, the Tet Mare would only shop in Christian businesses that sell only "Jesus' products". They rebuke their followers for watching secular TV stations and for letting their kids watch cartoons and other Disney shows (Disney is the *dyab*).

Additionally, they use Bible verses, seduction, indoctrination, and intimidation techniques to demand loyalty from their followers. They claim to have a higher calling and a special power from God, so their followers defer to them for decisions affecting their lives.

Not long ago, I attended a Haitian church gathering in Minneapolis, Minnesota. During a call for prayers, the pastor called on a *Tèt Mare* to pray. "We're going to have a special prayer, he said, "and only sister X can pray that prayer because we need to feel the power of the Holy Spirit."

Apparently, for this group of people, prayer is a spiritual gift given to a privileged few. It is such erroneous beliefs that lead spiritual leaders to boldly claim the right to play god in the lives of others.

Unfortunately, instead of trusting in the work of the Holy Spirit in their lives, followers of the *Tèt Mare* let themselves be zombified into a religious cult. Instead of being transformed into the image of Christ (2 Cor 3:18), they take on the character of their cult leaders.

Reward Theology

Reward theology is a theological concept that is centered on the belief that God rewards individuals for their good deeds and righteous behavior in this life and/or the afterlife. Haitian Protestants believe that when they die and after judgment day, they will be rewarded for the good works they have done on earth. But the rewards are in the form of heavy jewelry that the eyes have never seen before. They believe the harder they work for the Lord, the bigger their reward will be.

I was once talking to a hardcore believer of this doctrine about getting some rest, and she told me that she is working for the Lord to get as many crowns as possible. She said it would be a glorious day when Jesus put at least five crowns on her head. Here is a summary of our conversation:

"You need to take a break from all these church activities," I said to her.

"No, there is still work to do, and I don't want to lose my crowns," she responded.

"Your crowns?" I said.

"Yes, if you're faithful in working for the Lord, you can get at least five."

Then I said, "You would finally get rid of your headscarves?" (She is a *Tèt Mare*).

She smiled and said, "Yes, it will be a glorious day when Jesus puts these crowns on my head."

"But I'm afraid these heavy jewelry pieces will break your neck", I countered.

"Don't worry. You too can be rewarded if you serve the Lord well.

Then, right there in the middle of our conversation, she began to sing:

Pouki moun palè kristal sa-a	For whom is this crystal palace
Se pou mwen ak Jezu-Kri,	It's for me and Jesus
Pouki moun fotèy an nò yo	For whom are the golden chairs
Se pou mwen ak rachte yo	They're for me and the redeemed

At this point, I could not tell her about metaphor, context, and literal interpretation of a text. I could not even mention to her that knowing and following Jesus is the reward she is seeking. I could not explain to her that Jesus is the crown of righteousness because He is our righteousness.

To those who believe in reward theology, life in the kingdom, being the bride of Christ, and seeing Jesus in all His glory are all secondary. Getting the bling bling is the absolute goal.

Bibliolatry

Haitian Protestants revere and worship the Bible to the point that it takes precedence over Jesus. Bibliolaters have Bibles with the nicest cover, preferably leather with their initials engraved on it. Not only does the Bible need to be treated with reverence, but they venerate it as if it were God. If they could, the Protestants would wear the Bible on their neck as a talisman[126].

They will freak out if their Bible is accidentally dropped on the floor, and, in their zeal to protect the Bible, will rebuke you if you underline a verse. God will certainly punish you if you trash a worn-out Bible.

Bibliolaters think their Louis Segond is the original God-breathed Bible. They will defend their belief in its inerrancy and the infallibility of Scripture. These extra-biblical doctrines become a tool of spiritual abuse, psychological domination, power, oppression, and textual manipulation in the hands of bibliolaters.

In placing such belief and reverence in their Bibles, they forget that Jesus is the Word to which the Bible points to. Jesus warns about bibliolatry in John 5:39 (The Message). He said, "You have your heads in your Bibles constantly because you think you'll find eternal life there. But you miss the forest for the trees. These Scriptures are all about me."

My wife used to tell me that everything I need to live by is in the Bible. Was she right? Was the Bible written to you and me as an instruction manual, a rulebook, a blueprint to living? The Bible has

---

[126] Some people actually buy cross-shaped USB flash drive necklaces, download different versions of the Bible, and wear them around their neck.

wonderful life applications, but that is not its primary purpose, and while scripture is the Word of God, its foundation is Jesus (John 5:39). The Bible is a love story about God's redeeming humanity through Jesus. Jeremy Myers argues,

> The doctrine of the Inspiration of Scripture has led many to believe that there is power in the Word. But there isn't. It is not a book of magical words. It is not a book of secret power. It is not a book by which the full might and power of God is placed at our disposal. It is not a book where the ability to quote a few verses will help you defeat all temptations, persevere under every trial, and break down every stronghold.[127]

Bible: A Magic Book

The book of Psalms in the Bible is the most widely used scripture in Haitian Christianity. Its chapter and verses have served many purposes, from scripture reading during Sunday services, to protection against the devil, a talisman, and even magical prayers. Some Protestants use phrases like "*pase yon sòm*" (say a Psalm) as a form of protection against their perceived enemies.

Once, at a funeral I attended in a rural area near Les Cayes, a family member of the deceased tore up Psalm 91 from the Bible and placed it under the head of the deceased person before they closed the casket. It is believed that placing the Psalm under the dead person's pillow would prevent the reanimation of the corpse, a zombie.

In his book *365 Spiritual Warfare Prayers*, Gregory Toussaint affirms that because He and a few church leaders prayed Psalm 91,

---

[127] Jeremy Myers, "The Bible is not a Magic Book", accessed 1/19/23 https://redeeminggod.com/bible-is-not-a-magic-book/

God spared Miami from the threat posed by Hurricane Irma in 2017. He said that every hour for 24 hours they recited verses 7 and 8 as a formula prayer, and it worked. Actually, the storm did hit Miami, but not as bad as the Florida Keys, Fort Myers, and Naples, among others. Did Toussaint ever think of including those places in his prayers?

In his book *The Jesus Driven Life: Reconnecting Humanity with Jesus*, Michael Hardin argues, "When Jesus read or heard his Bible, he had a lens, a grid, a method of interpreting it. We not only want to know how he interpreted his people's writings but also how we can follow him in interpreting these Scriptures."[128] Although there are useful instructions in the Bible, it's not primarily a "how to" book and certainly not a magic book.

Conversion: Rantre nan Pwotestan

In 1884, the great Haitian thinker Louis-Joseph Janvier, pleaded urgently to the nation to convert to Protestantism. He argued, "*Le protestant est économe , respectueux de la loi, amoureux du livre, ami de la paix, riche de vaillant espoir, de persévérance.*"[129] (The Protestant is thrifty, law-abiding, book-loving, peace-loving, rich in valiant hope and perseverance.) He added, "*L'argent catholique est un mythe. Les nations reveuses, dormeuses, imaginatives, vite découragées, depensières, sont catholiques.*"[130] (Catholic money is a myth. The dreamy, sleepy, imaginative, quickly discouraged, spendthrift nations are Catholics.)

---

[128] Michael, Hardin. The Jesus driven Life: Reconnecting Humanity with Jesus. Lancaster: JDL Press, 2010, 37

[129] Louis-Joseph Janvier, Haïti aux Haïtiens (Paris, Typ. A. . Parent, 1884) 35-36

[130] Ibid

In their zeal to evangelize to the lost, Haitian Protestants use backward invitations as a prerequisite for conversion: *kite fimen, kite bwe tafya, kite jwe bòlèt, kite Vodou vinn jwenn Kris* (Get your life in order, clean up, and when you've got it all together, come on in.) In other words, the Haitian needs to leave his social life and make important behavioral changes before they can be accepted in the Protestant congregation. No more going to the gadyè (cockfighting), no smoking, no drinking, and especially no plaçage. By going after the behavior first, conversion simply becomes a change of religion.

The second method is the threat of hell. It goes like this: *Mwen ofri w levanjil, si w aksepte ou pral nan syel, si w refize ou pral tou dwa nan lanfè*. (I'm offering you the gospel, and if you accept it, you're going to heaven, but if you don't, you're going to hell).

A few years ago, I was riding a tap-tap (local bus) in Port-Au-Prince when the person sitting next to me asked me, "*Si w mouri jodi a, eske w konn kote w prale?*" (If you die today, do you know where you're going?) I told him that I'd be going straight to the morgue. While some people on the bus laughed, the "evangelist", did not find it funny.

In their hell-escaping messages, the ultimate goal is to get to heaven. These messages can be found in their sermons and songs, songs such as, *"An nou mache ak Kris...si nou rete fidèl na rive nan syèl"* (let's walk with Christ… if we're faithful, we'll get in heaven), sang by the popular gospel singing group, *Les Étincelles de l'Evangile*, and numerous songs in Les *Chants d'Éspérance*, such as *"Lemonn se pa lakay mwen, nan syèl la m prale"* (The earth is not my home, I'm heavenly bound).

There is this story about a man in the Artibonite Valley who put a machete under a man's throat, and he swore he would kill him if he did not repent and convert to Protestantism. In this case, the good news of the gospel is not so good after all for the man who was threatened.

Florent Toirac was visiting a church in Port-au-Prince. Before he preached, pastor Lozama made an altar call by asking first-time visitors and non-believers to raise their hands, and then called them hypocrites just for being there. For Lozama, "Only evangelical Christians who have repented of their sins and accepted the Lord Jesus Christ as savior can worship God, sing hymns, and pray."[131] In his diatribe, Lozama insisted, "Don't deceive us. God can't be deceived. If anyone tries to deceive us, he might be hit by a car and killed tonight as he leaves here, or lightning might strike and kill him."[132] Coercion and fear forced about 60 people to raise their hands and repent.

When a missionary was asked how he addressed honor and shame in his ministry in Haiti, he said, "Effective evangelism focuses on the guilt and fear aspects of the message."[133] While fear of God and hell can produce converts, it will not change their behavior as observed in many Haitian churches.

Conversion: A Hiding Place

Most Haitians use the idea of conversion as a hiding place for protection against perceived threats from people who want to harm

[131] Florent Toirac, A Pioneer Missionary in the Twentieth Century (Winona Lake: Florent Toirac, 1986), 526

[132] Ibid, 526

[133] See Culture profile of Haiti at http://honorshame.com/culture-profile-haiti/

them and their families. With little or no intervention, they bring themselves to the pastor, and after kneeling and having said the sinner's prayer, they claim complete protection. Usually, a family member's illness or death is in the rush to convert to Protestantism. Both my maternal grandma and my mother-in-law had similar experiences. When one of their kids died mysteriously (maybe some unknown illness), they took all the remaining kids to the Protestant church because they feared for their life and those of their kids from their husband's concubine. Even the local *ougan* told these women if they didn't *rantre nan pwotestan*, they would lose all of their kids one after the other.

In their magazine *Nouvelles de Côte d'Ivoire et d'Haïti*, the organisation *Mission Biblique* argues,

> Dans la mentalité haïtienne, le protestantisme représente un refuge contre les forces du mal assimilées à la frange magique du vodou. Beaucoup acceptent la foi protestante rien que pour s'y mettre à l'abri. D'autres sont attirés par la fraternité, le sens de communauté et de partage bien souvent absents dans les Églises catholiques, et une projection de vie morale et d'honnêteté.[134]

> [In the Haitian mentality, Protestantism represents a refuge from the forces of evil assimilated to the magic fringe of Vodou. Many accept the Protestant faith just for shelter. Others are attracted by the fraternity, the sense of community and sharing very often absent in the Catholic Churches, and a projection of moral life and honesty.]

---

[134] Cited in "Haiti et l'UEBH en quelques mots…" in Mission Biblique No. 237 3e Trimestre 2004

Misreading Scripture

In his sermon *Une Revendication pour la grâce*, Rev. Eden McGuffie of the *Église Évangélique Philadelphie* in Montreal said that he doesn't care about his titles in this life because when you get to heaven's gate, there are only two titles. It's either *"bon et fidèle serviteur ou dehors chien"*[135] (Come good and faithful servant or get out, dog). Haitian preachers have a habit of misreading Rev 22:15 in their French (Louis Segond) version of the Bible. They read *"Dehors les chiens, les enchanteurs…"* as if it was a command. The Creole version also translates the verse as *"mete nou deyò, bann chen…"* But the text is simply saying "Outside [the gate or the city] are the dogs and the sorcerers…"

In preaching on the seven churches mentioned in Revelation, Pastor Malory Laurent of the Salvation Church of God in New York claimed that the letters were addressed to the pastors of the churches. He wanted to make the point that a pastor of a church *"pa ka nenpòt moun"*[136] (a pastor needs to be someone special). Although his own Bible says the letters were written to the angel of each church, he deliberately said the pastor.

I was listening to a Haitian preacher, and in his sermon on the seven churches in Revelation 3, he claims, *"Bondye pral voye w jete tankou yon remèd anmè."* Meaning God will spit you out of his

---

[135] Calling somebody a dog is one of the most insulting things in Haitian culture. McGuffie imagines on judgment day everybody will be lined up in front of the throne by the gate of heaven. God will be calling people by saying "get in or get out". For more, see Rev. Eden McGuffie, "Une Revendication pour la grâce", 29 octobre 2023. Accessed 2/15/2024 https://www.youtube.com/watch?v=ATudE-Dl8w8

[136] See Yon Lidè Legliz Pa Ka Nenpòt Moun – Pasteur Malory Laurent, https://www.youtube.com/watch?v=x4mqsrakxkQ

mouth and send you to hell. Isn't that a misreading of Rev. 3:15-16? The Church of Laodicea was challenged not because they lost their salvation, but for lack of purpose.

My mother-in-law was from a coastal village where fishing was the main activity of the local men. Fish and other seafood are the main diet of the people there. I'm always amused by how women in that village eat their fish. They don't separate the bones from the meat. They would put a piece of fish in their mouth (bone-in), eat the meat, and spit the bones out one by one. Some people believe that God does the same thing with lukewarm believers. They are like fish bones. If you're not fully devoted, God will reject and deny your salvation. Unfortunately, this teaching ends up creating fear which is the dominant expression in the religious landscape of Haiti.

Biblical Formation

My dad was an avid farmer. He was also an expert in soil management and conservation. He was one of the few religious leaders who believed in protecting the environment for future generations. I learned from him how to grow everything related to Haitian agriculture, and I also remember that he had each student of two elementary schools bring seeds, sprouts, or saplings of any tree for his various reforestation campaigns. He had dedicated his whole life to fighting deforestation and soil erosion.

As a pastor in the conservative MEBSH, he surprisingly had a very good relationship with the local Catholic priest and even the local *ougan*. People were more important to him than their religious beliefs.

My father was way ahead of his time and had a way of getting everybody involved in the community's life. He befriended Catholics, and religious leaders of other denominations considered him a friend. He didn't care about one's religious affiliation. Some of his best friends were not Protestants, and he had no problem when he heard I was dating a Catholic girl.

When I was about eighteen, the girl he wished to be my girlfriend was Catholic and the daughter of a Freemason. His love for people crossed religious boundaries. I can still remember his countless jokes and conversations with the local Catholic priest and his Catholic neighbors. But what I remember most about him was the value he put on education. Wherever he was, he made sure that every kid in the neighborhood had access to quality education. Where there was no school, he would build one, and he would hire the best teachers he could afford. His office overflowed with books that he probably never read, but he was so pushy for his kids to read them.

One of the best pieces of advice he gave me was to "never throw out a piece of paper without reading it. Reading is knowledge," he said.

My dad knew the value of higher education, and until he died he didn't stop pushing people to be the best they could be. Unfortunately, some church leaders and organizations in Haiti don't believe in higher education. And this lack of interest creates a lack of knowledge. I was complaining to a church leader of MEBSH about the importance and the lack of quality theological training for church leaders and lay workers, and his response was, "The Holy Spirit is the best teacher. If you have the Spirit in you, he will reveal to you what you need to know." In other words, education is not important as long as you have the Holy Spirit. No wonder the intellectual elite wants no part of the Protestant churches in Haiti, especially those of MEBSH.

While I agree that God can use anyone's gifts for his purpose, it should not be an excuse for quality theological training for leaders in Haitian churches. Would you take your pregnant wife to an auto shop for a C-section? Would you go to a barber shop for a hernia because you heard the barber has the Holy Spirit in him? I hope not. Then why is it okay for a pastor to have mediocre training? Shouldn't your spiritual leaders have some kind of credentials?

MEBSH, for example, claims to have over 500 churches in southern Haiti and around Port-au-Prince. Over 80% of their pastors don't have a high school diploma, less than 5% have an equivalent of a Bachelor's degree, and roughly 30% can scarcely read and write. In his book, *La Mission Evangélique Baptiste du Sud d'Haiti (MEBSH): Un Octogénaire dans le Bicentenaire du Protestantisme en Haïti*, Lusson Napoléon, the current president of MEBSH and pastor of Bellevue Salem, a MEBSH mega-church in Port-au-Prince, acknowledges that there is no budget for training and their Bible school is subpar.[137]

Having the best seminary in Haiti has never been a priority for MEBSH. No budget means no qualified teachers, as their modus operandi is to wait for missionaries to come and teach for "free".

The problem is not only at MEBSH, but it is all over Haiti. In his book, *The Relevance of Christian Education for Lay Pastors in*

---

[137] Napoléon Lusson, La Mission Evangélique Baptiste du Sud d'Haiti (MEBSH): Un Octogénaire dans le Bicentenaire du Protestantisme en Haïti (Port-au-Prince: Imprimerie Media-Texte, 2016),280

Haiti: A New Vision, Fritz Olivier researches the deficiency of adequate formation for lay pastors. In a survey of 300 pastors, he found that 53% didn't finish high school, and only 7% had some type of theological training.[138]

When you go to a doctor's office, you expect that he/she is trained in a medical school and that he/she knows the tools of the trade. Shouldn't it be the same for pastors and church leaders? No wonder the Bible is interpreted literally. Most Haitian Protestants will read their Bible (Louis Segond) in French, but as they read, the meaning or interpretation is translated in their head in Creole. That's why a pastor will read a passage for his sermon in French, and then preach in Creole.

Consequently, the Creole translation of the text is also the literal interpretation. Back when I was in high school, I went to a church in Port-au-Prince where the pastor preached on Psalm 23:4. The pastor read "Your rod and your staff, they comfort me" in French *"Ta houlette et ton baton me rassurent."* but he translated *"houlette"* in Creole as *"yon ti wou."* *"Yon ti wou"* is a small wheel/tire or *petite roue* in French. So, what he ended up saying was, *"Bondye gen yon baton ak yon ti wou ladan, le l pran woule w, se pou di woule m Seyè"* (God has a staff with a small tire in it to roll over you. When he does, you should be saying roll on me, Lord).

Another pastor was preaching on Revelation 20:14, he translated the French *"étang de feu et de soufre"* as *"yon letan dife ak soufrans"*, meaning (fire and suffering) instead of fire and brimstone. In his sermon, he said, *"w ap boule, w ap soufri"* (you're

---

[138] Fritz Olivier, The Relevance of Christian Education for Lay Pastors in Haiti: A new Vision, 2007, p

burning, and you're suffering). And then this one is my favorite: The pastor read Psalm 37:4 in French, *"Fais de l'Eternel tes délices, Et il te donnera ce que ton cœur désire."* (Take delight in the Lord, and he will give you your heart's desires, (NLV)). But in Creole he said *"Se nan delis mo delisye soti. Sa vle di se pou fè bon bagay devan Bondye, lap ba w tout sa w merite."* (The word delights comes from delicious. If you do good things, the Lord will give you anything you desire.)

This one is the icing on the cake. In 1981, a deacon preaching at my dad's church wanted to make a point about the power of God. He used former Secretary of State Alexander Haig's name as an example of power in the U.S., but he didn't get the name right. In his sermon, he said, *"Eg la se yon bèt tankou malfini an Ayiti, men li pi pwisan. Nèg sa tèlman gen pouvwa, se pa yon sèl èg, se plizyè."* (The eagle is like the hawk we have in Haiti, but more powerful. This man is so powerful, it's not just an eagle, it's a bunch) He thought the name was Alexandre des Aigles (Alexandre of many Eagles).

The fact that the Bible is translated into Haitian Creole is irrelevant to most Haitians. What is the use of the Creole Bible if the Haitian who cannot read French most likely cannot read Creole, and reading the Bible in Creole does not require an interpretation? I wonder if the Creole Bible (Bib La) does more harm than good.

There are a lot of reasons why Bible colleges in Haiti do not attract recent high school graduates. Among other things, there are only a couple of seminaries with an equivalent of a four-year bachelor's degree in Haiti, and the handful of others are mediocre at best. Their research libraries are meager to non-existent, they have insufficient qualified teachers, and the internet is scarce and expensive.

I have met a teacher who has only a bachelor's degree, but he teaches Church History, Old Testament, New Testament, Hermeneutics, Missiology, and Evangelization.

Furthermore, most students have no way of researching and verifying claims in classroom lectures. Not only are there not enough materials in French and Creole, but also, the writings of renowned American theologians, other than Billy Graham, John MacArthur, and a few others whose books are translated into French, are excluded from their curriculum.

Moreover, their curriculum is not adapted to the Haitian worldview. Their theology is purely denominational and Western-style exegetical methods. In-depth research and study are non-existent. There are no specific courses on Haitian Vodou and Roman Catholicism. They prefer classes on big words such as soteriology, eschatology, and pneumatology. No effort has been made to do comparative studies of ATR, AICs, and the three main religions in Haiti.

The names and works of renowned African theologians, such as Ogbu Kalu, Alioune Diop, Bolaji Idowu, Laurenti Magesa, Kwame Bediako, John Mbiti, Lamin Sanneh, and Mercy Amba Oduyoye are unknown to Haitian theologians whose main textbooks are those of Alfred Kuen and René Pache.

Another major issue is that these schools train their students to be pastors. After their training, these students see pastoring a church as a profession, and as professionals, they need to get paid. Since most churches are not able to sustain their salary, they look for sister churches overseas.

To reverse this trend of biblical education, there needs to be a revolution, and the *"depi lontan se konsa nou jwenn li"* (it's been like that for a while) attitude needs to change.

Wall Builders

It's ironic that Haitian Protestants sing and preach about the crumbling down of the walls of Jericho (*Jeriko miray la kraze*), but they make a career out of building walls inside their churches and around themselves. The major Protestant denominations in Haiti are the ones mostly known for what they are against rather than what they are for. Take for instance mainstream denominations, such as the Baptists, the Pentecostals, the Adventists, the Methodists, and the Jehovah Witnesses, who are considered rival denominations split over doctrines, rules, rituals, and traditions. These denominations are known to fight and defend their biblical interpretations and rituals to prove their immutable creeds and doctrines. Even the Haitian Konpa band *Bossa Combo* doesn't understand these wall builders. They make this known in their smash hit *Religions,*

> *Pi gwo pwoblèm ki gen sou latè*
> *Dezinyon ki nan relijyon yo*
> *Katolik pa vle we batis*
> *Pankotis pa vle wè advantis*
> *Temwen jewova pa vle wè boudis*
> *Advantis pa vle wè jwif*
> *Yo tou ap sèvi menm Dye*

Men yo tout pa gen menm relijyon

The biggest problem in the world
Is disagreement in religions
Catholics don't like Baptists
Pentecostals don't like Adventists
Jehovah Witnesses don't like Buddhists
Adventists don't like Jews
They are serving the same God
But they don't have the same religion

Jules Casséus is the former president of North Haiti Christian University, and he claims that the Baptist tradition has no social class.[139] Is he serious? But how about the influencers? The people who have front seats in the church, who are in a men's club also known as the diaconate, who donate more to the building fund? Or who the pastor befriends and tries not to offend, and who has the means to bring the food for the church event, but will not do manual labor.

After the fall of Baby Doc, Casséus called for the *dechoukaj* (uproot) of denominationalism and traditionalism.[140] Claiming doctrinal certitude, Casséus' book, *Nous Les Baptistes*, is like a 10-foot wall between the Baptists and other mainline denominations where he portrays the Baptists as God's denomination. As one of the

---

[139] Jules Casséus, *Nous les Baptistes* (Port-au-Prince: La Presse Évangélique, 1985),46

[140] See Casséus, *Haiti: What Kind of Church…What kind of Freedom.*

largest denominations in Haiti, it's within the Baptist walls that I heard more of the distinction between "*ti pastè and gwo pastè*".

For example, at MEBSH you're a *gwo pastè* (affluent) if you have a big church, and you're living well. But you're a *ti pastè* (insignificant) if you're struggling and your church is way up the mountains. It's within their wall the poor have only one job: to clean the church on Saturdays. It's inside their churches that the poorer you are the further back your seat is. Is't among themselves that the poorer you are, the more likely you are to be invisible. No one notices if you have not been in church for a few weeks.

While the ministry of Jesus was dedicated to tearing down walls, religion keeps building them back up. And while Haitian Protestants want the walls in their life to fall, they keep raising walls between themselves and their neighbor. A revolution is indeed needed.

Tithes and Offerings

What's God got to do with it? Well, "*Sa nou bay nan ofrann nan, nou bay li pou Jezi*"(What we give during offerings, we give to Jesus), and "*Jezi bezwen lajan pou lèv li ka mache*" (Jesus needs money so his work can be done).

Haitian Protestants are often accused by their pastors and other church leaders of being poor tithers. In most churches, only 20% of their members participate in offering and they donate about 2% of their income. To remedy this, various schemes are used during church services to encourage church members to give more. I could write a separate book on the topic of tithing and offering, but that's not the focus here. At a MEBSH church I was in Les Cayes, a man and a woman held the offering buckets by the altar, instead of passing them along the pews like other churches do. Then, the deacons had each row come up front to drop their offering into the buckets. The men dropped their money in the men's bucket, and the women did the same in the women's bucket. Afterwards, a winner was announced. It was like a competitive sport. What a shameful tactic inside the church!

While shame and fear are the main motivating tools to collect money in all Protestant churches, some churches collect tithes by giving their members envelopes with their names on them. Using this method, church leaders know how much members give, and can track if a member does not return their envelope. Some will shamelessly ask such members for their envelopes.

Although the church should be the last place where fear is used as a motivator, it is mainly used to collect money. Instead of being a way to worship God, tithe and offerings have become a burden for the Protestants.

Haitian Protestants and Culture

Haitian Protestant churches tend to discourage their adherents from participating in anything related to Haitian culture. They use 1 John 2:15 (Do not love the world or anything in the world) to justify why their flock must abandon their social responsibilities and not take part in "worldly' activities. They associate the richness of the Haitian culture with the world (*dyab*). For the Protestants, it is sinful to hang in their house a piece of art created by a non-Protestant artist. (In Haiti, Protestants don't consider Catholics Christians).

In some denominations, it is still sinful to go to the beach, attend a concert by a non-Protestant artist, and dance to the rhythm of secular music. They argue that Satan and his demonic influence are everywhere and in everything related to Haitian culture.

Take music for example. Haitian Protestants are reluctant to listen to *konpa* because it's considered secular music. The irony of this thinking is that *Radio Lumière* Stereo 92, the prominent voice of Protestantism in Haiti, used to play mostly classical music. The hosts played Pyotr Ilyich Tchaikovsky and Benjamin Britten who were queer. They repeatedly played Nikolai Rimsky-Korsakov and Sergei Prokofiev who were known atheists. While the LGBTQ community is not welcome in their Protestant churches, their church choirs interpret Catholic composers' choruses such as Handel's *Hallelujah* and Haydn's *The Heavens Are Telling.* I wonder if they would still sing the *Messiah* if they knew Handel was a *masisi* (gay).

While most Protestants will listen to some Western secular music, they consider *konpa, rara,* and *troubadou* genres worldly rhythms. Is the devil the reason Tico Claude Pasquet is one of the best Haitian drummers? Robert Martino, André (Dadou) Pasquet, Ralph Conde, and Eddy Wooley[141] are in my view the greatest Haitian guitarists ever. Are they *"andyable"* (influenced by the devil) for being so talented? After all, the great Italian composer and violinist Niccolò Paganini was accused of selling his soul to the devil for being so gifted. But it was on Stereo 92 that I heard Paganini's *La Campanella* for the first time. I can assure you that if Beethoven

---

[141] Not necessarily in order of greatness. Other legendary Haitian guitarists include Amos Coulanges, Jean Claude Jean, Toto Laraque, Ignace Evens, Albert Chancy, Keke Belizaire, Claude Marcelin, Makario Cesaire, Frantz Casséus, and many more.

was Haitian, Haitian Protestants would not play or listen to his music.

Case in point: Carmen Brouard, the sister of the poet Carl Brouard, was a well-known Haitian classical composer who used to hang out with the great French composer, Maurice Ravel. Her symphonic poem, *Baron la Croix,* is played by the world's major ensembles.

Ludovic Lamothe, the most famous Haitian pianist, was so good that he was dubbed the "Black Chopin". One of his piano pieces, *La Dangereuse*, is frequently played on my local classical public radio (KSJN). Like Lamothe, Justin Élie was a legendary pianist and composer. He toured with Lamothe over the years, and he raised the roof of Carnegie Hall during his performance there in 1923. The rhythm of meringue and Vodou inspires some of his works.

You will never hear Brouard, Lamothe, and Élie's compositions played on *Radio Lumière*. They would not play either *Suite Folklorique* composed in four movements (Erzulie, Dambala, Interludio, Papa Simbi) by Haitian composer Werner Jaegerhuber.

Religion is such a monster. It can turn a Sorbonne graduate into the most ignorant human being.

While everyone is free to listen or not listen to whatever they want, to think that God is offended when a Vodouist or a Catholic glorifies his name in a song or a piece of art says more about who you are than who God is. Why is it a sin to sing Jean-Claude Martineau's love piece *Deklarasyon*? What is so offensive in TiCorn's *Sous le ciel d'Haïti*, Orchestre Tropicana - *Pran Pasyans,* Les Frères Déjean - *Bouki ak Malice*, Shoogar Combo - *Lèlène Cherie* (should be included in the national heritage), Harmonik –

Mwen Bouke, Tabou Combo - *Mabouya*, Klass – *Pale Pou Tét ou*, Colé Colé Band - *Symphonie Inachevée*, Magnum Band - *Libète*, Mizik-Mizik – *Lè Nap Fè Lanmou*, or Orchestre Septentrional – *Septen Dous*? Are you afraid to lose your "*Je crois en Dieu*" (faith)? Or is it because your religion keeps you in bondage?

Church and State

Throughout the history of Protestantism in Haiti, church leaders actively sought good grace and favor from the state. Missionaries wanted to meet with the head of state, and local leaders wanted to invite state dignitaries to their official events. Occasionally, local elected members such as mayors, senators, and deputies visited MEBSH's annual convention, and former President Jovenel Moïse made a pit stop at their 82nd meeting in 2018. Although the constitution guarantees every religion freedom of expression, as the Catholics did in 1860, the Protestants got their own "Concordat". In June 1985, they signed a pact with the government where the cross and the sword agreed to mutually use each other to the detriment of the Haitian people.

Violent War on Vodou and Catholicism

Throughout Haiti's history, there has been a complex and sometimes contentious relationship between Vodou and Protestantism. Protestant missionaries arrived in Haiti in the early 19th century seeking to convert Haitians to Protestantism and to eradicate what they saw as "pagan" practices like Vodou. The Protestant missionaries considered Vodou as devil worship and worked hard to eliminate it. Their efforts were met with resistance from Vodou practitioners who saw their religion as an essential part of their cultural identity.

In the 20th century, Protestantism gained more influence in Haiti, particularly with the growth of the charismatic movement. Some Protestant groups have continued to view Vodou as a threat to their belief and have been involved in efforts to eradicate the religion. In some cases, this has led to violence including murder against Vodou practitioners and the destruction of their places of worship. After Jean Claude Duvalier was overthrown, Haitian Protestants took to the streets and reacted violently by burning Vodou temples and religious objects. For days they went throughout the country killing the Vodou priests and priestesses in the name of their God.

Because of their perceived religious superiority over Catholicism and Vodou, the Protestants blame them as the main cause of Haiti's problems. For the Protestants, Catholics and Vodouisants are two sides of the same coin. Consequently, the Protestants demand from their converts a complete abandonment of Vodou practices and a total rejection of Catholic teachings. They see those religions as a challenge to their faith, therefore they wage a full-fledged war on these "idolaters and devil worshipers".

As their missionary mentors taught them, Haitian evangelicals stand against everything that goes against their belief system. Obsessed with a vengeful God, judgment took over their ability to love their neighbor. Instead of imitating Jesus by loving and serving people of their communities, they prefer to wage war on theological opinions and on those they consider unworthy of God's love. Forgetting their *raison d'être,* Protestant churches stand for wrong goals and wrong reasons as expressed in this lyric:

Bondye pral frape pye l sou moun k ap
Sèvi lwa, manbo ak divinò yo tout pral
Menm kote, yon sel bagay m ap di w, ou
Gen yon chans toujou. Kouri pran levanjil
Pou nanm ou ka sove[142]

God will put his feet down and strike
Those who are serving the spirits, the mambos, and the ougans
They are all going to the same place
But you have one last chance, accept the gospel
To save your soul

Top Ten Lies Heard Behind the Pulpit

Over the years, I've collected a tremendous amount of misguided statements from Haitian preachers. The majority of those lies are birthed out of ignorance, false religious concepts, misinterpretations of scripture, and a distorted picture of God. Eleven is more than ten:

1. *"Padon bon mache, men li pa gratis. Menm lè Bondye padone w, w ap peye sa kan menm."* [Forgiveness is cheap, but it's not free. Even though God forgives you, you will pay for what you did eventually.] I agree there's got to be accountability. While it's true that there are consequences for one's actions, the idea that God does not forgive for free is unfathomable.

---

[142] From a song composed in 1999 by Louisnord Fledger of Labiche MEBSH church for an end of the year conference (revival) sponsored by a small group of the church.

2. *"Gen de lè Bondye vle fè yon wout avè w, li pèmèt kèk pwoblèm rive w pou ka mache pi pre l."*(Occasionally when God wants to enlarge your vision, he permits a problem that will compel you to move closer to Him). This theology of blaming God for their problems is very common among Haitian evangelicals. One of the converts of the Baptist Haiti Mission in Fermathe prays, *"Bondye ap fè nou pase mizè pou li ba nou leson"[143]* (God is making our life miserable to teach us lessons).

3. *"W ap anba madichon Bondye si w pa bay ladim."*(God will curse you for failing to tithe.) I'm not surprised at this one.

4. *"Avan w wè Bondye touye yon moun, konnen li bouke avè w paske li ba w tan."* [Before God kills somebody, He probably has had enough with him/her because He gives you enough time to repent.] Ouch! 1 and 4 are from the same preacher. It's probably based on Job's distorted view of God's character.

5. *"Depi w ap dòmi ou wè w sou yon montay, konnen Bondye ap leve w. Montay vle di pouvwa, otorite, grandè. Yon pastè se tankou yon montay, li dwe elve an otorite."*[If you're sleeping, and in your dream, you see yourself on top of a mountain, know that God is going to raise you up. Mountains mean power, authority, and greatness. A pastor is like a mountain. He needs to rise up in authority.] Oh, Haiti! Land of mountains. Note there is nothing about being a servant.

---

[143] Eleanor Turnbull and Sandra Burdick, *God is No Stranger* (Durham: Light Messages, 2004), 98

6. *"Si w pa veye sou chè a, ou mèt te zele nan legliz ou pral nan lanfè tou dwat."* (if you don't watch over the flesh, you can be the most zealous person in the church, you're going straight to hell.) Again fear and hell are the two main themes in Haitian Protestantism.

7. *"Moun engra pap sove."* [An ungrateful person will not be saved] Fortunately, this preacher has no power over who is saved or not.

8. *"Bondye pral mande w kont pou nanm madanm ou ak pitit ou."* [God will hold you responsible for the soul of your wife and kids]. But they still believe that salvation is personal.

9. *"Si w pran kominyon an san w pa konfese, sak rive w, rive w. Ou ka menm mouri."* [If you take communion without confessing your sin, anything can happen to you. You can even die.] The fearmongering tactic of some preachers is to keep their flock in line.

10. *"Jezu ka pi bon zanmi ou byen lenmi ki pi kriyèl ou genyen."* (Jesus can be your best friend or your most cruel enemy.) Wow! This pastor was probably putting a new spin on one of Jack Chick's tracks. For most Haitian Christians, Jesus and *Bondye* are two different Gods who play different roles. While Jesus is more like a personal lawyer. Bondye is the ruthless judge who controls all things. So you need at least Jesus to be on your side. Haitians for the most part are not afraid of Jesus. For them, He is the good God. They fear Bondye (God the Father) who is seen as the One who punishes and condemns to hell.

11. *"Lè Jezu ap vini, li pap vinn chache savan ak zotobre."* (When Jesus returns, He is not coming for scientists and the well-to-do). This is a line from a popular song that some churches used to sing. The belief is that Jesus only cares for the poor. According to this view, the intellectual and the rich will not be in heaven even if they are followers of Christ.

CHAPTER 5

The Catholic Church in Haiti

———✦———

Si l'américain est l'adversaire de notre indépendance matérielle, le clergé blanc français est celui de notre indépendance spirituelle et un des moyens pour nous faire passer sous le joug colonial définitif.

(If the American is the adversary of our material independence, the white French clergy is the adversary of our spiritual independence and one of the means of bringing us definitively under the colonial yoke.)

Georges Petit, Elie Guérin, et Jacques Roumain

Fok ou yon bon katolik pou ka sèvi lwa byen

(To serve the spirits well, one must be a good Catholic)

(Popular Saying)

Pour être catholique, il ne suffit pas de ne pas être protestant.

(To be Catholic, it's not enough not to be Protestant.)

Robert Paul Samson Jean Marie

Bloody Sword - Silent Cross

At the end of the Papa Doc regime, a Haitian was asked about the position of the Church in Haiti, and he said, "The story of Haitian Catholicism is one of the saddest imaginable. In the course of the centuries, Catholicism has resulted in a real repression of Haitian consciousness, and as such of Haitian culture."[144] The history of the Catholic Church in Haiti is complex, spans several centuries, and has been marked by various events and changes.

In 1492, Christopher Columbus landed in Hispaniola and planted a cross at Môle St. Nicholas where he claimed at the same time both the land and the catholicity of the so-called New World.

It was also the beginning of a bloody conquest of the Indigenous people and eventually enslaved Africans by the sword-wielding Columbus and the legendary priest Bartolome de las Casas as the official cross-bearer. Among the early victims was Anacaona, the beautiful "Golden Flower" Queen of the Arawak Indians, who was raped and hanged by Nicolas Ovando. Guess who was watching all this? De las Casas was there, and he didn't say a word. Fast forward to December 1929. Marchaterre, near Les Cayes, was the scene of one of the worst massacres of unarmed Haitian civilians by the U.S. Marines. Jules-Victor-Marie Pichon, who was then the Archbishop of Les Cayes, was there and silent.

During the colonial period, the island had three important religious orders. After the Franciscans arrived in 1505, they were

---

[144] For his safety, an anonymous Haitian was interviewed in Paris in 1971 on the state of the Catholic Church in Haiti. For more see The Church in Haiti. Source: New Blackfriars, August 1971, Vol. 52, No. 615 (August 1971), pp. 363-36 in Stable URL: http://www.jstor.com/stable/43245298

followed by the Dominicans and the Jesuits in 1512.[145] The main role of the clergy was to baptize the slaves and to teach them obedience to their masters. With the introduction of the *Code Noir*, all other religions were forbidden, and instructions were given to get rid of the competition:

> We enjoin all of our officers to chase from our islands all the Jews who have established residence there. As with all declared enemies of Christianity, we command them to be gone within three months of the day of issuance of the present [order], at the risk of confiscation of their persons and their goods."[146]

Employment was also forbidden for Protestants in the French colonies. As Article V of the *Code Noir* of 1685 states,

> We forbid our subjects who belong to the so-called "reformed" [Protestants] religion from causing any trouble or unforeseen difficulties for our other subjects or even for their slaves in the free exercise of the Roman, Catholic, and Apostolic Faith, at the risk of exemplary punishment.[147]

As St Domingue became wealthy, the cross and the sword became one. French Capuchins and Dominicans owned massive sugar and coffee plantations and hundreds of slaves. These religious orders became plantation owners with a soutane:

---

[145] Anne Greene, *The Catholic Church in Haiti: Political and Social Change* (East Lansing: Michigan State University Press, 1993),74

[146] See Article I of the Black Code of 1685.

[147] See Article IV of The black code of 1685.

They bought and sold slaves. Some missions were just large agricultural and manufacturing complexes comprising sugarcane plantations, sugar mills and factories, and mules and cattle as well as black men, women, and children. Their prosperity was measured in terms of financial turnover, and the merit of a missionary was assessed in relation to his success or failure as a manager.[148]

When the cross is fused with the sword, there is always conflict. Then the cross loses her effectiveness and *raison d'être* in the fight for power and control.

The Concordat: Church and State

Among stupid treaties and contracts signed by the Haitian government after independence, the Concordat was probably the most irresponsible. Not only was the Concordat a self-inflicted wound to the Haitians, but the thought of paying priests to turn Haiti into France was foolish. *Le Petit Impartial,* a leftist journal during the American Occupation, rightly argues: *"Le Concordat est un carcan au cou du Peuple Haïtien."*[149] (The Concordat is a straitjacket around the neck of the Haitian people.) Even the

---

[148] Guitar, Lynne, Denis Verdier, J. C. Lespinasse, William Smarth, Fabio Chiarelotto, Olga Portuondo Zúñiga, Gaston Jean-Michel, Anny Dominique Curtius, Patrick Taylor, Elizabeth Wilson, C. D. Ooft, and Neville Smith. "Roman Catholic Church." In The Encyclopedia of Caribbean Religions: Volume 1: A-L; Volume 2: M-Z, edited by TAYLOR PATRICK, CASE FREDERICK I., and MEIGHOO SEAN, by LEUNG JOYCE, 817-85. University of Illinois Press, 2013. Accessed July 31, 2020. www.jstor.org/stable/10.5406/j.ctt2tt9kw.97.

[149] Cited in Lewis Ampidu Clorméus, "Des Leaders protestants haïtiens dans la vague anticléricale et nationaliste (1927-1929)" Journal of Haitian Studies, Fall 2015, Vol. 21, No. 2, Special Issue on the US Occupation of Haiti, 1915–1934 (Fall 2015), pp. 88-120

Catholic apologist Jules Caplan thought it was stupid for the Haitian government to take away the free will of the people by forcing Catholicism on them.[150]

With the Concordat, the Catholic church has become the most corrupt religious institution in Haiti to this day. The Concordat of 1860 was controversial for various reasons, but mainly:

a). Pledge allegiance to the state instead of to God

As Article 5 of the Concordat states:

Archbishops, Diocesan Bishops, as well as school headmasters with the right to succession, before commencing their pastoral mission, shall swear their allegiance to the nation before the Head of State in the following words: 'I promise and pledge my obedience and allegiance to the Constitution of Haiti for the pursuance of the good of the country and in defense of the Nation's interests.[151]

When Baby Doc named Jean-Baptiste Décoste as bishop of the new parish of Hinche in 1972, Décoste pledged: *"En me nommant au nouveau siège de Hinche, selon les normes du concordat et en accord avec le siège apostolique, vous me faites preuve de confiance, Monsieur le Président à Vie de la République, et je tâcherai de ne*

---

[150] For more, see Jules Caplan, *La France en Haiti* (Paris: Imprimerie F. Levé, 1904)

[151] See *"Concordat between Pius IX and the Republic of Haiti"* in https://www.concordatwatch.eu/haitis-first-concordat-1860-and-cardinal-antonellis-reply-text–t39311

pas vous décevoir".[152] [By appointing me to the new parish of Hinche, according to the norms of the Concordat and in agreement with the apostolic see, you are showing your confidence in me, Mr. President-For-Life of the Republic, and I will try not to disappoint you.]

Can you imagine Emperor Nero naming Apostle Paul as the bishop of Rome and Paul being so excited as he says thank you?

Being a state religion in a corrupt country, it did not take long for the Catholic Church to be one of the most corrupt institutions in Haiti. While visiting one of the cathedrals, Paul Magloire was greeted by the bishop with the words, "Art thou he that should come or do we look for another?"

After Jean-Bertrand Aristide was kicked out of the church for being elected president, that same church kissed the ring of the newly elected president by calling him "the new Moses"[153]. Go figure!

You can say what you want about the Duvaliers, but they mastered the uses of religion to consolidate their power. For Papa Doc, the Concordat had no binding effect. Notwithstanding that, he nominated the first six Haitian Bishops in 1966, and then was excommunicated by the Catholic church. Papa Doc was interested in the Indigenous leadership of the church, but it was his way of saying "Shut up".

---

[152] Sèl was a monthly journal published by expatriated Priests in New York. For more, see Sèl No 2. Moua-D Jin 1972, access 3/17/2024 Digital Library of the Caribbean, https://dloc.com/AA00089969/00002/images/20

[153] See Emile Jacquot, Les Spiritains en Haïti (1843-2003) : D'Eugène Tisserant (1814-1845) à Antoine Adrien (1922-2003) (Paris: Editions KARTHALA, 2010), 264.

b). The clergy became state employees.

Not only do the clergy and their dependents enjoy special protection from the government, but they also receive an annual salary and subsidies to run the seminary. The third article states,

> The Government of the Republic of Haiti undertakes to provide for and take care of archbishoprics and episcopates by way of a suitable annual allowance in excess of the usual state treasury funds.[154]

Although the Constitution of 1987 does not recognize the Catholic church as a state religion, the church still gets preferential treatment over the other major religions. For example, monthly stipends, diplomatic passports, and official license plates are still in effect.

The danger here is when the church is fused with the state, the church always loses its missionary duties and becomes morally bankrupt. As Jeremy Myers brilliantly points out here,

> When we exist by the permission of the state, we must turn a blind eye to the many abuses of that state, and how it robs the poor, silences the minority, and marginalizes the victim. When the government grants us the power of existence, we must allow injustice to go unchallenged so that we may continue to exist.[155]

---

[154] See *"Concordat between Pius IX and the Republic of Haiti"* in https://www.concordatwatch.eu/haitis-first-concordat-1860-and-cardinal-antonellis-reply-text–t39311

[155] Myers, Jeremy. Close Your Church for Good: Removing Religion to Reveal Jesus . Redeeming Press. Kindle Edition. Location 8572.

Catholics by Default

Haitian people do not need to convert to Catholicism. In Haiti, most people who are not members of a Protestant church consider themselves Catholics. For hundreds of years, it's been the state's religion and the religion in which they were baptized as infants. Article 48 of the 1816 Constitution of President Pétion states, "Roman Catholic Church, being for all Haitians, is the national church and its clergy is protected."

Unless one is born into a Protestant family, most Haitians would say that they are Catholics and/or Vodouists. It begs the question, who is a "true Catholic"?

God in Catholic Churches

God holds a central and profound place in Catholic theology and worship, embodying the ultimate source of all that exists and the focal point of faith and devotion. In Catholic belief, God is understood as a Trinity, comprising three distinct yet unified Persons: The Father, the Son, and the Holy Spirit. Each Person of the Trinity is fully and completely God, sharing the same divine nature, yet they are distinct in their relations to one another and their roles in the divine plan.

Haitian Catholics view God as a loving and merciful Father who desires a personal relationship with each individual. They believe that God is involved in the world and its affairs and that He is present in the sacraments of the Church. But, *"Se Bondye k konnen"*, meaning that Haitian Catholics attribute various life events and circumstances to God's will.

To maintain their faith, Catholics are encouraged to cultivate a personal relationship with God through prayer, participation in the sacraments, and living a life of virtue. This relationship is nurtured by regular Mass attendance, personal prayer, and reading of Scripture. Catholics also believe in the power of prayer to communicate with God and seek guidance and strength.

Through a deep relationship with God, mediated by the Church and enriched by the examples of the saints, Catholics seek to live out their faith in love, service, and hope for eternal life.

A Sunday God

In his book *Catholicisme et Vaudou*, Paul Robert argues, "Il est obligatoire pour professer le catholicisme d'assister à la messe tous les dimanches."[156] (To profess Catholicism, you must attend Mass every Sunday.) In his book *L'Église d'Haïti à l'aube du troisième millénaire: essai de théologie pratique et de sociologie religieuse*, the catholic priest Micial M. Nérestant argues that the main aim of Sunday is to find out who God is.[157] How about the other days? Can we inquire about God on a Monday?

For Nérestant there is a Sunday gospel as he puts it: *"Le dimanche, c'est le jour de l'espérance, le jour de la résurrection, le jour où le Seigneur s'est levé: c'est cela le plus important dans nos messes, c'est qu'elles donnent de l'espérance, qu'elles apportent une révélation."*[158] (Sunday is the day of hope, the day of resurrection,

---

[156] Paul Robert, *Catholicisme et Vaudou* (Cuernavaca: Sondeos No. 82, 1971), 170
[157] Micial M. Nérestant, L'Église d'Haïti à l'aube du troisième millénaire: essai de théologie pratique et de sociologie religieuse (Paris: Éditions Karthala, 1999), 300.
[158] Ibid, 300

the day the Lord rose: that's what's most important about our Masses, that they give hope, that they bring revelation.)

Church and the People

One of the staples of the Catholic church is the role of the priest among the parishioners. From colonial times up to the mid-1960s, the clergy was White and mostly Breton. Everything was done in French and Latin. The church's main role was to do a cultural cleansing among the lower class and to serve the government and the dominant class. Eugene Nida observes,

> In the Roman Catholic approach to a new society, primary consideration has usually been given to the upper class, though a number of instances can be cited in which a broad segment of the society has been approached. The tendency, however, has been for the Roman church to identify itself with the leadership of the society and through it to influence the lower classes.[159]

In firm control of the school system, the Church made sure that French thought and culture were being taught in the classroom. Haitian students knew more about Pierre Corneille's *Le Cid* than Jacques Roumain's *Gouverneurs de la Rosée*. Teachers would quiz and have their students recite La Fontaine's *Fables*, but not a word on Lhèrisson's *Zoune chez sa Ninnaine*. All the books that were in use in classrooms across the country were bookmarked F.I.C. (Frères de l'Instruction Chrétienne). The indoctrination was that bad. As a matter of fact, it was so bad that former students who

---

[159] Eugene Nida, Message and Mission: The Communication of the Christian Faith (South Pasadena: William Carey Library, 1972), 102

attended Catholic schools would proudly tell you, *"Se ka mè wi m te lekòl"* (I'm educated or I speak French).

As the clergy was becoming more Indigenous, some priests, seeing themselves as "serving dirty negros", refused to accept their Haitian counterparts as equals. On the pulpit a priest called women in plaçage wild pigs. In essence, the church was seen as the remnant of colonial power. Le Petit Impartial was so fed up that it did not mince any words:

> The French Catholic clergy has held us in its talons for over 70 years, and it's our robustness that has saved us... ... Having arrived in Haiti as a beggar, the Catholic priest has created an enviable situation for himself. But how? By getting involved in all the political hanky-panky and by engaging in agiotage, mercantilism, and exploiting the ignorance of the masses, whom his character led him to believe he was protecting. In the countryside, he sells confession and communion.[160]

While the priest is said to be representing Christ, he acts also as a middleman between the congregation and *Bondye*. But most priests have a compound mentality. You would not see them mingling with people in their neighborhood.

A Dying Church

Where are the parishioners? Citiene Toussaint was one of the few churchgoers who attended Mass during Ash Wednesday after

---

[160] Cited in Lewis Ampidu Clorméus, "Des Leaders protestants haïtiens dans la vague anticléricale et nationaliste (1927-1929) Journal of Haitian Studies , Fall 2015, Vol. 21, No. 2, Special Issue on the US Occupation of Haiti, 1915–1934 (Fall 2015), pp. 88-120

the earthquake of 2010. He said, "When there are things related to leisure and pleasure, everybody's there, but when it's time to celebrate Christ, there are fewer people."[161]

The Catholic church in Haiti has been on a downward spiral for years. Adult men do not attend Mass, and young men and women don't even try. If not for a few women, the pews would be empty on Sundays.

There was new life in the church with the emergence of the small church community known as TKL (*Ti Kominote Legliz*) in 1980, the charismatic renewal, the Pope's visit in 1983, and the youth movement in 1985, even so, the surge of the populist Catholicism to recapture lost ground is dead.

The church is losing members for various reasons, including corruption, irrelevance, and the rise of Protestantism. Between 1949 and 2019, the church lost 17% to 47% of its members in some parishes. The chart below shows the decline of the church in the major dioceses in Haiti for the last 70 years.

Decline of the Church[162]

Diocese	1949	2019
Cayes	96.8%	60.0%

---

[161] Cited in Catholic Review, "Haitians see Lent as a time to 'meet with God'", Accessed 2/18/2024 in https://www.archbalt.org/haitians-see-lent-as-a-time-to-meet-with-god/

[162] According to the Catholic Church's own statistics, Haiti was about 91.5% Catholic in 1949, but only 59% in 2019. In 2021, the Church lost five percentage points to finish the year at 54%. For more, see https://www.catholic-hierarchy.org/diocese/dlesc.html.

Cap-Haitien	97.7%	50.5%
Port-au-Prince	90%	70%
Gonaïves	95%	56.3%
Port-de-Paix	77.8%	60.1%

Rituals, Practices, and Dying Traditions

Haitian Catholic rituals are a unique blend of traditional Catholic practices and elements of Vodou, reflecting the country's rich cultural and religious symbiosis. Here are some key aspects of Catholic rituals in Haiti:

1. Mass and Sacraments: Like in other Catholic communities, attending mass is central to Haitian Catholicism. In Catholic teachings, the Mass is seen as a representation of Christ's sacrifice on Calvary, bringing the faithful into communion with God. Baptism, First Communion, Confirmation, Marriage, and Anointing of the Sick are important sacraments celebrated with vibrant local customs and community gatherings.

2. Feast Days and Saints: The celebration of feast days dedicated to various saints is prominent. Each saint often has a counterpart in Vodou, and celebrations may include both Catholic and Vodou elements. For example, St. Patrick's Day is linked to the Vodou spirit Damballah, and the Feast of Our Lady of Mount Carmel coincides with the celebration of the Vodou lwa Ezili Dantor.

3. Processions and Pilgrimages: Although a dying ritual, Processions during religious festivals, such as Easter, and the Feast of Corpus Christi, are common. Pilgrimages to sacred sites, like the shrine of Saut-d'Eau, still attract thousands of worshippers seeking blessings, healing, and spiritual renewal.

4. Vodou Integration: Many Haitian Catholics also practice Vodou, and it influences their approach to Catholic rituals. Vodou songs, drumming, and dance are now incorporated into Catholic worship, especially during major celebrations. This syncretism is seen in the veneration of both Catholic saints and Vodou spirits (lwa).

5. All Souls' Day (Fèt Gede): This day is significant in Haiti, combining Catholic and Vodou traditions. Families visit cemeteries to clean and decorate graves, offer prayers, and perform rituals to honor the deceased. Vodou ceremonies for the Gede spirits, who are guardians of the dead, are also held.

6. Easter and Holy Week: The observance of Easter and Holy Week is marked by a blend of solemn Catholic rituals and vibrant cultural expressions. Good Friday and Easter Sunday are particularly important, with special Masses, processions, and community gatherings. There were some beliefs and taboos associated with Easter. For example, you can't shower on Good Friday because you can turn into a fish. If a hen lays an egg on Good Friday, that egg will stay fresh for the whole year. As Roland Pierre argues in his editorial for Sèl, "We are dying

under the crust of debilitating religious traditions. When will we reject these alienating traditions so that, at last, life can be rediscovered?"[163]

Burden of Confession

"Tell me, my child, tell me everything," a command the priests used to give to their Haitian parishioners to control their behavior and to coerce them into confessing their sins. Confession or the Sacrament of Reconciliation also known as Penance has always been a central teaching of the Catholic church. Both the priest and the penitent believe that Penance is a sure guarantee that their sins are forgiven. In the confessional, either behind a screen or face-to-face, you tell a priest your shameful secrets, and he acts in the person of Christ to grant absolution by setting you free from your sins. Then the penitent is assigned a penance to complete the process.

Most Haitian Catholics don't go to the confessional anymore. In smaller parishes, there is a greater possibility for the priest to know who is in and out of the confessional. For this reason, many Catholics don't bother to show up. When they do, they choose sins that are less shameful to confess. Because Haiti is an honor and shame culture, confessing your sin to others becomes a burden. What could have been a conversation between the "sinner" and his/her Abba Father, religion makes it a hindrance and a thorn in the side of the parishioner.

While it's true "if we confess our sins, he is faithful and just to forgive us our sins and to cleanse us from all unrighteousness (1

---

[163] See Sèl niméro 8, Avril 1973 in Digital Library of the Caribbean
https://dloc.com/AA00089969/00008/images

John 1:9)," the erroneous teaching of the Catholic Church on sin is breaking the back of their flocks. It's a burden to go to the "sin list" to find out which ones are mortal, venial, or not a sin at all. It creates confusion and fear. At the end of the day, it doesn't matter how many Hail Marys you say, it's just an extra-biblical exercise. *"Fòk sa chanje"*.

Pentecostal Catholicism

Charismatic Renewal is a movement within the Catholic Church that emphasizes the experience of the Holy Spirit. It has gained popularity in various parts of the world and has been active in many Catholic communities. In Haiti, it is also known as Pentecostal Catholicism for its closeness to the Pentecostal movement stream of Protestantism. Some aspects of this movement include spiritual gifts such as speaking in tongues, prophecy, and healing.

It's not clear when charismatic renewal was introduced in Haiti. According to André Corten, it was started by Claire Gagné, a Canadian nun, in the coastal town of Les Cayes.[164] After the fall of Baby Doc and the rise of *Ti Kominote Legliz* (TKL), the movement expanded as a way for Haitian Catholics to break away from serving Vodou Spirits without the need to be converted to Protestantism.

Le Conseil du Renouveau Charismatique Catholique des Haïtiens d'Outre-Mer (The Council of the Catholic Charismatic Renewal of Haitians Abroad) is the main association of Haitian Catholics abroad. They have a yearly gathering or a congress where

---

[164] André Corten, Misère, religion et politique en Haïti.: Diabolisation et mal politique (Paris: Éditions KARTHALA, 2001), 98

a variety of speakers tackle different aspects of spirituality. They borrow practices such as hand clapping, speaking in tongues, waving hands in the air, and responding to the priest during sermons from the protestant movement. While attending this gathering a participant can experience corporate worship, healing, and the indwelling of the Holy Spirit.

Protestantism: A Danger

Haitian Protestantism was initially viewed with suspicion by the country's Catholic majority, who saw it as a threat to their religious traditions and cultural identity. Protestant denominations were called sects and people who switched religions were seen as heretics. In his book *Catholicisme et vaudou*, Robert Paul Samson Jean Marie observe; *"Comme il est douloureux pour nous de constater que l'une des principales raisons pour laquelle on se fait protestant: c'est pour échapper à la superstition."*[165] (How painful it is for us to realize that one of the main reasons for becoming a Protestant is to escape superstition.) He later concedes,

> "Haïti n'est plus exclusivement à nous, il faudra lutter pour conserver la foi intègre, dans nos mornes plus encore que dans nos villes. Léogane est envahi, Jacmel contaminé, Marigot, Bainet atteints, Côtes de Fer et Petit Goâve et Grand Goâve tiennent bon. La grande secte de ces quartiers est l'Église Baptiste; comme ceux-ci ne confèrent le baptême qu'aux adultes, nos gens des mornes font encore baptiser leurs enfants par les prêtres. Mais certains points sont tellement gagnés à

---

[165] Robert Paul Samson Jean Marie, *Catholicisme et vaudou* (Cuernavaca, México: CIDOC, Centro Intercultural de Documentación, 1971) 104

l'hérésie que c'est par plusieurs milliers (5 à 6 000 à Léogane, dit-on) que nos gens des mornes se font protestants."[166]

"Haiti is no longer exclusively ours, we will have to fight to preserve the integrity of the faith, in our hills even more than in our cities. Léogane is invaded, Jacmel contaminated, Marigot, Bainet affected, Côtes de Fer and Petit Goâve and Grand Goâve hold on. The major sect of these districts is the Baptist Church; as they only confer baptism on adults, our people of the mountains still have their children baptized by priests. But some areas are so won by heresy that it is by several thousand (5 to 6,000 in Léogane, it is said) that our people of the mountains become Protestants.

But the feeling is mutual. Florent Toirac who was a missionary in Haiti in the 1950s argues that Catholicism has failed the Haitian people. In his book, *A Pioneer Missionary in the Twentieth Century,* Toirac notes, "After one hundred years of its existence as the state church...Voodooism, spiritism, and black magic, with their raw paganism, dominated and afflicted the masses. Catholicism was only a religious system, deviating from the truth, filling a sociopolitical and commercial role."[167]

Violent Love: War on Vodou

It is odd that the Catholic church would talk about love and the cross during mass on Sundays, then turn around and express that

---

[166] Cited in Lewis Ampidu Clorméus, "À propos de la seconde campagne antisuperstitieuse en Haïti (1911-1912)", Editions Karthala | « Histoire, monde et cultures religieuses » 2012/4 n° 24 | pages 105 à 130

[167] Toirac Florent, *A Pioneer Missionary in the Twentieth Century* (Winona Lake: Florent D. Toirac, 1986), 319

love through the sword and other violent rhetoric. From the *Code Noir* of 1685 to the late 1980s, Vodou was under attack by the Catholic church. Various wars on Vodou have been waged in 1864, 1896, 1912, 1925–1930, and 1940–1943. During the colonial period, Catholic missionaries viewed Vodou as satanism or a pagan religion and worked to convert Haitians to Catholicism and to suppress Vodou practices.

In the 19th century, the Catholic Church was involved in efforts to ban Vodou practitioners from urban areas. In the 20th century, some Catholic leaders have been engaged in efforts to eradicate Vodou through legal and social means. In its war on les sortilèges, the Catholic church often used the state as an enforcer as the state made the church a transformer of society.

Although the church was concerned with the rise of Protestantism in Haiti, its arch-rival was always Vodou. The mulatto elite in their quest to keep the French cultural tradition used the Catholic church and the government to come down hard on Vodou.

With the signing of the Concordat of 1860, between Rome and Haiti, the official partnership between church and state was renewed to wage war against the sortileges. As Michel Laguerre notes, "When the Catholic church persecutes Voodoo, it does so on behalf of the elite and with the help of the government. When the state persecutes Voodoo, it does so because of pressure from the elite and always on behalf of the Catholic church."[168]

---

[168] Michel S. Laguerre, Voodoo Heritage (Beverly Hills: Sage Publications, Inc, 1980)

During this violent campaign, Vodouists were coerced to give up their religious objects. Vodou temples and their sacred materials were destroyed and burnt. William Smarth notes that "the campaign takes both the aspect of the inquisition by the severity of its disciplinary measures and its sanctions and the aspect of the crusade by its horsemen armed with weapons, sticks, torches, storming the vodou temples."[169]

It is important to note that in recent years, there has been an increased recognition and respect for Vodou as an integral part of Haitian culture and identity. While tensions and misunderstandings may still exist, efforts have been made to foster dialogue and understanding between practitioners of Vodou and Catholics.

---

[169] William Smarth, *Histoire de l'Eglise catholique d'Haïti 1492-2003: des points de Repères (Vol II)* (Port-au-Prince: Les Éditions CIFOR, 2015), 382

CHAPTER 6

Missions, Missionaries, and Religious Tourism

—————— ❦ ——————

Americans have a savior complex where we believe that everyone needs what we have to offer and we need to be the ones offering it.

Adam Moody

We are tired of false religions that enslave us, shady missionaries that dehumanize us, and NGOs that misappropriate our resources.

Celucien Joseph

A sense of superiority has been instilled in us since the day we learned to speak English. Our songs, sermons, educational system, and political speeches all reinforce this idea.

Glenn Schwartz

We know what's wrong with short-term missions. They're short. It's the brevity that reinforces stereotypes, perpetuates misperceptions about the poor, and feeds the quick-fix mentality. It's the brevity that leaves local Christians feeling shortchanged. The very notion that missions can be short plays into tourism.

Daniel Rickett

Failed Mission

Quite a few missionaries have contributed to the spread of Christianity in Haiti. While I critique the methods and motives of the missionary enterprise, I must acknowledge the role some missionaries played in touching thousands of lives. Some were instrumental in building hospitals, medical clinics, schools, and other social programs the country badly needed. Unfortunately, the Western missionary movement has also played a major role in the "split-level Christianity" and the religious bondage of the Haitians. In this chapter, I will look at the contributing factors of mission agencies and missionaries to the burden of religion in Haiti.

There are a few reasons for the failure of religion and the missionary movement in Haiti. Among others, the main causes are the deeply embedded racist theology of Western missionaries, the failure of the missionary movement in fulfilling the needs of the Haitians against perceived threats of evil spirits and demonic influences, the notion of seeing Haitians as objects of religious conquest, the insensitivity to the Haitian culture, the inability to understand honor and shame in the Haitian context, the lack of contextualization of the gospel, and the inadequacy of the message.

From her genesis, Haiti has been a "Christian country". Catholicism came to the country in 1492 with Christopher Columbus, and Protestantism was reintroduced to Haitians in the early 1800s, as history shows that some of the slaves were already Christians in Africa. Additionally, a lot of mission agencies have been in and out of Haiti for decades. For example, World Team, originally WIM (West Indies Mission), is a U.S. agency for missions that has been there since 1936. Yet, after more than eighty-eight years in the country, WT still claims in their two-page country's profile that Haiti is still captive of "spiritual warfare" and "spiritual darkness."[170]

First, contrary to WT's erroneous belief, spiritual warfare is not about a particular country; it's a reality in the life of the followers of Christ. Sadly, denigrating non-Western countries is embedded in the WT ethnocentric view, a fundraising technique, a self-righteous act, and a common xenophobic practice often used by the Western missionary movement. They engage in cultural warfare by destroying the cultures of other people. This practice is not even close to spiritual warfare. It is pure religious oppression.

Second, WT fails to realize that the whole earth is under the power of the ruler of this world (1 John 5:19). Consequently, spiritual warfare is, among other things, what the followers of Christ do by coming against poverty, racism, class, gender discrimination, and by taking every thought captive.

If Haiti is still in "darkness" and in need of evangelization, as WT argues, it's either the missionary movement was a major failure or Haiti has never been in darkness to begin with. I believe both statements are accurate.

The problem is that the early American missionaries embraced the idea of a special calling. Since they associated Christianity with whiteness, they thought they were "the light" that illuminated the heathen nations of the world. A clear example is in the writings of Dr. Dudley Nelson, a former WT/WIM physician in southern Haiti from 1946 to the late 70s. In his book, *As the Cock Crows*, he summarizes the state of a Haitian Protestant evangelical church

---

[170] *"Haiti: Land of Mystery and Spiritual Warfare"* World team.https://us.worldteam.org/uploads/files/N-Haiti.pdf, accessed 3/12/2020.

(MEBSH) as follows: "Sadly it was a carnal church, mainly because of its background. The Haitians had poor biblical knowledge, satanic and superstitious lifestyles, and pre-conversion fleshly lifestyles."[171] Ironically, it seems that Dr. Nelson forgot that he and his fellow missionaries were the teachers. What did he expect? The missionaries, who lacked adequate biblical training, were mainly nurses, medical doctors, carpenters, and auto mechanics who were more interested in cultural surgery than in the people themselves. Additionally, you can only teach what you know. Who is to blame if the Haitian church leaders had inadequate biblical knowledge? When Edwin Walker, a fellow missionary at that time, questioned the paltry curriculum at the Bible Institute, a veteran missionary professor answered: "None of us have ever been a pastor...how could we teach them?"[172]

The missionaries had a different agenda: doing missions the American way. Their task was to change the value system of the Haitians by doing a cultural cleansing while getting rid of what they perceived as witchcraft, satanism, and black magic in what they called the "primitive" Haitian culture.[173]

Instead of honoring and respecting the otherness of the Haitians, the missionaries tried to impose Western values as the biblical worldview. Consequently, after more than thirty years in Haiti, it was Dr. Nelson who failed to bring about the change he wanted, the American way. You can build hospitals, schools, clinics, and

---

[171] Nelson G. Dudley, *As the Cock Crows: Reflections of a Medical Missionary to Haiti* (Franklin: Providence House Publishers, 1997), 125

[172] Edwin S. Walker III, Astonishing Grace: A Mentor's Ministry in Haiti and Beyond (Bloomington: WestBow Press, 2015), 45

[173] Nelson's book is not only his autobiography, but it also reflects the ethnocentric attitude of the early missionary movement in Haiti.

orphanages, as a missionary, and you can go up and down the mountains thinking you're doing missions, but without a loving relationship with the people you're "ministering" to, you're only doing charity work. William Hodges observed this when he wrote,

> For the missionary who goes overseas, institutionalization is of the highest priority, for it seems to him that nothing permanent will come of his work unless he can set up churches, schools, seminaries, hospitals, and other social organizations which will be indigenous and will continue after him.[174]

Forcing American culture on others has nothing to do with sharing the gospel. Florent Toirac, the Cuban-born French missionary, who was an eyewitness to the American way of doing missions, observed in his book, "Instead of training and helping the nationals to grow spiritually many missionaries actually avoided being involved with the nationals...because they became a sort of "threat" to the status of the missionary."[175]

Robert Reese argues, and rightly so:

> Most of the world is moving into a postcolonial frame of reference, but frequently American evangelicals continue to operate with a colonial mentality...we tend to be "take-charge" people, too impatient to let the local Christians exercise initiative and leadership...Therefore we perpetuate stereotypes from the colonial period that regard local people as inferior and in need of our

---

[174] Hodges, "A Philosophy of Christian Mission", 68
[175] Toirac, "A Pioneer Missionary in the Twentieth Century"433

guidance and resources...but this is all a deception born of a long history of Western domination over colonial peoples.[176]

As Carter Godwin Woodson argues,

If you can control a man's thinking you do not have to worry about his action. When you determine what a man shall think you do not have to concern yourself about what he will do. If you make a man feel that he is inferior, you do not have to compel him to accept an inferior status, for he will seek it himself. If you make a man think that he is justly an outcast, you do not have to order him to the back door. He will go without being told; and if there is no back door, his very nature will demand one.[177]

Later in his book, Dr. Nelson admits that only 50% of the people understood his accented Creole. Imagine a medical doctor from the U.S. conservative Baptist tradition in 1946, who barely spoke the local language, and who had no clue of the host's culture, engaging himself in teaching "illiterate" Haitian peasants the Bible? What could go wrong?

For starters, the Haitians were not learning anything new about God. They were being trained to think and act as white men in black skins. They were being brainwashed to commit cultural suicide by being led to believe that their culture was satanic. To this day, missionaries and Haitian evangelicals are still promoting this

---

[176] Robert Reese, Roots & Remedies of the Dependency Syndrome in World Missions (Littleton: William Carey Library, 2010), 119

[177] Carter Godwin Woodson, *The Mis-Education of the Negro* (The Journal of Pan African Studies: 2009 eBook), 41

nonsense.[178] No wonder most religious leaders who are trained in a Western-style biblical school have lost and rejected their cultural identity.

So, why was the message of the gospel lost from the early missionaries? Racism, a distorted picture of God, and a lack of cultural intelligence were the main factors. Having drunk from the enlightenment stream, some missionaries believe, as Stephen Neill points out, "Only Western man was wise and good, and members of other races in so far as they become westernized, might share in this wisdom and goodness."[179]

It's harder for missionaries to immerse themselves in the Haitian culture when they think Haitians have satanic lifestyles.

> During my limited stay in Haiti, my heart was greatly moved by the sin, superstition, and suffering of the multitudes. Every country on earth dominated by Roman Catholicism is under a curse, for every such country is given to idolatry, and idolatry is in God's eyes rated as the most hateful and hideous of all sins.[180]

This is what G. T. Bustin, a former missionary with the Evangelical Bible Mission wrote, after just a few days of being in the country.

---

[178] See for example the "News and Updates" section website of Emmaus University in Acul du Nord. In "even the pig did not die", and "Let us see what God will do…" are examples of sensational stories of Haitians and satanism and how their prayers lead to God's action to block satan at Bois Caiman (November and December 2020). For more, see https://emmaus.edu.ht/news-and-updates/

[179] Stephen Neil, *A History of Christian Mission* (Rev. for the 2nd ed. The Pelican History of the Church. New York: Penguin Books, 1986 [1964], 220

[180] G. T. Bustin, *My First Fifty Years* (Intercession City: Wesleyan Heritage Publications, 1997), 56

While it is normal for missionaries to bring their culture with them on the mission field, it is never appropriate for them to impose it on others. And that's exactly what they did in Haiti, they came to change and westernize the locals from their "barbaric" ways. As Toirac notes, "The missionaries wanted to plan the work themselves and then impose the decisions on the national."[181] These missionaries were more interested in the westernization of the Haitian culture than the Haitianization of Christianity.

Daniel Hill, the author of *White Awake: An Honest Look at What It Means to Be White*, said someone told him, "When white culture comes in contact with other cultures, it almost always wins."[182]

Lingenfelter Sherwood and Marvin Mayers in their book *Ministering Cross-Culturally: An Incarnational Model for Personal Relationships*, counsel, "We must love the people to whom we minister so much that we are willing to enter their culture as children, to learn how to speak as they speak, play as they play, eat what they eat, sleep where they sleep, study what they study, and thus earn their respect and admiration."[183]

In addition, Western missionaries did not know how to approach a culture mainly based on oral tradition. The missionaries deliberately avoided the elite and the educated class, claiming not

---

[181] Toirac, "A Pioneer Missionary in the Twentieth Century"434

[182] Daniel Hill, White Awake: An Honest Look at What It Means to Be White

[183] Lingenfelter, Sherwood and Mayers, Marvin K., Ministering Cross-Culturally: An Incarnational Model for Personal Relationships (Grand rapids: Baker Book House, 1986), 25

to "feel comfortable with them."[184] Instead, they went after the poor in the countryside, and they complained that they were "primitive", mountain people, uneducated, lower-class peasants, and slow learners, even as they ridiculed them in private and in their field reports.

In his book *Anthropological Insight for Missionaries* Paul Hiebert argues, "It's important for us as missionaries to realize that many national leaders with whom we work may appear to be "ignorant," or lacking large amounts of knowledge, but in fact, they may be wise in their handling of church situations."[185]

Religious Conquest

The missionary movement of the 19th and 20th centuries in Haiti can be summarized as an asymmetrical relationship. Because most missionaries considered themselves soldiers in a foreign land, being in the mission field was seen as a task: "*We went to this devil-worshiping country. Life was hard, but we "fixed" them,*" meaning we showed them our ways. When he was asked how he would describe the Church of the Nazarene missionary strategy, Howard Culbertson, former missionary to Haiti, responded, "The Church of the Nazarene views its missionaries as assault troops"[186]. Is it one of the reasons U.S. military conquests go hand in hand with religious conquests? No wonder mission agencies use military language in their recruitment booklets. For example, on a mission agency

---

[184] Edwin S. Walker III, Astonishing Grace (Bloomington: WestBow Press, 2015), 45

[185] Paul Hiebert, *Anthropological Insights for Missionaries* (Grand Rapids: Baker Books, 1985), 136

[186] Q & A "Mr. Missionary, I have a Question", Howard Culbertson. Accessed 3/10/2020 http://home.snu.edu/~hculbert/mr6.htm

website, the process is as follows: identify, activate, develop, and deploy. It's similar to the U.S. Army process: enlistment, basic training, activate, deploy. Since everything about the mission is task-oriented, missionaries use language like "soul winning" and "church planting" which put the focus on tasks, activities, and results.

This did not happen only in Haiti. Evangelization was also established by violence in a lot of places around the world, particularly in Africa. They also used spirituality in much the same way as territorial conquest: coercion and force. The systematic eradication of indigenous lifestyles and beliefs has always been one of the most powerful weapons used to oppress indigenous people. It is still alive today in the religious zeal of some evangelical missionaries. Commenting on an article on Yahoo, a user wrote,

> Proselytizing by its very nature must include deception, coercion, emotional manipulation, threats, and even bribery. Traveling Jesus-peddlers are culture junkies looking for their next fix (conversion) in order to feel good about themselves. And if preaching involves exploiting extremely vulnerable people and disrespecting the existing religions of targeted populations, so be it. After all, the "primitives" need to have their souls "saved," whether or not they want the Protestant white man's church and creed in their village.[187]

In her book, *Called as Partners in Christ Service*, Sherron Kay George, notes "Through the years our sense of "evangelical"

---

[187] Freethinker, "He paid the ultimate price': the grisly fate of the missionary who met the last 'uncontacted' tribe https://www.yahoo.com/lifestyle/paid-ultimate-price-grisly-fate-080000262.html

responsibility has been tainted by pride and has developed into an offensive hegemony with arrogant imperialistic assumptions about our unique leadership role in the world."[188]

The Theology of the Curse

The theology of the curse is a doctrine based on the Western myth that anyone descended from Ham and Cush (black people) is cursed and therefore subhuman. For centuries, Western Bible teachers have been making this unjust interpretation that the Cushite were inferior because of their dark skin, therefore they are a slave race. Africa was then considered a dark land, inhabited by dark-skinned heathened people, uncivilized, and without religion.

By treating blacks as subhumans, it is easier not to have any guilt in abusing them. To justify this thinking, the German theologian Count Nicolaus Zinzendorf says, "God punishes the first negroes by making them slaves, and your conversion will make you free, not from the control of your masters, but simply from your wicked habits and thoughts, and all that makes you dissatisfied with your lot."[189]

The colonial Christians, in their attempt to civilize the slaves, brainwashed them into accepting their social condition as fulfilling the will of God.

After he had called Haiti the devil's territory, Florent Toirac said, "God allowed Haitian slavery to bring about His purpose."[190] It makes one wonder if it was God's purpose that, during World War

---

[188] George Sherron Kay, Called as Partners in Christ's Service: The Practice of God's Mission (Louisville: Geneva Press, 2004), 53

[189] Cited in Noel Leo Erskine, *Decolonizing Theology* (Trenton: Africa World Press, Inc, 1988), 30

[190] Toirac, "A Pioneer Missionary in the Twentieth Century", 318

I, Toirac's immediate family in Cuba bought at least five hundred Haitians as slaves at $250 a head to work in their banana groves and tobacco farms.[191]

White Supremacy and Cultural Imperialism

There is no place where white supremacy is more prevalent than within the Western missionary movement. The racist attitude of some missionaries is hidden in plain view. It's in their actions, their conversation, and their writings. For hundreds of years, missionaries were teaching the Haitian peasants that sin and the blackness of their skin are all the same.

As a result, some Haitians have low self-esteem, and they think their blackness is not worthy of God's love. It's not a surprise to hear one of the Turnbulls' converts at the Baptist Mission in Fermathe pray: "Lord, our skin is black, but our sins are blacker; but you have delivered us from Satan and made us white."[192]

This hymn, inserted in the popular Haitian hymn book, *Les Chants d'Éspérance*, says it all:

> Voyez, voyez! Les voici!
> En foule accourent ici:
> De leurs cités innombrables
> **Les mystérieux Chinois,**
> **Et les Hindous misérables**…
> Tous regardent vers la croix.
> Voyez, voyez! Les voici!
>
> Lentement s'approche aussi

---

[191] Ibid, 226
[192] Anderson, "Beyond All This", 202.

L'Africain noir et sauvage.
Aux pieds du Crucifié,
Son long et dur esclavage
Sera bientôt oublié![193]

See, see! Here they are!
In crowds flock here:
Of their countless cities
The mysterious Chinese,
And the miserable Hindus ...
All are looking towards the cross.

See, see! Here they are!
Slowly approaching too
The black and savage African.
At the feet of the Crucified,
His long and hard slavery
Will soon be forgotten!

Most missionaries came to Haiti with their assumptions and preconceived attitudes toward the Haitian people. Having linked Haitians with "dark" Africa, they believed Haiti was a backward nation, inhabited by wild, lazy, slow, irrational, and immoral people. In *Crusading in the West Indies*, Jordan William says, "Backward as Haiti is, she has discovered that Bible readers, those

---

[193] There are various versions of this song in both French and English. However, this particular French translation does not do justice to Wakefield's English version, but the translators could not resist the urge to show their superiority over non-Europeans. Wakefiel wrote; "From the wild and scorching desert, Afric's sons awaked from sleep." After many complaints, the French version was revised to change the language and add the remaining verses. See *Les Chants d'Espérance* #242, original translation of J. Wakefield MacGill "Coming, coming, yes they are", Public Domain, https://hymnary.org/text/coming_coming_yes_they_are.

who profess to live by the principles laid down in the Book, are the only people to be depended upon."[194]

Linda Crow, a former missionary with the Church of the Nazarene in Haiti, in her book *Haiti I Love You*, writes, "I've heard the eerie voodoo drumbeats, the chants of the devil worshipers, and seen your sons and daughters gripped with heathenism, and thought how mysterious you are."[195]

Mildred Anderson, in *Beyond All This*, called Haiti "the darkest corner of our hemisphere"[196] and a "primitive land."[197]

Most missionaries accepted their racial and cultural superiority as a given. For some missiologists and missionaries, the West is by default Christian. No wonder in missionary literature on how to communicate Christ to other cultures, it's hard to find a chapter on the Western worldview.

In a speech given in 1993 at the Road to Victory Conference of the Christian Coalition, former presidential candidate Pat Buchanan confirmed this when he said: "Our culture is superior. Our culture is superior because our religion is Christianity and that is the truth that makes men free."[198]

On this note, Lingenfelter and Mayers caution,

---

[194] Jordan, "Cruisading in the West Indies", 109-110

[195] Linda Crow, *Haiti I Love You* (Kansas City: Nazarene Publishing House, 1970), 9

[196] Anderson, "*Beyond All This*", 214

[197] Ibid, 133.

[198] See "*Pat Buchanan in His Own Words*", quoted in https://fair.org/press-release/pat-buchanan-in-his-own-words/

While every culture is imperfect and may be used by individuals in it for good or evil purposes, each one is the integrating point of reference by which people comprehend themselves and others. So if we are to minister successfully to the members of a different society, we must learn about and participate in their culture; we must even learn to do things their way rather than our own.[199]

Kosuke Koyama rightly argues, "I doubt strongly whether the idea that the "people over there are enemies of God" is central to the Spirit of Christ. The Spirit of Christ does not support the spirit of greed to conquer others and self-righteousness to demonstrate our superior piety."[200]

Missionaries in Haiti have a pattern of denigrating the country and its people. They are the ones who decide which customs and beliefs are profane and superstitious. It is white supremacy that led Mildred Anderson to say that "Satan is the prince of this world, but headquartered in Haiti."[201] It's her ethnocentric view the reason she argues that fear "had held the primitive minds [of the Haitians] in bondage from man's emergence from the jungle."[202] Some missionaries acted as if they were the ones who brought God and Christianity to Haiti, and they played god as if God was not already at work in the hearts of the Haitians. Listen to Wally Turnbull,

---

[199] Lingenfelter and Mayers, "*Ministering Cross-Culturally*", 122

[200] Cited in Bryant L. Myers. *Walking With The Poor: Principles and Practices of Transformational Development* (Revised and Expanded Edition). Orbis Books. Kindle Edition. Location 6142.

[201] Anderson, "*Beyond All This*", 84

[202] Ibid, 42

Look, they are starving and we give them food. They're dying and we give them medicine. Medicine that works. Isn't that Christian? This country is poor because of voodoo. These people have no responsibility. The gods did it they tell you. They're so stupid. To us, it looks like utter stupidity, but that is the African mind.[203]

Considering the Turnbulls were in Haiti for over seventy years taking advantage of the "stupidity" of the "mountain people" in Fermathe, the old lie[204] perpetrated by some missionaries to enrich themselves must be true. Bryant Myers, as if he was debunking Turnbull's claim, in *Walking With the Poor* argues, "The assertion that the poor are ignorant and stupid does not survive any informed knowledge of real poor people. The depth and breadth of their indigenous knowledge frequently astound us."[205]

In *We Are Not The Hero*, former missionary Jean Johnson notes,

When Western missionaries use their ethnocentric influence and economic affluence in ministry, they inevitably birth ministries that are carbon copies of their expensive, Western form of Christianity. This action makes it nearly impossible for local disciples of Christ to implement effective evangelism,

---

[203] Cited in Amy Wilentz, *The Rainy Season: Haiti Since Duvalier* (New York: Simon and Schuster, 1989), 190

[204] To stay in the country longer and to hold on to their power, some missionaries used to tell their supporters and mission agencies that Haitians are worthless, stupid, and unteachable.

[205] Bryant L. Myers, *Walking With The Poor: Principles and Practices of Transformational Development* (Revised and Expanded Edition). Orbis Books. Kindle Edition.

discipleship, worship, acts of compassion, leadership training, and church planting by mobilizing their own local resources and cultural expressions.[206]

Paul Orjala, just two months in Port-au-Prince as a missionary, picked up on the theme and noted, "With just a little water, almost anything will grow like a weed in Haiti — in fact most growing things are weeds."[207] Seriously?

Orjala forgot that he was in a suburban area near a ravine where wild things naturally grow. It seems that Haiti was not even his choice. He cemented that thought by writing in his diary, "We [he and his wife] have often wondered how the board happened to send us here instead of a more mature couple with missionary experience."[208]

Later, he described the Haitians as "like the Spanish "mañana" with their "demain" when it comes to work. If you get one piece of business done, why crowd another into the same day? You might not have anything to do tomorrow."[209]

As Jerry Mander points out in *The Absence of the Sacred,* "Our assumption of superiority does not come to us by accident. We have been trained in it. It is soaked into the fabric of every Western

---

[206] Jean Johnson, *We Are Not The Hero* (Sisters: Deep River Books, 2012), 17

[207] Kathleen Spell, *Haiti Dairy: Compiled from the Letters of Paul Orjala* (Kansas City: Bacon Hill Press, 1953), 27

[208] Ibid. 52

[209] Ibid. 52

religion, economic system, and technology. They reek of their greater virtues and capabilities."[210]

G. T. Bustin was from Mississippi, and he went to Haiti as a missionary in 1945. He was visiting the village of Source Matelas when he came in contact with the death of a child. He had this to say, "We went into the mud hut where the little thing lay on the cold ground with a few banana leaves as its bed."[211]

Bustin was so blinded by racism and his sense of superiority that he failed to see that the "little thing" he was talking about was made in the image of God. Whether this precious child was lying on banana leaves or his wife in a "beautiful mahogany casket,"[212] both of them are loved by God, and they were worth Jesus dying for them. The sad thing is that Bustin's ethnocentric view is the norm among missionaries rather than the exception.

When I was living in Haiti, I knew quite a few missionaries who had used dehumanizing language to describe Haitians. Derogatory words such as primitive, barbarian, retarded, simple-minded, and savage were common usage.

By presenting themselves, their culture, and their religion as superior, and by reducing Haitians to subhuman, it makes it easier for these missionaries to hunker down in their mission compound. Instead of affirming the Haitians as bearers of the image of God, the missionaries wanted to make them in their image. Haitians are not more stupid than the followers of QAnon and the hundreds of

---

[210] Jerry Mander, *The Absence of the Sacred* (San Francisco: Sierra Club Books, 1991) 209

[211] Bustin, "My First Fifty Years", 69

[212] Bustin grieved the death of his wife in Haiti where she was also buried in a mahogany coffin made by Haitians. Bustin, "My First Fifty years", 74-75

followers of cult leaders such as David Koresh and Jim Jones. Every culture and every country has groups of people who let themselves be duped into believing some type of theory.

Ivah Heneise and her husband Harold were missionaries in Haiti with the American Baptist National Ministries for over thirty years. They are credited for implementing the Baptist Seminary in Limbé and other social programs in the area. Her book, *By The Light of My Kerosene Lamp*, is a series of letters to her mother with whom she shared her experiences in Haiti from 1947 to 1982.

"On a Sunday afternoon", she writes, barely three months in the country, she invites people over for a meeting, and she describes them to her mom: "I wish you can see how poor and ragged the people are"[213], and a year later, "people are as thin and ragged as ever"[214]. She continues fourteen years later, "Most people are ragged and half naked. All are poor and underfed."[215]

On his second day in Haiti, Jordan William describes a security guard as, "A half-starved, dirty, ragged, unkempt, barefoot negro boy soldier is on guard, sitting in the dirt nearby."[216]

While describing the people in a village, Bustin says, "a motley crowd of half-dressed natives with bleary, scornful, sleep-sodden eyes."[217] When you read books and reports written by field missionaries in Haiti, you would think the whole country is as they depicted it. The picture folks get back home is that everybody in

---

[213] Yvah, Heneise, *By The Light Of My Kerosene Lamp* (Valley Forge: International Ministries, 1982), 8
[214] Ibid., 11
[215] Ibid., 30-32,
[216] Jordan, *Crusading in The West Indies,* 93
[217] Bustin, "*My First Fifty Years*", 69

Haiti is poor, uneducated, half-naked, and living in mud homes. This is a deliberate act of defining people by what they have instead of who they are. Listen to Heneise again describing her "Haitian neighbors," "ragged mothers whose starving babies are huddled to empty breasts, naked little children with matchstick legs and swollen stomachs, emaciated fathers with desperate eyes."[218] With this attitude, the missionary will fail to closely examine local folklore as Eugene Nida observes:

> When an American goes to a foreign country, however, he tends to judge all situations by what he has known at home. He does not appreciate the significance of the existing contrasts, because his eyes have not been opened to them. He therefore lumps all groups together and proceeds without reference to basic differences.[219]

In his book *Cultural Insights for Missionaries*, Paul G. Hiebert notes,

> As missionaries, we compare our culture with the cultures in which we serve: cars versus oxcarts and cycles, electricity versus oil lamps, gas stoves and refrigerators versus campfire and dried foods, and sanitary toilets versus the bush. And we conclude that we are more civilized.[220]

---

[218] Heneise, "By The Light Of My Kerosene Lamp", 26

[219] Eugene A. Nida, Message and Mission (South Pasadena: William Carey Library, 1960),121

[220] Paul G. Hiebert, Anthropological Insights for Missionaries (Grand Rapids: Baker Book House, 1985), 116.

In San Francisco, California, at the time of this writing, there is a mile long of people sleeping on the sidewalks, in makeshift tents, and under bridges. Every big city in the U.S. has something similar. There is an area of downtown Los Angeles that is home to one of the largest homeless populations in the United States. An estimated 3,000 to 6,000 homeless people reside on the sidewalks in cardboard boxes and tents. If I were a missionary to these places, I would write back home to say: "The people here in the U.S. have no homes, and they all sleep on the side of the road." Would I be doing justice to the United States as a whole?

Like the sensationalist travelers, the early missionaries were no different when they talked about their heroic adventures in a land of "darkness". Their sacrificial picture is painted as white missionaries getting stuck in the mud with their trucks, crossing raging rivers, and living with no electricity nor running water, no Christmas trees, taking cold showers, and critters running in and out of their house. Their heroic feats feel like one is reading the adventures of Robinson Crusoe or The Swiss Family Robinson. All for Jesus.

One can be moved to do missions by reading about the heroic adventures of missionaries *From Jerusalem to Irian Jaya,*[221] but being a missionary without love is self-serving. The apostle Paul was indeed beaten, imprisoned, shipwrecked, and eventually put to death, but this is not how the early church remembered him. Jesus "endured the cross for the joy that was set before him (Heb 12:2)."

---

[221] *From Jerusalem to Irian Jaya* is a popular book on Christian missions' history by Ruth A. Tucker.

When missionaries go to a respondent culture, they tend to judge that culture through the lens of their own culture. Most of the time, judgment will put observing and learning on the back burner, making them miss the beauty of missions. Robert Reese once said,

> North Americans tend to judge other cultures based on their technology or economy and military with our own and generally find them lacking. At the same time, we may omit to compare their social systems and family structures with ours, as we value hardware perhaps more than relationships."[222]

As James Heisig points out, "Most missionaries do not give up home and land and civilization; they carry it with them and systematically resist radical change in the cultural biases of the religion they are propagandizing for."[223]

No wonder it took Heneise twenty-five years to realize that she and her husband didn't bring "civilization" to Haiti. In her book she notes, "All the time there has been here a kind of "civilization" -a deep courtesy, a sincere hospitality, a love of family, a spiritual sensitivity, a basic dignity."[224]

At the end of her time in Haiti and thirty-five years later, by then, her daughter had married a Haitian (Jules Casséus), a former student of the seminary, and they had given her two grandchildren. What does Heneise think of Haiti now [1982]? She says,

---

[222] Robert Reese, Roots and Remedies of the Dependency Syndrome in World Missions (Littelton: William Carey Library, 2010), 147

[223] James Heisig, "Christian Mission: The Selfish War", accessed 10/10/2020, https://nirc.nanzan-u.ac.jp/en/files/2013/07/JWH-Christian-Mission-Selfish-War.pdf

[224] Heneise, "By The Light Of My Kerosene Lamp", 47

A misty green hump in a tropical sea. Cloud-capped mountains, deep valleys, and a scalloped trim of emerald plains. Nights filled with the perfume of orange blossoms and the work song of the peasants...The feeling of comradeship, of warm oneness that laughs at discomforts and philosophizes at hardships...the road filled with brightly dressed young people.[225]

What happened to the half-naked people and the "strange and haunting rhythm" of the Vodou drums in this "God-forsaken island"? Did she clothe them? Did she feed them? I don't think there were many deep changes in the lives of the Haitians during her time there. The orange trees have always blossomed, and the peasants have been singing to the beats of the drums since colonial times. I believe the veil of her prejudice had been lifted, and she was able to smell the perfume of the orange trees, enjoy the songs of the peasants, and see that young people had been "brightly dressed" all along.

If you want to see white supremacy at work, look into the mission field. I can't even understand why some missionaries would spend twenty to forty years in Haiti, yet show such disdain for the people and their culture. Maybe it's because, as Bernice Johnson, a former nurse missionary said, "Haiti fits my picture of a mission field--poor and sick."[226] In other words, being a missionary was about her.

---

[225] Ibid, 70

[226] Johnson, "She Did What She Could", 9

And she would be one of the many Florent Toirac was talking about when he argued that there are some missionaries "who never should have been allowed to go to serve in a foreign country."[227]

Oligarch Missionaries

As it is with a dozen elite families who control 85% of the wealth in Haiti, there are also a handful of family enterprises in the mission field in Haiti. Some would call them veteran or seasoned missionaries because they have been in the country for more than thirty years, but a more appropriate term would be oligarch missionaries. In these family enterprises, the business of missions is passed down from generation to generation while enriching themselves on the poverty of the Haitians. If the original idea was to preach the gospel while assisting the "poor", over the years it became a social enterprise to enrich themselves under the guise of sustainability and development, so that now the missionary movement is more beneficial to the missionaries than it is to the responding culture.

In addition, the oligarch missionary families know the ins and outs of the Haitian government. Not only do they influence some of the decisions made by the U.S. Embassy and USAID in Haiti, but they also co-opt their mission by meddling with corrupt local politicians and public institutions. While they complain daily to their donors and supporters about corruption in Haiti and how Haitians cannot be trusted, they take advantage of a corrupt system by robbing the Haitians of their honor, their pride, their dignity, and their culture.

---

[227] Toirac, "A Pioneer Missionary in the Twentieth Century", 429

Under the guise of social programs such as medical clinics, schools, and feeding programs, they exploit the poor while throwing at them some breadcrumbs. And what their supporters get in return are some crafty newsletters to include touching and uplifting stories with supporting pictures as evidence of what God is doing in Haiti. Sad!

Missionaries and The Great Commission

A young Haitian man knocked at the door of a missionary's house and asked him if he could borrow his truck for a short trip in town. The missionary told him that he couldn't do that because the truck was assigned by his agency for mission work only. The young man replied: "Am I not your mission?"

Unfortunately, cases like that are quite common in the mission field. Missionaries are trained to forget that mission is as much about being and doing. Former missionary to Haiti (MEBSH) Ed Walker recalled one of those instances where a Haitian pastor's wife was having difficulty during childbirth. The pastor ran to a missionary for help transporting his wife to the hospital. But the missionary asked to be paid first.[228]

The first wave of missionaries of the 1930s came to "fix" the Haitian "backward culture". They took advantage of the Haitian radical hospitality, but they closed their doors and lived in isolation from the people they were supposed to serve. Few are the ones who believe they need to immerse themselves in the local communities. Ed Walker was probably one of the few missionaries who resented

---

[228] See Ed Walker, "Astonishing Grace", 52

163

what he called a "missionary-compound mentality".[229] I knew of a few missionaries at MEBSH who were recalled by their sending agencies because other missionaries reported that they were too cozy with the Haitians.

Interestingly, Toirac was himself a victim of discrimination. Although he was white of French descent, he was considered a Cuban and, therefore a national. Consequently, the WIM didn't want to support him financially, and he was shunned for marrying Dorothy Lee, a white American missionary he met in Haiti. He was eventually forced out of MEBSH after thirteen years of ministry because he didn't want to break up her relationship with Dorothy. He claims, "Over and over again I had been humiliated and discriminated against by some of the missionaries because I was a national."[230]

No wonder books written by fellow missionaries in Haiti barely mention Toirac and Curtis Holmes, an African-American from Michigan who was at MEBSH for years. It's not surprising that one of the main reasons for attrition among missionaries is relationship problems with other missionaries and their sending agencies.

Bernice Johnson, who went to Haiti in 1946 with the West Indies Mission and Andrews Memorial Baptist of Graham, NC, tried a few times the Haitian hospitality and conceded in her testimony that:

> Haitian hospitality is beautiful. I loved it. They are such friendly, easy-to-love people and they treated us royally, putting me to shame over and over again. Getting out in the country

---

[229] Edwin S. Walker III, "Astonishing Grace", 45
[230] Toirac, "A Pioneer Missionary"

and into their homes was a tonic for me. Sitting at their tables, eating their food, and sleeping in their beds gave me an entirely different view of the people.[231]

Still, after 23 years in Haiti, she could not resist sharing her prejudice. In an interview with Bob Minnis of the Daily News in 1969, she described her mission field as follows: "Suffering, poverty, sickness, and superstition characterize the Haitian people. But they are a people resigned to their way of life and seemingly happy even in these adverse circumstances. They don't know any better."[232] Johnson is not alone. I've met missionaries in Haiti who, after 30 years in the country, still feel like total strangers. They're not comfortable spending time with the local people. Their neighbors are other missionaries like them. Even when they attend a local church service, they don't mingle with the local congregation. As soon as the service is over, they sprint out. When I asked a former missionary why he went to Haiti, he told me there is something in missionary circles called "white love" and white guilt". You go on a mission to fix what you think is wrong and at the same time alleviate the guilt of being privileged. It's no wonder they don't want to go back home, as if they were on a perpetual vacation. Of course, some missionaries do not follow the status quo, but unfortunately, they don't have a loudmouth.

---

[231] Bernice Johnson, She Did What She Could: The Missionary Journal of Bernice Johnson, 82
[232] Ibid, 31

Converting the Converted

"Jezi renmen ou" (Jesus loves you) is the only evangelism phrase missionaries can say in Creole. Otherwise, they have to rely on social services to evangelize "the lost". If one were to browse mission agencies' websites and read reports from field missionaries, one would think there are no more "lost souls" in Haiti.

From baptizing 3000 people on a given Sunday, 600 converts on the last day of the evangelism crusade, to churches multiplying by the hundreds, their reports are filled with astonishing numbers on what God is doing in Haiti. Hand of Hope, a division of Joyce Meyer Ministries, claims that 2371 souls were saved out of 21,971 patients seen at their short-term medical ministries.

What the statistics don't show is how many of those were already converted. When social services are used as a means, especially at health care facilities, to attract people to Christ, then conversion is only a transaction, an exchange of goods between the parties. If today Haiti is said to be 45% Catholics and 52% Protestants, isn't she a Christian nation? The Joshua Project, a research organization engaging in highlighting unreached people groups around the world, says in their latest update (2019) that Haiti was 94.8% Christians.[233]

One of the main verses used by the missionaries in the 50s and 60s was "Therefore if anyone is in Christ, he is a new creature; the old things passed away; behold, new things have come (2 Cor 5:17 NASB)."

---

[233] See https://joshuaproject.net/countries/HA#languages

When Linda Crow wrote, "I was haunted night and day by the beat of the voodoo drums in the village,"[234] she automatically assumed that Haitians are devil worshippers. When Wallace Turnbull purchased a piece of land previously owned by a Vodou priest in Fermathe, it was presumed to be a victory over darkness. For Elizabeth Turnbull, the granddaughter of Wallace, it was "A Vodou stronghold claimed for Christ."[235] By characterizing Vodou as purely satanic, a lot of missionaries were emphasizing what this "new creature" in Christ was supposed to look like instead of nurturing who the Haitians were.

For them, the "new creature" had to undergo cultural surgery. Consequently, the uniqueness of Christianity took precedence over the uniqueness of Christ. As G. Parrinder points out, "The old attitude of missionaries was usually destructive; the indigenous religion was not studied, it was not thought to have any divine revelation or inspiration, and little effort was made to use any part of it as a basis for fuller teaching."[236]

As a result, converting became just a change of religious expression. These missional activities resulted, as a consequence, in Western formalized theology, western hymns and liturgies, demonization of indigenous culture, and the identification of Christianity as the religion of the white man. As Herbert Kane

---

[234] Linda Crow, *Haiti, I Love You* (Kansas City: Nazarene Publishing House, 1970), 37.

[235] Elizabeth Turnbull, *Say To These Mountains* (Durham: Light Messages, 2017), 47

[236] G. Parrinder, "Theistic Beliefs of the Yoruba and the Ewe Peoples of West Africa," in African Ideas of God: A Symposium, ed. Edwin W. Smith (London: Edinburgh House Press, 1950), 239.

argues, "The Third World churches got the theology we gave them, not the theology they needed."[237]

Haitian Vodou can be compared with the theology of the OT. In essence, the Vodouist mental picture of God, their understanding of the cosmos, their creation care, their sacrificial system, and their liberation theology are no different than the ancient Israelites. When you fail to understand that Christ can redeem the Haitian people within their own culture, you end up preaching Christianity instead of Christ. Consequently, converting became just a change of religion. Therefore, the church is full of people who are simply religious. And what makes the missionary think that God is not actively working in Haiti? We know Vodouists already believe in the existence of a good God (Bondye). There is no point in trying to prove the existence of God as a means to coerce them to accept Jesus as their savior. In his book *Miracles, Mission, and American Pentecostalism*, Gary McGee notes,

> The gospel is often presented to people in alien cultural forms. Then the missionaries are resented and their message is rejected because their work is seen not as an attempt to evangelize but as an attempt to impose their own customs and way of life. Where missionaries bring with them foreign ways of thinking and behaving, or attitudes of racial superiority, paternalism, or preoccupation with material things, effective communication will be precluded.[238]

---

[237] J. Herbert Kane, *The Christian World Mission: Today and Tomorrow* (Grand Rapids: Baker Book House, 1981), 191

[238] "The Willowbank Report: Consultation on Gospel and Culture", Lausanne Committee for World Evangelization, https://www.lausanne.org/content/lop/lop-2

In his book, *The Myth of a Christian Nation*, Gregory Boyd rightly argues:

> Instead of respecting the integrity of people's beliefs, and building on what is true about them, we simply point out what we think is wrong. Rather than looking for the best, believing the best, and hoping for the best, we zero in on what we believe is the worst. Rather than serving people by taking the time to understand their worldview, we assume they think like us and speak to them from within our own worldview. Consequently, we unwittingly undermine the credibility of the gospel and do not communicate the central thing we are called to communicate — Calvary-quality love.[239]

And Eugene Nida observes, "Too often the minister or missionary regards himself as an intermediary of a superior message from God, and hence not aware of or dependent upon the feedback that should come from the congregation."[240]

Gospel *Pèpè*, Coercion, and Missionary Medicine

Gospel *Pèpè* (foreign) is when the good news of the gospel is co-opted with the "gospel of goods". It's when the new missionary movement ships containers of food, medicine, and clothes, and uses STMs to distribute the goods to attract thousands of people to Jesus. When the shipping containers stop coming the new converts are nowhere to be found.

---

[239] Gregory A. Boyd, *The Myth of a Christian Nation* (Grand Rapids: Zondervan, 2005), 159

[240] Eugene A. Nida, *Message and Mission: The Communication of the Christian Faith* (South Pasadena: William Carey Library, 1960), 99

It is well-known that one of the bait-and-switch tactics used by the Western missionary movement is to use social programs to attract people and hope they will convert and accept the gospel. After the 2010 earthquake, the gospel *pèpè* model was on full display. As U.S. churches and organizations poured into the country, they gave away toys, food, and clothes throughout Haiti while claiming many converts. In missionary circles, they say the end justifies the means. However, the desire to see people come to Christ should not be coercive or manipulative. Wealth should not be a tool to manipulate the poor into accepting the gospel.

Another tool in the missionary toolbox is missionary medicine. In Haiti, as it is in various parts of the world, medical missions are of great value. However, the problem arises when missionary nurses and doctors are putting more emphasis on God being the healer in lieu of the medicine they prescribe. While it's true that God is the ultimate healer, it's wrong when missionaries suggest to their patients that antibiotics, pain relievers, and other drugs have no effects on the fever, the infection, and the worms.

In her book, *Victory over Voodoo*, Linda Crow recounted several stories of Haitians who have been delivered from the "darkness of Vodou" to victory in Christ.[241] As I was reading the book, one particular story caught my attention. Crow recalled the story of Jacqueline, a young Haitian woman, who thought she was

---

[241] Terry Read was a missionary in Haiti in the 1960s. He recorded on tape the interviews for Linda Crow. As the author acknowledges, this book is written purely from a missionary point of view and as a missionary marketing propaganda. While it is possible for a missionary to have a working knowledge of a respondent cultural system, it is very difficult for him/her not to fall into the trap of cultural relativism. Linda Crow, *Victory over Voodoo* (Kansas City: Nazarene Publishing House, 1975), 8.

cursed by bad spirits and demons who wanted to kill her. A few days after Jacqueline had given birth to a baby boy, delivered by the local midwife, she had a fever, and the local ougan could not treat her. Then the local pastor and the missionaries came to the rescue. She was healed, and there was victory over Vodou.[242] The following is a lengthy excerpt from the story:

> When the baby was nine days old, I became ill with abdominal pain and a high fever. The fever was so high that at times I was irrational. So finally the decision was made to visit the voodoo priest.
>
> Gilaine, the old voodoo priest, saw us coming and instructed the men who were carrying me to bring the chair onto the cement-floored, metal-roofed porch that surrounded two sides of his house. My mother, Ibo, who is a mambo (a voodoo priestess), stepped up to the tall hollow-eyed man and made the sigh of the voodoo cross. She felt Gilaine's powers were much greater than hers and that he would be able to prescribe a successful treatment for my illness…
>
> In a calm yet mysterious voice, Gilaine proceeded to tell my mother the necessary procedure for my healing. It would involve a sacrifice of live animals, a voodoo ceremony, herbal medicines, and of course a high payment to be made in advance to Gilaine.[243]

---

[242]These types of miracles and deliverance stories from Vodou are abundant in missionary literature. Usually, these testimonies are far away from the truth, as they always portray the missionary as the "savior". A natural illness has nothing to do with Vodou spirits. While the patient may have to go to the ougan for some herbal medicines, it doesn't have to be *dyab* related. See for example, "*Sauvé de la sorcellerie pour servir le Seigneur*" in Le Courrier Évangélique Mai 2003, p.16-18, or missionary stories from Haiti, such as, Linda Gouge, *Esther's God and the Witch Doctor*, and Ruth Harner, *Ti Fam: Witch Doctor's Daughter.*

[243] Crow, "Victory over Voodoo", 31-32

Two observations with this story. First, fever and abdominal pain were a relatively common occurrence for women in the postpartum period in rural Haiti, especially in the 1960s. Jacqueline most likely had a microbial infection of the uterus which caused the high fever, and her abdominal pain was probably caused by a rare condition of the HELLP syndrome, similar to pre-eclampsia. It is also likely she suffered from Postpartum Psychosis, which made her confused, delusional, hallucinate, and depressed.

Second, one of the missionaries, Mrs. Ford, was a registered nurse, and she knew exactly Jacqueline's condition was not related to evil spirits. Jacqueline said they gave her medicine, probably some antibiotics, quinine, and cafenol pills (similar to ibuprofen), and after a few days of rest, she was well. Instead of telling her she was infected by the midwife and poor sanitary conditions, the missionaries reinforced Jacqueline's fear of "bad Vodou spirits". To coerce her into conversion, the missionaries made it about a battle between the force of "good" (white people and God) against the force of evil (Vodou and the *manbo*).

Consequently, Jacqueline was healed only because the God of the missionaries was more powerful than the gods of Vodou, reinforcing Jacqueline's worldview.

While the missionaries might have claimed victory over Vodou, in their hearts they knew a little antibiotic could work magic. Although Jacqueline and her family may end up devoted followers of Christ, fear and missionary medicine should not be used to manipulate and compel people to convert.

As Linda Crow points out, "The most important part of the dispensary program is that it is a tool for winning the lost."[244] This disastrous strategy is, among others, one of the reasons for the "split-level Christianity" in Haiti. By hiding their true intention under the guise of missionary medicine, the missionaries presented a distorted image of God among their converts, and at the same time, they affirmed Christianity as the "miracle" white man religion.

Yes, healing was part of Jesus' ministry, but He did it out of love. When Jesus heals and casts out demons, not only was he demonstrating the kingdom of God, but He was also coming against the Powers. He was not coercing people into conversion.

Bernice Johnson was a missionary nurse in Haiti for over 37 years from 1946 to the late 70's. It was a time when some diseases like TB (tuberculosis), malaria, and yams were rampant in the countryside, but still unknown to the average Haitian. In her journal, Johnson recalled her visit to a young woman who had TB. She said when she got to the woman's house, a *manbo* was already summoned, and she was at work to break what they thought was a curse. Johnson said she noticed what was going on, and she did not mince her feelings,

> Now, you have to choose between our treatment and yours. Go on with your program, and I will wash my hands of the whole affair and you will be responsible for her. Choose our treatment and outgo all the others, the witch doctor, and the whole works. We cannot work together, it is one or the other.[245]

---

[244] Linda Crow, Haiti I Love You (Kansas City, Nazarene Publishing House: 1970), 59

[245] Bernice Johnson, She Did What She Could:The missionary journal of Bernice Johnson (Graham: Andrews Memorial Baptist Church, 2002)

Like all of the missionaries before and after her, Johnson accuses Vodouists as devil worshipers. In her conversation with the family, she said the *manbo* is not working with God, "She's serving Satan...She is a deceiver and she is a servant of the Devil."[246] As a common trend in these stories, the *manbo* was dismissed, and within a week the missionary medicine worked like magic. The young woman recovered from TB, and the whole family became Christians.

Based on their worldview, the Haitian peasants rightly believed that all diseases were of material causes, the devil, and bad spirits. While they may not have the right approach to treatment and while science and modern medicine were foreign concepts to them at that time, it is wrong to blame their ignorance on worshiping the devil.

While medical missionaries failed to see any value in Haitian traditional medicine, the Haitians' uses of plants and tree bark do not have to be of the devil. While I'm grateful for the care and treatment missionaries provide in the countryside, their goal was not to exchange medical knowledge with the Haitian leaf doctor. As Lauren Elizabeth Hamblen points out in her thesis, *Be a Missionary Every Day": Evangelical Missionary Stories and the Mission Field at Home,* "Their ultimate goal, however, was not to replace the traditional spiritual worldview of native cultures with that of modern science, but rather to replace it with an alternative, yet still

---

[246] Ibid,

thoroughly spiritual worldview, teaching them to turn from their false gods to the one true God."[247]

But isn't it audacious to think that, as foreigners, you can just show up and erase hundreds of years of beliefs and practices? Change takes time, love, and building lots of community relationships.

Bernard Diederich argues that judgment made it difficult for missionaries to show kindness and love when he wrote the following:

> Compassion and love don't always come easy to missionaries hardened by years of tough rural life in Haiti. Too many and too often these missionaries, no matter how deserving, look down on their patients or "victims" as primitive pagans, devil-worshippers...The missionaries drum it into the Haitians that to serve Vodou bring down the wrath of God on their heads...The Haitian peasant suffers mental fatigue from all the holly brainwashing.[248]

Bad Policies, Rules, and Rituals

The second wave of American missionaries who came to Haiti in the early 40s up to the late 80s were mostly fundamental Baptists from the conservative South (U.S.A). They were known for their rigorous discipline and their profound disdain for the Haitian culture. Influenced by the teachings of fundamentalist pastors such

---

[247] Hamblen, Lauren Elizabeth, "Be a Missionary Every Day": Evangelical Missionary Stories and the Mission Field at Home" (2017). All Theses. 2809.https://tigerprints.clemson.edu/all_theses/2809

[248] Bernard Diederich, The Asson and the Cross (Port-au-Prince: Henri Deschamps, 2014), 171-172

as W. A. Criswell, Billy Graham, and others, they brought with them the patriarchal ideas of their theological traditions.

In 1951, my dad and my mom were in their late teens when they attended the Bible school run by the missionaries in southern Haiti. Over the years, I have collected testimonies from my parents and former students who have had firsthand experience with the missionaries during that period.

According to witness accounts, rigorous rules were in place on campus. Women were only admitted so that the lucky ones could be pastors' wives and teach Sunday school. There were numerous cases of forced and arranged marriages. There are other instances where it was not who you love, but whom the leaders approved of and who could make you a better ministry partner. One of these women told me, *"Se entel mwen te renmen, men mwen te fòse marye ak entèl."* (I loved someone else, but I was forced to marry my husband). Overall the newly indoctrinated pastors were forbidden to marry a woman who was not trained in their biblical school. This policy has led to abuse, remorse, lack of respect for their spouse, and loveless marriages. The women were told that their role was to take care of the house and to respect and obey their husbands blindly.

Additionally, I have met and talked to former pastors who were kicked out of the church for sexual sins committed by their kids. Not only is the offending kid forced to marry, but also the whole family is shamed out of the church. And if a woman got pregnant out of wedlock, she wouldn't get married inside the church.

As a kid, I witnessed one of those weddings being celebrated under a tree in the churchyard. The woman was forbidden to wear a white dress and a veil. After the wedding, the couple came to church the following Sunday and they sat on a designated two-seated bench called the discipline bench. For six months, they were not allowed to participate in church activities and to partake in communion. However, the elders gladly took their tithes and offerings. "Hah!", they said, "You're a sinner, banned from church activities, but we will gladly take your money." Sad!

Hopital Lumière in Bonne Fin is the flagship hospital of MEBSH. The missionaries used to have a policy that said you had to be Protestant to work there. Because of this policy, the local church was full of "new converts" every Sunday. They finally discontinued this practice when church leaders realized that their church had become more of an employment center than a community of believers.

Apre Bondye Se Blan

Some Haitians, including the peasantry and the marginalized urban poor, have been dehumanized to the point of believing *apre Bondye se blan.* I know of a pastor who made repeated altar calls after his sermon on a Sunday night. When no one came forward, he said: *"Blan ki blan konvèti, ale wè pou nou menm ayisyen."* [The superior white man has converted...you Haitians, who are nothing, should know better.] As of this writing, the pastor is ordained in the Baptist tradition of MEBSH, and he still has a big church and social services sponsored by a couple of U.S. churches and faith-based organizations.

The *"apre Bondye se blan"* is a colonial-era belief of the superiority of the white man, reinforced by the Western missionary movement. As soon as the missionaries establish themselves in an area, they make sure Haitians are in awe of and impressed with their power, superiority, and *savoir-faire*. In that way, God is presented to the Haitians as white. The Father, the Son, the Holy Spirit, Moses, Abraham, David, Mary, Joseph, and other important personalities of the Bible are all white in the mind of the Haitian.

Sadly, this belief is still prevalent in the Haitian society. At any time one can hear a Haitian say, *ou viv tankou blan*, (Life is good or you're a good person); *se lè blan w genyen*, (you're always on time); *mwen manje tankou blan*, (I had a good meal); *blan an pap fè erè sa a* (white people don't make mistakes); *blan an pap ba w manti*, (a white person won't lie to you), *se po m ki nwa men mwen gen kè blan* (my skin is black but my heart is white or I'm a good person). Or, as this Haitian businessman from Les Cayes, who boasted to a white man, said, "I thank God every day because I have the strength of a Negro and the brains of a white?"[249]

Haitians tend to believe what the white man says as nothing but the truth. Since the white man says Haitians are an animistic society, and Vodou is devil worship, then it must be true. In the '70s up to the late '90s, if you want your church to have new converts, all you have to do is invite a *blan* to preach. Not only does the blan draw a big crowd, but also God, heaven, and hell are who and what the *blan* says they are.

Time-oriented vs Event-oriented

One of the major sources of tension between the old-school missionaries in Haiti and the locals is time. If time is money in the

---

[249] Cited in "FOCUS in Haiti, 63.

West, it is not so in Haiti. Haitians are unfettered by the clock, and everybody knows *ayisyen pa janm a lè*.

In his diary, Paul Orjala with the Church of the Nazarene complains "It takes so long to do everything here. Scarcely anyone goes by the clock."[250] The Haitian use of time is in a sense healthy because it reduces stress associated with chasing after stuff. This is not the case in the Western world. There, they tend to be time and task-oriented, while Haitians are more event and people-oriented. In Haiti, a two-hour delay is normal. While the missionary may be frustrated and annoyed by this apparent lack of respect, it's not as simple as unethical behavior. It's embedded in the Haitian culture. For the Haitian, it's not when, but who and what.

The Western missionary is frustrated by someone being 15 minutes late to a meeting or event. Because missionaries like efficiency, timely synchronized schedules create tension with the host culture. Consequently, when time creates tension, there is a communication breakdown. Judgment takes over your ability to communicate lovingly, and you end up saying "Those Haitians" and "What a waste of time".

The use of time in Haiti was the major complaint of Orjela during his first year in the country: "There is no earthly way of doing anything fast in Haiti...It gets on your nerves if you aren't careful."[251] He later describes the Haitians, "They are like the Spanish "manana" with their "demain" when it comes to work. If you get

---

[250] Kathleen Spell, *Haiti Dairy: Compiled from the Letters of Paul Orjala.* Kansas City: Bacon Hill Press, 1953. p23
[251] Ibid, 73

one piece of business done, why crowd another into the same day? You might not have anything to do tomorrow."[252]

In their book, *Ministering Cross-Culturally*, Sherwood Lingenfelter and Marvin Mayers note, "A missionary must devote his or her time and life to personal interaction. This means the task-oriented individual must consciously allocate significant amounts of time to sit and talk with people."[253]

Unfortunately, rushing to judge the respondent's culture without a good grasp of that culture is one of the main mistakes made by missionaries.

That was then. Now, the new missionaries waste more time than the locals. They are on a perpetual vacation. I asked a "veteran" missionary why she was still in Haiti after more than 45 years, she said, "This is home". I can only imagine what she is telling her supporters.

Poverty Tourism and Short-Term Mission

In a critical article, *Les Touristes de Jesus*, the Haitian daily newspaper Le Nouvelliste argues that there is nothing missional in most STM trips to Haiti. According to the American Embassy, there are about 200,000 Americans who annually take an STM trip to Haiti at a cost of about half a billion dollars ($400,000,000). Consequently, STMs are, for the most part, a money-making scheme for some and a waste of resources for others.

---

[252] Ibid, 73

[253] Lingenfelter, Sherwood and Mayers, Marvin K., Ministering Cross-Culturally: An Incarnational Model for Personal Relationships (Grand rapids: Baker Book House, 1986), 88.

In his article, *Two Awesome Problems: How Short-Term Missions Can Go Wrong,* missiologist Glenn Schwartz points out, "The purpose of short-term mission trips is to provide a positive spiritual experience for both the givers and the receivers."[254] The desire, he says, is to show that the trip was worth it and the money was well spent, we took pictures and put on a slide show for the folks at home. The folks at home watch the slideshows and they say: "I've never seen so much poverty", and, "They have nothing but they are so joyful", or "These people are happy with anything." When you're ministering to people out of charity rather than out of love, you're hurting both yourself and the people being served. And your charity is as short as your STM trip.

I'm not saying STMs are not beneficial, but it's usually you, the short-termer, and the sending organization who have more to gain. Robert Lupton argues, "Contrary to popular belief, most mission trips and service projects do not: empower those being served, engender healthy cross-cultural relationships, improve quality of life, relieve poverty, change the lives of participants [or] increase support for long-term missions work."[255] "What's in it for me" would be a better assessment of the reasons for some STM trips. The way some mission agencies and parachurch organizations advertise their STMs reflects exactly their motives. The following are from websites

---

[254] "Two Awesome Problems: How Short-Term Missions Can Go Wrong", Glenn Schwartz, accessed 1/6/2019,
https://ijfm.org/PDFs_IJFM/21_1_PDFs/27_34_Schwartz.pdf
[255] Robert, Lupton. Toxic Charity: How Churches and Charities Hurt Those They Help (And How to Reverse It)

of churches, Christian NGOs, and mission agencies working in Haiti.[256]

Take one for the team:

"We can help turn a week into a team-building experience that will galvanize your group. When they return home, they will view the world, your organization, their peers, and themselves differently."

"Let us help you customize your trip to meet the needs of your group depending on the amount of time you have available, the number of members, and the aspects of service you'd like to experience."

"Enter into a life-changing experience by volunteering in Haiti...a trip can open your team's eyes to a new culture and give the opportunity to serve our neighbors in Haiti!"

"A unique opportunity to show the people of Haiti how much we care. Once we are able to show ourselves as true followers of Christ, we can win many souls for His kingdom."

Sometimes it's about the place:

"The Caribbean is a special destination for a mission trip: aqua blue water, crisp breezes, lush jungle, and rich history create a scenic backdrop for a host of our locations."

"Less than two hours from American shores lies the most impoverished country in the Western Hemisphere."

---

[256] I choose not to name these organizations and churches because it's beyond the point. But a quick Google search on STM trips and Haiti will give you thousands of hits.

But most of the time it's about you:

"You will see the face of Jesus, you will be the hands and feet of Jesus, you will have your heart broken and your eyes opened, you will leave a piece of your heart in Haiti and you will go home changed."

"Each short-term mission trip to Haiti is tailored to the gifts and abilities of those in the group."

"We believe that a trip [with us] will not only leave a lasting impression on your life but will possibly change your life forever! Whether you are doing a work detail, loving on the kids at the Orphanage, attending a church service or just getting some alone time with God, you will most definitely feel rewarded, refreshed, and renewed."

"It is our hope this will be a rewarding experience for you and your team."

Some Christian organizations function as middlemen and travel agencies. For example, "Our staff at Praying Pelican will help you every step of the way, from picking a location to renewing your team's partnership for the next year after you return home. Your mission team's ministry opportunities will be tailored to fit the local church's needs."

"The Caribbean is a special destination for a mission trip: rich history, breathtaking ocean, and mountain landscapes, and a vibrant

Church create a scenic backdrop for a host of our locations here at Praying Pelican"[257]

I have been on both ends of the STM movement. My dad used to host STMs in his church, and I've been on a couple of trips myself. In my experience as the host family, when the women on these trips let local kids play with their hair, the group throws candies to the kids from the back of a moving truck, a local boy is given a soccer ball, or when they repainted the church and fixed a couple of benches, there was no life-giving and transformative experience on the people and the local congregation. You might say that they blessed the local folks by repainting the church and fixing the benches, but my dad left those tasks undone so that the trip leaders, who said they needed something to do during their visit, had something to do.

There is a big difference between doing something for the people and doing something with the people.

When you pay around $2000 for a trip and your main activity is to open the valve of a water truck so that the local folks can fill their containers with water, do you think they have no other means to get water and that they are in that desperate of a state?

Or when you pay that much money to go to an "orphanage" so that you can hold a couple of kids in your arms, what is the point? Did you know that those kids have at least one living parent? Did you know you may unintentionally participate in child abuse, organ harvesting, and child trafficking rings? Would you let a stranger

---

[257] For more see *"Caribbean Mission Trips"*, https://www.prayingpelicanmissions.org/caribbean-mission-trips, Accessed 12/17/2020.

come to your house and start holding and playing with your kids for seven days? Why do you think it's okay to do that in Haiti? Did you know 95% of orphanages in Haiti are a big scam? Is yours one of them?

After the earthquake of 2010 in Haiti, the outpouring of support was overwhelming. Millions of dollars were raised, but unfortunately, the people who needed help the most were never part of it.

The problem lies in funneling the generosity directly to the victims. A 2016 survey of fly-in medical missions estimates the cost of those trips at $3.7 billion annually.[258] The average short-term medical mission trip to Haiti is about $30,000. When a team goes once a year, some people may have received the care they needed, and it was probably a lifesaver for some local people. But it is only once a year. Who is doing the follow-up?

On my STM trip to the Nahuatl Indians in the mountains of Texhuacan, Mexico, I struggled to answer honestly why I was going. Was it beneficial to the people? Was it really about sharing God's love? Or was it about me? I was curious. I wanted to feel the emotions others had during their STM trips to a "poor" area. I enjoyed it not because of my contribution to the cement slab for a basketball court, not because I shared my testimony with the local church or building simple wood chimneys over the open fire pits in the kitchens of a dozen homes, but mostly because the landscape of Texhuacan is similar to the countryside of Haiti. Because the

---

[258] Caldron, Paul H et al. "Economic assessment of US physician participation in short-term medical missions." Globalization and health vol. 12,1 45. 22 Aug. 2016, doi:10.1186/s12992-016-0183-7

Nahualts' daily life is comparable to my own culture, I felt at home. When I looked around the rugged terrain, the mountain trails, the people preparing the land for their crops, and the living conditions, I felt that I was at my grandma's village in southern Haiti. I was not a stranger. I felt that I was one of them. I was at home flipping tortillas on the open pit and buying tamarind juice from the street vendor.

So, it was mostly about me. I was purely a tourist in the name of Jesus. Still, as anyone who has been on STM trips, I took pictures, and I shared them with my house church community. And then when I shared the pictures on Facebook, Instagram, and other platforms, I asked myself, 'What and whose story were they telling'? 'What was the likelihood they were being used without context to potentially stereotype and sensationalize'?

There are some pictures I wish I hadn't taken, because when you look at them, they don't tell the whole story. Unfortunately, whoever is in the position of power controls the narrative.

Money, Power, and the Western Mission Movement

As Jesus was sending his disciples on a mission, he instructed them: "Don't take any money with you, nor a traveler's bag, nor an extra pair of sandals. And don't stop to greet anyone on the road (Luke 10:4 NLT)." In essence, Jesus was telling them not to worry about their life, and to trust in God to supply their needs.

Going against this advice, the Western missionary movement in Haiti not only took the purse but also held on to it tightly and used it to control Haitians. Sure, there are costs associated with living abroad. But keep in mind that over 98% of missionaries in Haiti are in leadership positions, and most of them manage non-profit agencies and other para-church organizations. As the saying goes, he who controls the purse makes the rules of engagement. Being poor in Haiti is good for the Western mission enterprise. Just as the U.S. Marines did with the Haitian government for over fifty years, American mission agencies, such as WIM and WT control the finances of MEBSH. Haitian pastors are scattered all over the southern part of Haiti with no salary, left to their own devices to fend for themselves in places that are for the most part unlivable. Most of these pastors are living in inhumane conditions, and their kids could go years without a decent education. The worst thing is that their 40-member churches are poorer than they are.

When the mission board transferred my dad to a new area in 1974, the average weekly offering was five gourdes, which was about $1 at that time. This was ten days after my mom had given birth to my little brother in a two-bedroom shack that leaned on one side. My parents' furniture was trashed and broken during the move. There was a Haitian board, but just as it was for the Haitian government during the U.S. Occupation, the board members were all puppets of the mission agency. Even after WT relinquished control to the Haitian board, the pattern of dehumanization of their pastors and lay workers persisted.

The board learned the hard way that when you're dependent on foreign aid, you cannot make independent decisions. But just because Haitians are perceived as poor and different does not give anyone power over their lives. Some new missionaries won't even leave for the mission field until their fundraising goal has been met. I know of a missionary who complained about her $6000 a month support in Haiti. That was in the mid-90s, and she was single.

When you read the history of thousands of religious organizations working in Haiti, most of them have the same genesis. It is usually after an STM trip, and overwhelmed with "compassion", the story goes like this:

"We saw a need to establish an orphanage in Haiti and to meet the spiritual, physical, and educational needs of the people."

We saw the need to help the starving and dying children in the remote mountain villages of Haiti.

We feel a deep compassion for the Haitian people. This ongoing compassion drives [our] desire to improve the lives of the Haitians in a manner that is meaningful, respectful, effective, and that will benefit future generations in Haiti.

If you're a foreign NGO or independent mission agency, and if you love Haiti, stop solving problems with money.

Sister Churches - Twinning

The concept of sister churches consists of pairing Western churches to churches in mostly non-western countries. In Haiti, most Catholic and Protestant churches have a sister abroad. Some of them have multiple foreign siblings.

One organization said, *For the Haitian church a tremendous opportunity opens up to them for progress in their ministry.* When Haitian churches look for sister churches overseas, it is usually done with a "what can I get from them" attitude. The Haitian church usually thinks she doesn't have anything to offer. One of the reasons for that is that the request for sisterhood usually comes from the big sister. The phenomenon of having sister churches in a third-world country has nothing to do with cultural exchange and growing together in Christ. It's always out of necessity. It's always a utilitarian relationship. It's more like a mother/daughter relationship which creates total dependency. It is also about you, the big sister:

You'll have the blessing of working side by side on various projects and ministries...You'll be able to personally visit your sponsored school children...you'll discover that much of the ministry occurs in your own life as well as the life of your Sister Church, and you'll return home transformed with a new worldview.

We have had a special relationship with our sister church...Money is sent annually to help with the needs of the Church and community.

Most sister church relationships do not produce any kind of cross-cultural relationship. In my research, I have not seen any contribution of the Haitian church to its U.S. counterpart. As Janel K. Bakker points out, "Just as merely having a sister doesn't mean you have a good sibling relationship, so too merely having a sister church does not automatically entail a good sister church relationship."[259]

In his interview with *Christianity Today*, Paul S. Williams argues "Christians in the West cannot possibly learn from or speak to Christians in other cultures unless we're willing to recognize our essential spiritual equality."[260] In her research, Dr. Bakker finds that

---

[259] Janel Kragt Bakker: "Sister church relationships and the friendship principle", https://faithandleadership.com/janel-kragt-bakker-sister-church-relationships-and-friendship-principle

[260] See Elliot Clark interview with Paul S. Williams, CEO of the British and Foreign Bible Society in The 'Over There' Era of Missions Is Over Nowadays, the Western church needs to send ambassadors to its own culture. MARCH 16, 2020 Christianity Today

"bad behavior on both sides" can be a source of conflict. At MEBSH, for instance, there is nothing reciprocal in their Reciprocal Ministry. It's always about the needs of the Haitian church, as the local church doesn't know the needs of its foreign counterpart.

Hundreds of Catholic parishes in the U.S. have developed the same approach of sister churches, best known as twinning. According to the Parish Twinning Program of the Americas (PTPA), their purpose is to create "lasting sister parish relationships between parishes in the U.S. and a parish in a Caribbean country or Latin America. Parishes in the U.S. often raise funds and send resources to their twin parishes and help with various special projects."[261] The Diocese of Norwich Outreach Program in Connecticut explains their understanding of the twinning relationship:

"While each twinning carries the same promise of mutual support in faith and desire for cultural exchange, every union is unique. The program does not require specific exchanges of funds or materials; rather each partnership determines how its connection will be fostered."[262]

The Holy Redeemer Catholic Church in Webster Groves, Missouri twins with the Catholic church of St Jean du Sud, Haiti. They argue that "Most families have a very humble thatched or tin roof home without running water or electricity. Their only means

---

https://www.christianitytoday.com/ct/2020/april/paul-williams-exiles-mission-over-there-era.html

[261] "Give back Parish Twinning", https://www.parishprogram.org/

[262] For more see https://outreachtohaiti.org/programs/twinning

of survival comes from selling produce from the small plot of land they farm".

I've traveled to St Jean du Sud numerous times, and I know a lot of families there. This is not the village that I know. No wonder their parish twinning mission statement states: "We are dedicated to 1) establishing a supportive relationship between Holy Redeemer parish and our twin parish St. Jean du Sud, by providing assistance and support for their spiritual, financial, medical and educational needs, and 2) raising awareness of the plight of the Haitian people in general."[263] In other words, you're so poor, we're going to help you out. It's more like a mother/daughter relationship which creates an acute dependency syndrome.

The Dependency Syndrome

Haitians live in three timeframes at once. They are still using colonial-era tools and techniques for agriculture; the infrastructure and education system are from the nineteenth century, and some people have the latest iPhone and Samsung Galaxy. This is the perfect scenario for the spread of the dependency disease.

> In his book, *Roots and Remedies of the Dependency Syndrome in World Missions*, Robert Reese argues that dependency syndrome is the result of,

>> The use of colonial mission methods, from financial subsidies by missionaries to local evangelists and pastors, from missionary paternalism, from short-term mission teams, and from partnerships between Christian organizations from various countries...Above all, it's a

---

[263] "*Haiti Newsletter_7.11*", https://holyr.org/?page_id=285

spiritual dilemma, indicating a shift of the gospel message from new life in Christ to dependence on materials and technology. [264]

In Haiti, there are over 10,000 NGOs for a population of over 11,000,000. After the earthquake in 2010, the number of NGOs operating in Haiti, mostly illegally, skyrocketed. As the number of social institutions grows, so does poverty. If one were to survey the thousands of religious organizations working in Haiti, one would find that all of them use the same cliché in their literature: "Haiti is the poorest country in the western hemisphere". The irony is that some of these organizations have been in Haiti for over 40 years, and they have raised millions of dollars annually in the U.S. If thousands of NGOs are doing the same thing, forever in Haiti, why is it that the condition of the people never changes? Why is Haiti getting worse? Is it because poverty is good for business? Who would have thought that dependency begets corruption at all levels, including the mission field?

I browsed the website of an organization working in Haiti which claimed to have a total expense of $60,477,393 in 2018 and a payroll of over $2,000,000. Their primary focus is feeding "starving children".

There is no sustainable plan in place, otherwise they wouldn't be doing it for over 30 years. As Glenn Schwartz points out, Westerners "thrive on the need to be needed."[265] Craig Smith calls

---

[264] Robert, Reese. Roots and Remedies of the Dependency Syndrome in World Missions (Littelton: William Carey Library, 2010), 89

[265] "How Missionary Attitudes Can Create Dependency", Glenn Schwartz from the May-June 1998 issue: The Mission to the "Aucas", accessed 1/30/2020,

it "plight-based" ministry. It's a kind of ministry where a missionary goes to a poor country, stays there forever, and lives off the support of U.S. churches as long as he/she provides a steady stream of newsletters about the plight of the people there.[266] Reese called codependency: "While missionaries supply subsidies out of their prosperity, the converts feed the missionaries' self-esteem as they set them on a pedestal."[267]

As with most need-based ministries, there is money to be made. If I were to question the merit of some U.S. organizations in Haiti, their Haitian staff would cut off my head. In a country where the unemployment rate is over 50%, it's understandable. Their livelihood depends on these jobs. By presenting Haiti at its worst, one would think that there are not enough schools in Haiti, kids are running around naked, people are eating dirt, and all the houses are made of cardboard. It's all a big fundraising scheme.

While I'm sure there are many needs and some well-intended people, by presenting Haiti at its worst, it's easier to ask for money to support their programs. It's insane to think that you are saving lives and ending hunger by raising millions of dollars in the U.S. to cook rice and beans in Haiti and by taking kids out of their homes and villages so that you can have an "orphanage".

In their 2018 financial statement, one organization in Jacmel spent $173,000 on travel alone while they paid their Haitian staff (about 15 employees) a meager $29,000. Meanwhile, multiple

---

https://www.missionfrontiers.org/issue/article/how-missionary-attitudes-can-create-dependency

[266] Craig Smith. *Whitemans's Gospel* (Winnipeg: Indian Life Books, 1997), 68

[267] Reese, "Roots and Remedies of the Dependency Syndrome in World Missions", 120

reports suggest some expat salaries can be as high as $200,000 a year.[268]

The dependency syndrome works both ways. It keeps the local church in need and hungry for more, and it helps the missionaries, the supporting churches, and organizations stay alive as these programs give them a sense of doing mission work and a reason to be needed.

The Western missionary movement has a long history of forcing locals to rely on foreign funds. In *We Are Not the Hero*, Jean Johnson notes,

> When Western missionaries use their ethnocentric influence and economic affluence in ministry, they inevitably birth ministries that are carbon copies of their expensive, Western forms of Christianity. This action makes it nearly impossible for local disciples of Christ to implement effective evangelism, discipleship, worship, acts of compassion, leadership training, and church planting by mobilizing their own local resources and cultural expression.[269]

As Schwartz points out,

> The challenge is to figure out how to function as an insider without bringing into the situation the power, authority, and resources of the outsider which everyone knows we have as Westerners. Unless that is avoided, the seeds of the dependency syndrome are sown and it may be next to impossible for anyone

---

[268] See Miami Herald /2012/01/09/v-fullstory/2581629/many-question-whether-haiti-quake.html; CGDEV: Postcard from Haiti, https://www.cgdev.org/blog/postcard-haiti-life-after-2010-quake; Foreign Policy in Focus, https://fpif.org/are-foreign-ngos-rebuilding-haiti-or-just-cashing-in/
[269] Jean Johnson, *We Are Not the Hero: a Missionary's Guide to Sharing Christ, Not a Culture of Dependency* (Sisters: Deep River Books, 2012), 17.

in the future to break the addiction to outside resources which develops.[270]

This dependency syndrome is based partly on the benevolence and racist paternalism of the West. In *Toxic Charity*, Robert Lupton cautions, "Give once and you elicit appreciation. Give twice and you create anticipation. Give three times and you create expectations. Give four times and it becomes entitlement. Give five times and you establish dependency."[271] While I'm not advocating for Christians to stop being generous, don't let your generosity create dependency. As Craig Smith points out, "Having a heart for a people is biblical, keeping them as perpetual receivers is not."[272]

The average tuition for registered nurses in private institutions in Haiti is about $2000 a year. Meanwhile, a seven-day STM medical trip costs about $30,000. Perhaps that money would be put to better use if it were loaned to students/nurses from the villages where your mobile clinics are held. Would you consider sustainability? Would you let the parents invest in their kids' education?

Haitian parents would rather go hungry to pay their children's tuition. That was before every NGO had a child sponsorship program. Now with free money from abroad, both parents and kids have gotten lazy. Would you let the Haitian people be what they

---

[270] "How Missionary Attitudes Can Create Dependency", Glenn Schwartz from the May-June 1998 issue: The Mission to the "Aucas", accessed 1/30/2020, https://www.missionfrontiers.org/issue/article/how-missionary-attitudes-can-create-dependency

[271] Lupton, Robert D. Toxic Charity: How Churches and Charities Hurt Those They Help (and How to Reverse It). New York, NY: HarperOne, 2011. p130

[272] Smith "*Whitemans's Gospel,*"71

were known for before you came? Haitians are known for their hospitality, caring, and sharing of resources. As a commenter on Le Nouvelliste rightly argues, "*Yo pa kite w jwenn vè d'lo a, lè yo wè w swaf twòp yo lage de gout nan gòj w pou w ka jwenn youn rezon di yo mèsi e di kou w ka kite yo peze kou w nèt ale.*"[273] [They (blan/ white people) won't let you get a glass of water, but when you're thirsty, they will give you a few drops so that you can say thank you, and you will be forever at their mercy.]

---

[273] See Kuri comment on the news that Haitian students could study in Spain in Le Nouvelliste "L'Espagne s'ouvre aux étudiants haïtiens", accessed 3/7/2020 https://lenouvelliste.com/article/212877/lespagne-souvre-aux-etudiants-haitiens

CHAPTER 7

Religion in the Haitian Experience: A Burden

———————— ✵ ————————

Religion is a thief that's delighted to clean us out. Religion plots to rob us of our religious possessions and our sense of security. Oh, religion is happy to drop by our doorstep later to offer it all back.

Andrew Farley

J'ai heurté mon front à tous les barreaux de la vie, il n'y a qu'une issue: la religion.

(I have hit my forehead against all the steel bars of life, there is only one way out: religion.)

Carl Brouard

Nous aimons le violon, Autant que le tambour. Nous aimons l'Église, Et nous adorons le Vodou

(We love the violin, As much as the drum. We love the Church, And we love Vodou.)

Franck Fouché

Dual Allegiance

Among the many pitfalls of the bondage of religion in Haiti, none is more obvious than the dual allegiance in Haitian Christianity. This phenomenon, also known as split-level Christianity or riding two horses, is "the coexistence within the same person of two or more thought-and-behavior systems which are inconsistent with each other,"[274] according to the Jesuit psychologist and priest Fr Jaime Bulatao. He argues that:

> The split-level person at one level professes allegiance to ideas, attitudes, and ways of behaving which are mainly borrowed from the Christian West. At another level, he holds convictions that are more properly his own ways of living and believing which were handed down from his ancestors. These flow into action now and then.[275]

This two-value system is due to not only the Haitian worldview and his brutal colonized past, but mainly because of a distorted picture of God, a lack of contextualization, the tendency of the missionaries to label Vodou as superstitions, and the constant diabolization of the Haitian culture. This dual allegiance makes it possible for a Haitian Protestant to go to the doctor's office, solicit prayers from fellow Protestants, and consult the bòkò (diviner) for the same issue. Bryant Myers' book *Walking With the Poor* calls it "folk Christianity."[276]

---

[274] Cited in Tony La Viña, "Philippines: Land of split-level Christianity", accessed 6/12/2020 https://www.rappler.com/thought-leaders/80855-philippines-split-level-christianity#:~:text=Decades%20ago%2C%20the%20eminent%20Jesuit,are%20inconsistent%20with%20each%20other.%E2%80%9D

[275] Ibid

[276] Myers, "Walking With the Poor", Kindle Location 6766.

Although Haiti is at least 90% Christian, Vodou's beliefs and practices continue among the believers of the Christian faith. It's not a surprise that Christian songs and prayers are used during Vodou services. Words such as *fidèle and serviteur* are used to describe both Protestant and Vodou adherents. Haitian oral and written literature, music, and visual art are full of slogans depicting the co-existence of the two belief systems.

Theologians have forever mistakenly labeled Vodou a syncretic religion. As an oppressed religion, Vodouists juxtaposed elements of rituals such as Christian songs, holidays, saints, and prayers during Vodou services to survive. But they are more ritual than syncretic (see Appendix A).

Frederic Wise was a Colonel with the U.S. Marines during the occupation. In his book *A Marine Tells It to You*, he observes:

> You can meet a Haitian who has been educated at great world capitals, who speaks four modern languages fluently and has a really French appreciation of music and art and literature. You can meet a Haitian living in a shack in the jungle, half-naked, supported by his group of wives, each one of whom works a small clearing with primitive implements. All of them are supposed to be devout Catholics. But whether the man wears clothes from one of London's Bond Street tailors and the woman frocks from Paris, or whether they wear rags in a jungle clearing, the ancient Voodoo of the Congo is a living thing to them.[277]

Theodore Junior Beaubrun, the son of the iconic Haitian comedian Theodore Beaubrun, aka Langlichatte, confirms in an interview with *Le Nouvelliste* that, *"Bien que protestant, mon père*

---

[277] Wise, Frederic May, 1877-; Frost, Meigs Oliver, 1882-. A marine tells it to you (Kindle Locations 2580-2584). New York, J.H. Sears & Company, inc.

savait danser et connaissait les rythmes de folklore national. Il n'a jamais, malgré sa foi chrétienne, renié ses origines culturelles.[278] (Although Protestant, my dad knew how to dance, and he knew the rhythm of the national folklore. Despite his Christian faith, he has never repudiated his cultural origins.)

The famous Haitian writer René Depestre, at a young age, admits, *"Adolescent, j'ai eu le vaudou dans mon collimateur, en même temps que la foi catholique."*[279] (As a teenager, I had Vodou in my sights, along with the Catholic faith.)

In his book, *The Asson and the Cross,* B. Diederich argues that at *Seau d'Eau,* a religious pilgrim village, "A Vodouisant has no trouble lighting a candle to Damballah at the foot of the cascade's giant white fig tree...and the very next day light a candle to the Our Lady of Mount Carmel in the Roman Catholic Church."[280]

In his book *L'Heritage Sacré,* J.B. Cineas exposes the dual allegiance of Doctor Benfield and Brother Osiris[281]. It's the same people who are adherents of both Vodou and Christianity. Cinéas concluded, *"Aux danses et à l'église, même assistance. A la Sainte Table et au houmfort, les mêmes devots."*[282] (At the dances and the

---

[278] Pierre Clitandre, "Boukman Eksperians et la Musique racines", in Haiti recto Verso, http://haitirectoverso.blogspot.com/2007/09/boukman-eksperyans-et-la-musique-racine.html

[279] « René DEPESTRE », Cultures & Conflits [En ligne], 84 | Hiver 2011, mis en ligne le 15 mars 2013,
consulté le 04 mai 2019. URL: http://journals.openedition.org/conflits/18265; DOI: 10.4000/
conflits.18265

[280] Diederich, *"The Asson and the Cross",* 254

[281] J. B. Cineas, *L'Heritage Sacré* (Port-au-Prince: Editions Henri Deschamps, 1945) 81

[282] Ibid, 81

church, the same attendance. At the Holy Table and the hounfour, the same devotees.)

Antoine Innocent in *Mimola*, argues, *"Le culte d'un Dieu n'excluait pas celui des autres divinités."* (The worship of one God did not exclude that of other deities.)

Leslie Desmangles in *The Faces of the Gods: Vodou and Roman Catholicism in Haiti* points out that,

> They will attend a Vodou meeting that begins on a Saturday evening and lasts throughout the night; and while their clothes are still wet with the perspiration caused by the exhausting contortions of their sacred dances, they will walk directly from the ounfò to the four o'clock Mass on Sunday morning.[283]

Kate Ramsey in *The Spirits and the Law: Vodou and Power in Haiti* argues,

> These practices, which in former times hid themselves in shadowy dens in the mountains and were only carried out under the darkness of night, now display themselves in broad daylight . . . , and what can only be said with tears in the eyes, the very people who claim themselves Christians and who frequent the sacraments are not afraid to participate in them, as if they could serve Jesus Christ and the devil at once."[284]

Tonton Georges, one of the main characters in the Marcelin brothers' novel, *The Pencil of God*, doesn't see any conflict

---

[283] Leslie G. Desmangles, *The Faces of the Gods: Vodou and Roman Catholicism in Haiti* (Chapel Hill: University of North Carolina Press, 1992), 6

[284] Ramsey, Kate. *The Spirits and the Law: Vodou and Power in Haiti* (p. 101). University of Chicago Press. Kindle Edition.

whatsoever between a *manbo* and a priest who are using the same God to heal Mrs. Cyprien: "Both of them are counting on God to save your daughter, and I can't see why the efforts of one should conflict with those of the other."[285]

This is exactly why the famous Haitian band *Skah Shah* can sing about God's protection in their well-known classic piece *Yahve* and sing about a lwa in another piece, *Ouanga Nibo*. The *rasin* group *Boukman Eksperyans* praised God in *Bay Bondye Glwa* and acknowledged *Legba,* the guardian of the gate. *Les Frères Déjean,* one of my favorite *konpa* bands, have no problem singing about their faith in both God and Erzulie in *La Foi* and *L'univers.* And the group Magnum Band prayed to God in *Jehovah* and also called on the *lwa* in *Ashadei.*

Lamartine Petit-Monsieur, in his book *Vers un Nouvel Echo d'Haiti,* shows the to and fro movement within the three religious systems. In his book, he argues that, "L'Haitien converti évacue donc son état de catholico-vaudouisant pour devenir "catholico-vaudouico-protestant.""[286] (The converted Haitian leaves his catholico-vaudouisant state to become catholico-vodouisant-protestant.) Consequently, for Petit-Monsieur, the Haitian is born Vodouisant, baptized Catholic, converted Protestant, and has become Catholico-vaudouico-protestant.[287] In essence, the Haitian

---

[285] Thoby-Marcelin, Phillippe and Marcelin Pierre, *The Pencil of God,* trans. Leonard Thomas (Cambridge: The Riverside Press, 1951), 66

[286] Petit-Monsieur Lamartine, Vers un Nouvel Echo d'Haiti (Xlibris corporation, 2011), 176-177

[287] Petit-Monsieur has laid very nicely a table of this triple religious affiliation of the Haitian. For a graphic detail, see *Vers un Nouvel Echo d'Haiti,* 177

struggles to adapt to his adopted Christianity, therefore he uses all three religious systems as needed.

The dual allegiance can be summarized through this diagram:

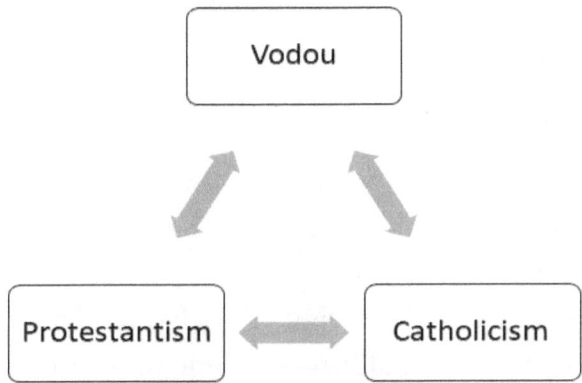

Figure 1: While some Haitians move back and forth across the main religions, the central religion is Vodou.

Appeasing a Ruthless Tyrant

Throughout the history of religion in Haiti, God is always presented not only as a loving God but also as a distant and ruthless tyrant. To appease Him and to win his favor, various types of sacrifices are offered to him. The name of God instills fear, and as such one must do everything to appease his wrath and anger. For the Catholics, God is simply God. For the Vodouists God is good but distant. However, for the Protestants, God is both good and cruel.

In Vodou, Vodouists try to appease God in several ways such as *manje lwa* and animal sacrifices. In Christianity, since most Haitian Catholics and Protestants are also Vodouisants, the Catholics appease God not only through Vodou sacrifices but also by the Holy

Sacrifice of the Mass. The Protestants, on the other hand, to win the love of God try to live a life of sacrifice. They see God's love as something to be earned. Therefore, they don't want to rob God by giving their tithes and offerings, missing a church service, and so forth.

Fear of Fear

All three major religious movements in Haiti rely on fear to keep their adherents in check. The use of fear is so alarming that, as a consequence, most Haitians suffer from a phenomenon called phobophobia. The fear of fear is an anxiety disorder characterized by the intense and irrational fear of experiencing fear itself. People with phobophobia are afraid of the physical and psychological sensations associated with fear, such as a rapid heartbeat, sweating, trembling, and the feeling of losing control. This fear can become debilitating and may lead individuals to avoid situations or triggers that they associate with fear, even if there is no real threat present.

In some cases, religious teachings and beliefs can contribute to the fear of fear. Certain religious doctrines or interpretations may emphasize the consequences of fear, portraying it as a lack of faith or as a sin. This can create a vicious cycle where individuals feel guilty for experiencing fear, leading to increased anxiety and fear of divine punishment. I was at a church service on a Sunday morning, and the pastor wanted to encourage people to come to the evening service when he said, "If you love Jesus, you don't want to miss this service."

Some Protestant denominations in Haiti offer guidance and teachings on how to cope with fear and anxiety. These teachings often emphasize faith, trust in a higher power, and seeking solace through prayer, meditation, or religious rituals. Individuals who experience phobophobia may find comfort in their religious beliefs and practices, using them as a source of strength and support to overcome their fear.

When Bertrand Russell said in his 1927 lecture at the Battersea Town Hall that "Religion is based primarily and mainly upon fear," one would think he was talking to the Haitian people. In his lecture, Russell argues why fear is the foundation of religion:

> It is partly the terror of the unknown, and partly, as I have said, the wish to feel that you have a kind of elder brother who will stand by you in all your troubles and disputes. Fear is the basis of the whole thing—fear of the mysterious, fear of defeat, fear of death. Fear is the parent of cruelty, and therefore it is no wonder if cruelty and religion have gone hand-in-hand. It is because fear is the basis of those two things.[288]

As Lyonel Paquin argues in his book, *The Haitians: Class and Color Politics,*

> The Haitian is inordinately preoccupied with himself. He is also paranoid. Life and experience have proven to him abundantly the uncertainty of life. He perceives the world around him as inhabited by hostile forces. The Haitian is always en garde against somebody or something. He is constantly protecting himself against some malevolent force.[289]

---

[288] "Why I Am Not a Christian (1927)", Bertand Russell, accessed 1/2/2020, https://users.drew.edu/~jlenz/whynot.html

[289] Lyonel, Paquin. The Haitians: Class and Color Politics (Brooklyn: Multi-Type, 1983), 228

It's with reason that the number one burden of religion in Haiti is fear. Among many fear-mongering thoughts holding the religious mind captive, there are also:

Fear of following Jesus the wrong way

Fear of out-sinning God's love and forgiveness

Fear of going to hell

Fear of losing salvation

Fear of displeasing God

Fear of spiritual failure

Fear of missing a church service

Fear of withholding tithes and offerings

Fear of Satan

Fear of other people

Fear of offending the *lwa*

Fear of having doubt

The Religion of Do's and Don'ts

Religion can be a heavy load when it is presented as a list of rules and regulations such as no smoking, no alcoholic beverages, no gambling, no swearing, and so forth. As a teenager, I used to listen to the popular bands of my time (I still do), such as Rico Mazarin and Les Fantaisistes de Carrefour, Les Frères Déjean, Tabou Combo, Shoogar Combo, Les Shleu Shleu, Gerard Daniel and DjetX, Skah Shah, Magnum Band, Alix Jacques and his "Konpa

Philharmonic Orchestra" Colé Colé Band, Les Gypsies de Pétion-Ville, Les Difficiles de Petion-Ville, Scorpio, and D. P. Express. Was that a sin? Does listening to secular music preclude me from following Christ?

Unfortunately, religion has robbed Haitian Protestants of their ability to appreciate the richness of Haitian culture. I understand that "We are allowed to do anything, but not everything is good for us to do. We are allowed to do anything, but not all things help us grow strong as Christians (1 Cor 10:23 NLV)". But still, I like to listen to the screams of the pipes of Bach's Fugue. I cry whenever I listen to Puccini's Nessun Dorma. Are you so religious that the Ginette Reno hymn to love *L'Essentiel* turns you off? Frank Viola, in his book *Insurgence*, says, "Listen to a gorgeous piece of music enough times, and you will grow weary of it."[290] Is he kidding me? I can never get enough of Orchestre Septentrional hit *Mariana*. I'm sure, as a Haitian, you wouldn't mind playing over and over *Anita* of Orchestre Tropicana d'Haiti or *Mambo Instrumental* of Shleu Shleu. The point is some of the music you enjoy, do you care if the composer is a Christian?

Religion and Money

One of the main accusations of missionaries in Haiti against Vodou leaders has to do with money. They claim that the *ougan* and the *manbo* are milking out the peasants out of their meager earnings. Bernice Johnson, a former missionary nurse to Haiti argues that, "A witch doctor will not work unless he is assured of his fee. And sometimes that means the person must sell his livestock or

---

[290] Frank Viola

a piece of land to pay it."[291] It's not just Vodou. The Catholic church does not do anything for free. From their first-class wedding price plan to their fifth-class funeral, there is always something to pay for. Listen to Gerard Gayot,

> We give ... we give to the offering collection on Sundays, we give to build the cathedral, we give to the Vatican ... we give for the acquisition of bells, we buy rosaries, we buy images, we buy sacraments, we buy statuettes and even statues, we buy grace, we pay for the rest of our deceased mother, we buy salvation, we buy eternal life, we buy God himself.[292]

The Protestants collect tithes and offerings at every gathering, even prayer services. Tithing is the greatest religious robbery inside Haitian evangelical churches. I know several families who got evicted from their houses because a pastor told them to give their rent money to Jesus. Religion is an expensive enterprise, and money is what keeps it alive. How many church leaders use the bible to shame people into giving? How many church leaders and other manipulators use tithes and offerings as a money-back guarantee? Are they any better than the ougan?

I was at a church that was still under construction in Les Cayes, and the pastor told me they were inviting another pastor for a weekend revival because he is a specialist in fundraising sermons. Another church nearby pits men against women during offering time. Wives would compete against their husbands in this

---

[291] Bernice, pg87
[292] Gérard Gayot, *Clergé Indigène* (Montreal: Imprimatur Gérard G. Gayot, 1955) https://ufdc.ufl.edu/UF00074431/00001/2x., 121

fundraising scheme, and every Sunday the winner of the competition is announced.

I know of a woman in Les Cayes who was convinced that the reason she always got denied a U.S. tourist visa was that she was not faithful in her offerings. Her church leaders would tell her that "you reap what you sow, and you will never get a visa until you pay in full what you owe God."

Money is not just Vodou-related, as Jeremy Myers argues, it's a problem with religion. Myers argues that Christianity is no different than the other religions. He says, "We are not much different from most other religions in the world. We all struggle for money, popularity, and power. We all pray and worship in relatively similar ways, with all of us believing that our God hears and answers our prayers, while pretty much ignoring everybody else."[293]

Have you had any encounters with *machann priyè* (prayer sellers)? Someone or a group of people walks the neighborhood, knocks on people's doors, and says something like "I come to offer you prayers". Like an accomplished salesman, they subtly let you know it's an exchange for food or money. There is no such thing as a free religion. A better question is which religion is more expensive to its adherents?

During the Coronavirus in Haiti, instead of motivating their flocks to be safe and practice recommended hygiene, the church leaders were complaining about their inability to collect tithes and offerings. Meanwhile, the *rasin* (roots) group RAM put out a widely acclaimed music video, "*Ayisyen leve*" encouraging people to

---

[293] Myers, Jeremy. Close Your Church for Good: Removing Religion to Reveal Jesus. Redeeming Press. Kindle Edition.

change their behavior. While the Protestants claim the coronavirus is proof that the end of the world is coming, the Vodouists are saving lives. While the protestant religious leaders are worried about their church services and their pocketbooks, the Vodouists are sensitizing Haitians to be accountable to one another. Strange!

Religion and Poverty

In an opinion piece for the New York Post, Jonah Goldberg says, "Haiti isn't simply that it is poor, but that it has a poverty culture...Haiti will never get out of grinding poverty until it abandons much of its culture."[294]

The Catholic priest Roger Riou, who was a missionary in Haiti for more than 35 years said, "Anyone who has studied the problem in depth, who's lived with it, will acknowledge the fact that voodoo is one of the causes of Haitian poverty and underdevelopment."[295]

Clinton Eugene Lain was a compound-based missionary who never assimilated with the Haitians, and after spending many years as a missionary in northern Haiti argues, "A lack of creativity is built into the social structures of Haiti."[296]

Riou, Lain, and other missionaries, who failed miserably in Haiti, scapegoated Vodou for their failure after decades of unsuccessful missions. As a supposedly Christian country, the same argument can be made about both Catholicism and Protestantism

---

[294] Jonah Goldberg, *"Haiti's true curse"*, accessed 12/20/2020.
https://nypost.com/2010/01/20/haitis-true-curse/

[295] Riou, *"The Island of my Life"*, 145

[296] Clinton E. Lain, *Church growth and Evangelism in Haiti: Needs, Problems, and Methods"*, Doctoral diss., (Asbury Theological Seminary, 1998)

in Haiti. In *Deux siècles de protestantisme en Haïti (1816-2016)*, Rosny Desroches boasts,

> *"l'Église méthodiste et le protestantisme en général ont apporté une contribution majeure au développement spirituel, moral, social et économique du pays, au cours de ces deux derniers siècles. Pourtant le pays demeure le seul pays moins avancé de la région, l'un des pays les plus pauvres et les plus inégalitaires de la planète, avec un taux encore important d'analphabétisme, un taux de perception de corruption parmi les plus élevés dans le monde."[297]*

[The Methodist Church and Protestantism in general have made a major contribution to the spiritual, moral, social, and economic development of the country over the last two centuries. Yet the country remains the only least developed country in the region, one of the poorest and most unequal on the planet, with a high illiteracy rate and one of the highest rates of perceived corruption in the world.]

In his book, *La Mission Evangélique Baptiste du Sud d'Haiti (MEBSH): Un Octogénaire dans le Bicentenaire du Protestantisme en Haïti* Lusson Napoléon, the current MEBSH president, claims that after the independence, Haiti had 10 - 20% Catholics and 0% Protestants, and in 2013, Haiti was 49% Catholics and 45% Protestants.[298] If Haiti is, as Napoleon argues, 94% Christian, I'm tempted to ask if the country would have been better off without Christianity.

---

[297] See Deux siècles de protestantisme en Haïti (1816-2016)
[298] Napoleon, "*La MEBSH*", 269

Gérald Guiteau, a Pentecostal pastor of the Church of God, believes that Haiti is under a divine curse for being free. As a prosperity gospel preacher, Guiteau firmly believes that poverty is a curse and wealth a blessing. In his doctoral thesis, *La mission intégrale des églises pentecôtistes dans le contexte haïtien influencé par les traditions du vaudou: Cas de l'Eglise de Dieu*, Guiteau argues, *"Pour qu'Haïti soit délivré des liens de la pauvreté, la malédiction doit être enlevée. Le salut d'Haïti sur le plan économique requiert la consécration de la nation entière à Dieu et la mise en pratique des commandements de la parole de Dieu."*[299] (For Haiti to be delivered from the bonds of poverty, the curse must be removed. The salvation of Haiti on the economic level requires the consecration of the entire nation to God and putting into practice the commandments of the word of God.)

The Pentecostal church is the fastest-growing denomination in Haiti, but it also has the poorest of the poor as members. As poverty grows, so does the church, and as the church grows, so does dependency. While the church is inviting the nation to be under God, they are preaching that it's okay to be poor because God has a plan for the poor.

Guiteau later admits, *"Le mouvement pentecôtiste haïtien a commencé comme un puissant mouvement des pauvres. Le Pentecôtisme ne s'adresse pas aux couches prolétaires en tant que groupe, mais aux individus en général pauvres"*.[300] ("The Haitian Pentecostal movement began as a powerful movement of the poor.

---

[299] Gérald Guiteau, La mission intégrale des églises pentecôtistes dans le contexte haïtien influencé par les traditions du vaudou: Cas de l'Eglise de Dieu, p 107
[300] Ibid, 153

Pentecostalism is not aimed at the proletarian classes as a group, but at poor individuals in general.)

And I could not agree more with Celucien L. Joseph who argues that:

> Haitian Protestantism does not play a social role in Haitian society as to improving the Haitian condition and the life of more than 85% of the country's population that lives in dire poverty. Haitian Protestantism rejects the social vision of Christianity but emphasizes its pietistic spirituality.[301]

In *Walking with the Poor*, Bryant Myers defines poverty as broken relationships. For Myers "Flawed relationships—with self, others, the environment, and God—result in violence, conflict, greed, racism, poverty, oppression, and marginalization."[302] In other words, If you want to keep Haiti poor, bring in more religion. Conversely, if you want to get rid of poverty, restore broken relationships with God, others, self, and creation. It's not something you do by being religious, it's a gift of the Spirit of God.

Religion out of Duty

Growing up, I didn't like the nightly devotions that my dad compelled my siblings and me to participate in. For my dad, you have to use certain words when you pray. Because of this, I have dreaded prayer for a long time, particularly, being asked to pray in

---

[301] Celucien L. Joseph, *"Redefining cultural, national, and religious identity: The Christian– Vodouist dialogue?"* Theology Today 2016, Vol. 73(3) 241–262

[302] Bryant L. Myers, *Walking With The Poor: Principles and Practices of Transformational Development* (Revised and Expanded Edition), (Orbis Books. Kindle Edition), Location 5870.

public. For most Haitian evangelicals, spiritual disciplines, such as reading the bible, praying, and going to church, are activities one ought to do out of obligation. The majority of Haitian Christians feel that they are required to attend church regularly. This compulsory participation has taken a toll on the adherents of the Christian faith. For Protestants, this obligatory participation is more of a burden than they can bear.

Take for instance a few burdensome practices within the church. In most Protestant churches, members are not given communion if they don't attend members' monthly meetings. They also cannot receive communion if they're not active in the church. In most churches, attendance is taken, and the membership card is hole-punched. What should have been a load lifter became a burden in the Haitian religious experience.

I've seen countless times when verses from the Bible are being used to compel people to "work for God". For example, a leader will quote, "No one who puts a hand to the plow and looks back is fit for service in the kingdom of God (Luke 9:62)." This verse is usually used against people who backslid in their responsibilities. It can be a choir member who missed a couple of rehearsals, a Sunday school teacher who could not make it on a given Sunday, a member who did not attend the monthly meeting, or someone who did not show up for a prayer meeting.

Although Catholics are required by their dogmas to attend all masses and special ceremonies, they are more lenient as the priests don't have such direct contact with their members. Still, some priests will refuse to celebrate a mass, a funeral, or a special ceremony if the person is not a regular attendee.

In Vodou, some ougans and manbos admit that they became priests, priestesses, and practitioners against their will. They claim that they cannot resist the demand of the lwa. Being *sèvitè* becomes a burden since there is fear of being cast out by the lwa if some ceremonies are not performed.

Are you following your religion because you were born into it? Were you coerced into accepting your family's religious traditions?

Religion and Sexual Abuse

One of the least talked about abuses of religion in Haiti is sexual abuse. Although this issue has timidly been exposed, it's been going on for a very long time without impunity. According to a 2020 report, 4% of teenage girls between the age of 14 and 17, and 8% of women are victims of sexual violence.[303] If Haiti is 94% Christian, a majority of these sexual acts are done by Christians, including the clergy, missionaries, leaders of NGOs, and religious tourists. The majority of abuses of minors and men and women are done by Haitian pastors, missionaries, Christian agencies, aid workers, and ougans. It's well-recorded that Catholic priests have been sexually abusing their maids, nuns, and other church workers for centuries. In some cases, Catholic priests impregnated their maids and used them as common-law wives.

There have also been reports of abuse being covered up by church leaders or ignored by church authorities, which has made it difficult for victims to receive the support and justice they need.

---

[303] For more see EMMUS IV survey cited in Caleb Lefèvre, "Quand les violences sexuelles restent impunies", accessed 1/9/2021, https://lenouvelliste.com/article/225033/quand-les-violences-sexuelles-restent-impunies.

This is a widespread problem that requires action from both the church and wider society to address.

Haitian women usually won't report if they are victims of sexual abuse, and their abusers know that. Some cases of sexual abuse are well-known since they were investigated and tried in a court of law. For example, the pastor of the Eglise Evangélique de la Restauration who was accused of multiple sexual assaults of a church member,[304] the Ohio-based mission worker who confessed several instances of immoral sexual relationships with boys,[305] the Jesuit priest who abused homeless boys for over a decade in Cap-Haitien,[306] and the pastor of a ministry in Haiti who exploited the girls for sexual favors.[307]

Numerous cases of sexual abuse by STMs and orphanage workers who are engaged in trafficking children for sex. Jeriah Mast admitted to molesting over 30 boys while working for Christian Aid Ministries in Petit Goave. He was sentenced to nine years in

---

[304] Mark Price, "Pastor sexually assaults woman during 'spiritual revival' ceremony, Florida cops say" in Yahoo News, https://www.yahoo.com/news/pastor-sexually-assaults-woman-during-170330753.html

[305] Jeriah Mast was with Christian Aid Ministries and Shining Light Christian Fellowship in Ohio where he confessed of his sins. He was sentence to nine years in prison. For more, see https://www.post-gazette.com/news/faith-religion/2019/06/12/Christian-Aid-Ministries-Haiti-Mennonite-Amish-sexual-abuse-covernigs/stories/201906110110

[306] A class-action lawsuit was settled for $60 million against the Society of Jesus of New England and others. The abuser, Douglas Perlitz is serving a 20-year prison sentence. https://apnews.com/article/03a0f20918d94f2b936cc0ca7acb4413

[307] Pastor Larry Michael Bollinger of North Carolina was charged in abusing four young girls between August 1 and November 18 of 2009. For more, see *Pastor denied bond after sexual abuse allegations against Haitian children*", https://www.wbtv.com/story/18575871/pastor-denied-bond-after-sexual-abuse-allegations-against-haitian-children/

prison.[308] Michael Geilenfeld was arrested and accused of abusing young boys in his orphanage for more than five years.[309] In his article, *La vie sexuelle secrète des prêtres catholiques haïtiens,* Emmanuel Moïse Yves concludes, "In Haiti, cases of pedophilia involving missionary priests are rife. Local churches, whether Catholic or Protestant, have always been in the spotlight due to sexual abuse by senior officials, sometimes plunging victims into acute trauma."[310]

Religion and Women

Women have always played a significant role in the religious history of Haiti. One cannot silence the past by ignoring the role that Cécile Fatiman played as a Vodou priestess at Bois Caïman. In Haiti, women outnumber men in attendance at any religious setting. I dare to argue that without women, there would not be a church in Haiti, especially a Catholic church where over 80% attending Sunday masses are women.

However, it is also inside the church that women are oppressed and marginalized the most. Not only are they spiritually to be submissive to male leadership, but they are also subjected to all types of rules. For example, some places of worship kept women out

---

[308] See "An Open Letter from the Board of Directors of Christian Aid Ministries Regarding the Case of Jeriah Mast." Christian Aid Ministries, June 17, 2019. https://christianaidministries.org/haiti-abuse-case/public-statement-haiti-investigation/, Web accessed May 18, 2023.

[309] For more, see the press release of the Office of Public Affairs regarding "U.S. Citizen Arrested for Traveling to Haiti with Intent to Sexually Abuse Minors", accessed 02/4/2024 https://www.justice.gov/opa/pr/us-citizen-arrested-traveling-haiti-intent-sexually-abuse-minors

[310] Emmanuel Moïse Yves, *"La vie sexuelle secrète des prêtres catholiques haïtiens"* accessed 4/10/2021 in https://ayibopost.com/la-vie-sexuelle-secrete-des-pretres-catholiques-haitiens/ 16 novembre 2019.

of the pulpit. They are forbidden to wear makeup, pants, nail coloring, sleeveless blouses, and jewelry, and they must wear hair covering while inside the church building. Some churches used to take it to the extreme by sitting women on the left side and men on the right.

Although in most places of worship, the majority in attendance are women, they are relegated to supportive roles such as cleaning and cooking. In Haiti, it is only in Vodou that both men and women of the clergy are considered equal.

Unfortunately, religion has put an undue burden on these women, and spiritual leaders are for the most part responsible. In a male-dominated clergy, women are reduced to second-class citizens. Church leaders don't care that women are also filled with the Holy Spirit. They don't even believe that God equally gifts both men and women.

Although numerous gospel accounts described how Jesus showed love and respect for women, and how he elevated them, religious leaders choose not to recognize women as members of equal standing. They forget that the good news of the resurrected Christ was given first to two women (Mary Magdalene and the other Mary). They brush off stories of women leaders such as Lydia of the community of Philippi and Priscilla, Euodia, and Syntyche whom Paul called co-workers in ministry. They ignore that Moses's sister Miriam was the first Hebrew prophet. They don't care if Huldah was prophesying concurrently with Jeremiah and that she was a great teacher of men during King Josiah's reign.

In a patriarchal society like Haiti, women inside the church are reduced to being glorified maids. Not only are they sexually abused by religious leaders, but they are also restrained in expressing their spiritual gifts. Less than a tenth of a percent of women are accepted in Bible colleges, and they are trained not for the work of ministry, but on how to become good wives.

It's not a surprise then in their code of ethics, MEBSH has their pastors pledge the following: "My wife will always be my marital partner, the mother of my children, the mistress of my house, and she will serve in the church in the same capacity as the other women."[311] Translation: *My wife will give me sex when I want it, and she will bear me a lot of kids (6 to 8) while taking care of the house, and she will sit quietly in church like the other women.*

The Church of Nazarene in Haiti used to encourage their Bible students to marry women not out of love, but to "find wives who could teach Sunday school classes, be active in church work, keep clean homes, and be good mothers."[312] While in rare cases religion can elevate the status of Haitian women, it is also their worst oppressor.

Religion and the Environment

A lot of Haitian Protestants believe that God created the world for their enjoyment. But they also believe that this earth will burn down on their way to heaven, as they watch the Vodouists and the Catholics crying for help while they say to them "*Mwen te pale w*" (I told you so). They see natural disasters as a sign of God's

---

[311] See MEBSH - "Code of Ethics for Pastors"
[312] Linda Crow, Haiti I Love You (Kansas City: Nazarene Publishing House, 1970), 50.

imminent return, and they reason "Why care about the environment"?

Their literal reading of the forthcoming new earth is, for them, an incentive to trash the old one. Who would have thought that Vodouists would care more about the stewardship of the earth than Christians? In response to their role in healing the nation of COVID-19, the Haitian Vodou's supreme leader said "My hope is that after corona... instead of transforming all we touch, transforming nature, we look instead to live in harmony with it,"[313]

Power and Pulpit Bullies

Haitian spiritual leaders tend to have a significant influence when it comes to the everyday lives of their members. These leaders use fear, pointed sermons, and intimidation to power over their members and to keep them into submission. Some leaders even control the emotional and social aspects of their members' lives. Haitian Christians are mostly made up of people who have been indoctrinated in their respective denominations, and they have been told what to believe and to never question religious authorities.

Additionally, some religious leaders claim to be representing God on earth, and they believe the Bible gives them that authority. Consequently, they demand to be put on a pedestal, and they are proud to be called "Berger" (Shepherd), Reverend, Bishop, "Papi" (Daddy), "Serviteur"[314] (Servant), "Homme de Dieu" (Man of

---

[313] Andre Paultre and Robenson Sanon, "Haiti voodoo leaders prepare temples for coronavirus sufferers", https://www.yahoo.com/news/haiti-voodoo-leaders-prepare-temples-193859033.html

[314] In this context, Serviteur means 'faithful servant of God' not someone who is serving others.

God), and "Oint de l'Eternel" (Anointed of God). Some insist on being called "Reverend Doctor" even if their fake doctorate diplomas were acquired from honorary sources and diploma mills[315]. They usually have an inflated ego and a *folie de grandeur.* Their wives cannot even call them by their first names, only by their titles.[316]

When they are in a room full of people, they believe they should be the most important person in the room, and they should be treated accordingly. The less educated they are, the more they need to be esteemed. Their flocks are scared to talk back to these earthly "saints" for fear of retribution from God.

Instead of serving others, they lord it over others by twisting scripture. On Sundays, they can peach about how Jesus was a poor Galilean carpenter to teach their members about humility, while at the same time, using the pulpit as a bullying platform and boosting their bloated egos. They forget that real power looks like calvary love as displayed on the cross (1 Cor 1:18). Instead of serving God and their neighbor, religion becomes their servant.

Religious Rules, Rituals, and Traditions

I've seen my share of religious bondage among Haitians, and I have witnessed their lives ruined because of religious rules, rituals, and traditions. Some years ago, I was at a friend's wedding in Port-au-Prince as the designated photographer. The wedding was held at

---

[315] For prestige and power, some religious leaders in Haiti pay a lot of money to get fake doctorate diplomas in Florida and elsewhere.

[316] Usually when talking about or to her husband, a pastor's wife would say, "Pastè a pa la non" (the pastor is not home), or "Past, men yon ti ji wi" (I bring you some juice pastor)

one of the most well-known churches of the Church of God denomination in Haiti. A family member of the bride, obviously not a member of this particular church, wore a nice two-piece pantsuit to the ceremony.

As the invitees were standing up to receive the bride, the officiating pastor noticed the woman's outfit since she was standing in the front row. Through the microphone, the pastor said, "There is a woman wearing pants inside the church, she needs to get out now, otherwise I will not celebrate the wedding. Women are not permitted to wear pants in this church".

Confused and ashamed, the woman was hesitant to leave at first, but as the pastor insisted a second time, she shamefully strolled out of the church. Sadly, this is too common in our Haitian churches. This is another one of the many burdens of religion on church leaders. The pastor was so blinded by his religious rules and traditions to be enforced that judgment took over his ability to love.

When religious rules and traditions are more important than people, religion becomes the focus while Jesus is put on the back burner. As Bruxy Cavey points out, "His [Jesus] life's works were about undoing the knots that bound people to ritual and empty tradition."[317] Jeremy Myers agrees when he says,

> If in our efforts to protect our "rites" and our "rights," we are ruining our witness and destroying the clarity of the gospel, this is an indication that we have made idols of such things, and they need to be brought once again into subservience to Jesus Christ. The gospel of Jesus Christ is not about defending our

---

[317] Bruxy, 44

religious rites or our legal rights, but about sacrificing everything for the sake of others.[318]

Another burden of religion on Haitians is around rules and traditions associated with Communion. While each denomination has its own ritual, the rules and traditions are the same. Communion is usually celebrated on the first Sunday of the month in the quasi-totality of Protestant churches in Haiti. It's a high-attendance Sunday that members don't want to miss. People dress in their best, and even what they cook at home matters. In some churches in the big cities, it's a fashion show. I know people who sometimes would not go to church that day if they could not find something new to wear. Most senior pastors would not give up the pulpit to other pastors. What was supposed to be a celebration became an idol.

Additionally, there are also rules and traditions attached to this ritual. For example, communion is given only to baptized members who are in good standing with the church, and visitors need to show a membership card from their church if they want to participate. Only deacons and other pastors can pass the elements, and they must wear a suit and tie. Before taking communion, members are asked to examine themselves if they are worthy to participate. This penance is required to realign their soul with the will of God.

If for some reason, a member does not partake in communion, he/she is denounced by the deacon and is subjected to shame and church discipline. To avoid sanctions and gossip, a member would

---

[318] Myers, Jeremy. Dying to Religion and Empire: Giving up Our Religious Rites and Legal Rights (Close Your Church for Good Book 3) (p. 14). Redeeming Press. Kindle Edition.

pretend to participate by taking the elements of the ritual, but discard them on the floor pretending as if it were an accident.

Until a few years ago, most Protestant denominations did not permit inter-communion. Nowadays some churches are more lenient on their rules by letting those who are free to receive Communion in their churches partake in communion. What is supposed to be a celebratory event becomes a stumbling block and an undue burden on Haitian Protestants.

The Catholic church, as a general rule, won't give the Eucharist to anyone who should not be conscious of grave sin and normally should have fasted for one hour. It's also unlawful for Catholics to take Communion from a Protestant minister. In the Catholic Church's view, those eligible to take the Eucharist are those who are living "in communion with" Catholic teaching. Additionally, married people outside the church, such as civil ceremonies, are not eligible for the Eucharist. It would not happen either way because the church in Haiti is so caught up in the what and how of the rituals that they miss the point. As Bruxy points out, "The cup is more important than the water."

Another area of religious burden is from the religious organizations. Thousands of Christian organizations in Haiti have discriminated against Haitians who do not share their beliefs. For example, Hospital Lumière in Bonne Fin, a Baptist (MEBSH) missionary hospital in a rural area of Les Cayes, used to have a policy of hiring only Protestants.

The best nursing school in Haiti (Ecole Nationale d'Infirmières des Cayes) is in my home town of Les Cayes. Although a state-affiliated school, it used to be run by Canadian and Haitian

Catholic nuns. Not too long ago, to be admitted, a prospective student must be Catholic and must adhere to Catholic rules and principles. I know of a few Protestant students who lied to get in. They told the nuns they were Catholics, and then forcefully attended masses and all Catholic religious activities and rituals.

A pastor of a well-known Baptist church in the capital used to force the women in his church to do a pregnancy test in his office before agreeing to celebrate their wedding. Pregnant women would trick him by bringing someone else urine and pouring it in the empty vial for the pastor.

One of my friends who is an Adventist was kicked out of her church because she married a non-Adventist, someone outside of her denomination.

I certainly agree with Bruxy Cavey who argues that "Religion uses rules to force our steps, guilt to keep us in line, and rituals to remind us of our failure to live up to those rules. In doing this, religion adds more weight to those who are already burdened with life's hardships."[319]

A Case Study

A few years ago, in conversation with some church leaders in Haiti, I presented to them this case study:

Robert was a Catholic while he was previously married to Sabine, and, for some reason, he divorced his wife. As Robert and Sabine have gone their separate ways, they have found new love, and they have been since remarried. From frequent conversations

---

[319] Bruxy The End of Religion, p14

with their Protestant neighbors, Robert and his new wife, Rosette, have accepted Christ as their savior. When I asked three pastors in leadership positions at MEBSH what would they do if Robert and his wife wanted to join their church, and after a brief discussion among themselves, here is how they answered me:

First Pastor: *"Robert would have to leave his new wife and go back to his previous wife before I would welcome him in my church. I'm big on church discipline".*

Second Pastor: *I would accept them, but they would never play any roles in the church nor participate in any activities. I would not baptize them either.*

Third Pastor: *Since Robert and his wife became Christians[320] after his divorce, I would welcome them not as baptized members, but as believers.[321] In this case, I would never let them participate in communion or be a member of any group in the church.*

Don't you find it odd that they gave me slightly three different answers although they are leaders in the same denomination? At MEBSH, the body of Christ would never experience Robert and Rosette's God-given gifts. Other than collecting their tithes and offerings, the church would have no use for them. When you make Protestantism or any religion about rules, rituals, and traditions, you end up creating more rules by wrongly interpreting the Bible to accommodate your opinion. Then what you have is a zombie church. As Edwards Tyler in *Zombie Church* points out, "When

---

[320] Note that Protestants don't consider Catholics as Christians.

[321] The MEBSH tradition has two groups of people: members (baptized) and believers (not yet baptized). Only baptized people are allowed to take communion. In most MEBSH churches, if you're a visitor, you need to show the membership card of your church to partake in communion.

we make Christianity about rules and routines, we destroy relationships. The church moves from being a revolutionary, world-changing force to being a lazy social club that exists to keep on existing."[322]

NGOs and Conversion

You may have heard that Haiti is a country of NGOs. Over 9000 parachurch organizations with roots in the U.S. are working in Haiti. Their websites, field reports, and individual testimonies tell the story of how Haitians are hungry for the gospel, and how their souls are being delivered from Vodou. It's not a surprise that their social enterprises are fused with a social gospel that produces a lot of "converts". Free health clinics, free food, and free clothes will deliver the goods.

The problem is that Haitians are people who live in the now, especially those who are the recipients of the missionary social enterprise. When they attend these drive-by social activities, the questions they ask themselves are "How is it going to benefit me today?", "Would saying yes to Jesus let me see the doctor quicker"? Would I get a bigger bag of rice or more used clothes? How can this activity benefit me socially? Therefore, they don't have any problem saying "yes" to Jesus for a day.

Fatalism and Free Will

Is the Haitian by default deterministic? Maybe, since *"Que sera sera"* could have been the motto of the Haitian flag. Still, the idea that Haitians do not have an entrepreneurial spirit and no sense of

---

[322] Edwards, Tyler. *Zombie Church* (p. 44). Kregel Publications. Kindle Edition.

personal responsibility is misguided. Haiti's issues are not because of Haitians' lack of effort, imagination, passivity, laziness, and resigned attitude. The Haitian's fatalistic worldview is rooted in religion and a distorted picture of who God is.

The Haitian believes God is so powerful that He does what He wants, and He doesn't care what others think. Therefore, God's purpose takes precedence over human will. In his poem *Haiti Cherie*, Othello Bayard says it well,

Lor en Haïti, ou pas jam manqué temps pou souffler
Ca qui pas faite jodi, ou cap fait li demain si ou vlé.
Quand demain river, qu'il bon ou qu'il pas bon,
Ca pas fait engnin toute moune pas jam désespéré
Moune gangne la foi lan gnou Dié qui pas jam menti
N'ap fait jodi quand demin pas assuré
À la bon pays, oh mon Dié, ce Haiti![323]

When you're in Haiti, you never panic.
We'll do tomorrow what hasn't been done today,
And tomorrow, whether it works or not,
We don't worry, we're never discouraged
We have faith in an infinitely good God
We take care of the present and leave the future in God's hands.
What a good country Haiti is, my God!

Consequently, God is blamed for inequalities, suffering, and evil in their world. For example, God is accused of being unjust in

---

[323] Cited in Maximilien Laroche, Portrait de l'Haïtien (Montréal: Les Éditions de Sainte-Marie, 1968), 60

this expression: *"Bondye bay, li pa konn separe"* (God knows how to give, but He is an awful distributor).

Claire Payton was interviewing a survivor of the 2010 earthquake who believed that it was a way for God to punish evil in Haiti. He said,

> There is a lot of evil in this country all around. Evangelists preach everywhere, but the people don't listen. Because Cod, when he does his work, he come to those who are the most evil. He says "That's your problem," and then he destroys. That is the will of Cod .... There is so much evil everywhere in Haiti. A lot of sacrifices happen here. Cod says, "Well, I'm going come, and there is nothing that can keep me from striking, and I am going to destroy." It happened in Chile, it happened in other places without so much destruction. It's clear that he destroyed the place where there was the most evil.[324]

The Haitian's experience with colonialism has also given the Haitian a fatalistic worldview. The colonial powers and the Catholic priests had taught their ancestors that it was God's will for them to be slaves, and both Catholic and Protestant leaders have preached a theology of resignation for over three hundred years as a result. This is evident if you listen to the lyrics in their hymn book.

"Konsole w frè mwen, reziyen ou zanmi mwen" (console yourself, my brother, resign yourself my friend) is on the lips of every Christian.

---

[324] Cited in Claire Payton, *"Vodou and Protestantism, Faith and Survival: The Contest over the Spiritual Meaning of the 2010 Earthquake in Haiti,* The Oral History Review, Summer/Fall 2013, Vol. 40, No. 2 (Summer/Fall 2013), pp. 231-250

Expressions, such as, "*Si Bondye vle*" (God willing), and "*Bondye k konnen*" (God who knows) are in every conversation. Public buses are named to reflect their worldview: *Dieu Qui Décide* (God Who Decides), *La Volonté de Dieu* (God's Will), and *Volonté Divine* (Divine's Will) are just a few examples. This worldview is also evident in the following everyday expressions:

1. *L'homme propose, Dieu dispose.* (Man proposes, God disposes). In this expression, why make plans since God controls everything?

2. *Je tiens le volant, c'est l'Eternel qui conduit.* [I hold the steering wheel, but God is the driver.] In this case, anyone can drive as long as one can get a hold of the steering wheel.

3. *Je soigne, c'est l'Eternel qui guérit.* [I give care, but it's God who heals.] The doctor sheds all responsibilities. Your healing depends on God's mood. Knowledge and science are useless.

4. *Dieu dirige mes affaires.* [God manages my businesses]. God decides if my business fails or grows.

In a survey done by the Faraday Institute for Science and Religion at the University of Cambridge to assess the emotions and beliefs in Haiti after the earthquake of January 12, 2010, the researchers found that 80% of Haitians believe the earthquake was God's will, and 51% think that it was a punishment that God has inflicted on sinners.[325]

---

[325] "Pour plus de 50% d'Haïtiens le séisme de 2010 était une punition de Dieu", accessed 1/15/2020, Le Nouvelliste, https://lenouvelliste.com/article/211092/pour-plus-de-50-dhaitiens-le-seisme-de-2010-etait-une-punition-de-dieu

The well-known Haitian poet, Alcibiade Fleury-Battier, expresses his fatalism and his view of God in his poem *Sur la Mort de Mon Père.*

Mais puisque c'est Dieu seul qui retire et qui donne,
Selon sa sainte volonté,
Qui juge en souverain, qui punit, qui pardonne,
Et qui règle l'éternité;
Mais puisque c'est ce Dieu qui veut bien que tout tombe,
Depuis l'enfant jusqu'au vieillard;
Qui garde pour lui seul les secrets de la tombe[326]

But since it is God alone who takes away and gives,
According to his holy will,
Who judges in sovereign, who punishes, who forgives,
And who rules the eternal;
But since it is this God who wants everything to fall,
From the child to the old man;
Who keeps for him alone the secrets of the grave

For the Protestants, God is behind everything, good or bad. He rewards you if you're good, and he punishes you when you're bad. After all, one of their favorite verses is *"Bondye chatye pitit li renmen"*. (Because the Lord disciplines the one he loves, and he chastens everyone he accepts as his son (Hebrew 12:6-7)).

Contrary to the Haitian evangelicals, Vodouists don't blame God for evil. They know there are competing evil spirits in the world.

---

[326] Alcibiade Fleury-Battier, *Sous les Bambous: Poésies* (Paris: Imprimerie typographique Kugelmann, 1881).

CHAPTER 8

A Way Out: Let My People Go

———— ·⚜· ————

The problem with organized religion is not that it is organized.
The problem with organized religion is that it is religious--
believing that its own set of rules, regulations, rituals, and routines
are the exclusive way to God.

Bruxy Cavey

The kingdom of God is built on the cross, not on bread and
butter.

David Oginde

What you fellows don't understand is that you must get a man
through his religion and not through yours.

George Bernard Shaw

In a country in which the prime human struggle is to climb
out of the deep morass of poverty and powerlessness, the church is
of no help if it is itself poisoning the people with the virus of not
taking responsibility for its own affairs.

Kritzinger J. J

Things Must Change

The great Kenyan theologian and scholar, John Mbiti, once told the New York Times in a 1971 interview, "The days are over when we will be carbon copies of European Christians. Europe and America Westernized Christianity. The Orthodox Easternized it. Now it's our turn to Africanize it."[327]

By the same token, the Haitianization of Christianity is long overdue. The Catholic church and Vodou were introduced in Haiti at the birth of the nation. The Protestant church celebrated a few years ago, two hundred years in Haiti. There are churches on every street and corner in Haiti. Religion is doing its job, but a bad one. Missionaries and parachurch organizations quadrupled following the earthquake. Yet, there are no significant changes in the lives of most Haitians. Like Pope John Paul II said when he visited Haiti in 1983, "Things must change."

It's time for the Haitian religious experience to be centered on the cross. As promised, I'm proposing a way out of the woes of religion, and it starts, among other ideas, by getting the right picture of God, having self-expression, moving away from religion to follow Christ, rethinking the role of missionaries, getting off dependency, and switching from institution to a covenant community.

Getting the Right Picture of God

I was a good boy growing up. Ask my mom. I was a bit clumsy, shy, and sloppy at times, but that didn't seem to warrant the fact that

---

[327] *"John Mbiti, 87, Dies; Punctured Myths About African Religions"*, New York Times, accessed 2/12/2020 https://www.nytimes.com/2019/10/24/world/africa/john-mbiti-dead.html

my dad was always ready to punish me for every perceived mistake or imperfection. Other authority figures, including the teachers in my young life, were mean most of the time. I was constantly living in fear. I wish I could say it was different from my faith, but as discussed in previous chapters, I was taught from an early age that God was also mean, and He could strike me anytime he wanted to. My mental picture of God did not change when I said the sinner's prayer.

The first time I was "converted"[328] I was about twelve. Every summer, at my dad's church, the missionary ladies would come for a week of summer Bible school, also known as Vacation Bible School. They would narrate Bible and missionary stories while flipping through the pages of an oversized picture book[329]. This particular summer, one story was about a black devil king who wanted to kill and eat a white missionary who came to his island to share the good news of the gospel. The other story was about how people were going to burn in hell if they didn't ask Jesus to come into their lives. It was a scary seven days. I was scared. Out of fear, I surrendered my life to Christ to avoid hell.

Throughout my teenage years, my mental picture of God did not change much. Like most Haitian Protestants, I grew to know Jesus as my loving savior, but God the Father as the punisher. I was involved in religious activities, such as youth groups, summer camps, and church choir, but my relationship with God was

---

[328] I probably re-converted at least 50 times at evangelism campaigns, open-air revivals, conventions, youth meetings, crusades, and altar calls or whenever I felt convicted of my sin.

[329] After my dad passed, I went into his archive, and I found, 40 years later, *Devil-Kings and Cannibals: 5 Missionaries stories, a picture book from the life of John Paton.* It brought back memories.

nonexistent. I believed that I was a good person, and as long as I didn't do anything crazy, I was saved and bound for heaven where a golden crown was waiting for me. And that's all I needed to know. However, I was still living with the fear of going to hell if I didn't have time to repent of my last sin. I was in an eternal state of recommitting and rededicating my life to God by reconverting over and over. I was relating to God, as Cavey points out, "through systems of doctrines, codes of conduct, inherited traditions, or institutions of power."[330] In other words, I was following the religion of my parents, but I was not following Jesus.

When Jesus reintroduced Himself to me during my adult life, it was a game changer. I have learned to rethink, critically consider, and double-check my beliefs. My story may be similar to yours. Maybe like me, you were raised to keep up with the rules and traditions of your family's religion and to make everything possible to avoid the wrath of God. Maybe like me, you grew up in a religious environment but not in Christ.

Maybe you are around someone or you are part of a group that uses God and religion to instill fear in yourself and others to control your life. To you, God is like a tyrant or your mean earthly father always looking for an opportunity to punish you. That's what religion does. It often paints a scary picture of God. But I can assure you that our Abba Father is nothing like that. God cannot love you more than He loves you now, and there is nothing you can do, good or bad, for Him to love you less.

---

[330] Bruxy, 44

Self-Expression

The last fifty years have seen the emergence of African Indigenous Churches (AIC) in Africa. Not only is this rapid growth due to the rejection of the European mission but also from the desire to appropriate Christ to the African worldview. In the same way, another Haitian revolution is needed for Haitians to be free from the grip of the Western mission hegemony that undermines the Haitian people's culture, self-expression, and openness. Glenn Schwartz rightly argues in *When Charity Destroys Dignity*,

> An indigenous church should look and sound like the society of which it is a part. In other words, it should not stand out as something culturally different or foreign...It out to be seen as a group of people concerned to carry out God's priorities in their communities. Believers should stand apart from the average person in the neighborhood because of their obedience of God's Word. But the church should not look like a culturally foreign institution.[331]

When the missionaries came to Haiti during and shortly after the U.S. Occupation in 1915, they translated into French and Kreyòl old hymns from, among others, *The Missionary Message, Making Melody,* and the *Old Baptist Hymn Book.* Years later, the Haitian people compiled them into their hymnal book called *Chants d'Espérance,* from which they've been singing ever since. For some Haitian Protestants, it's a second Bible.

The problem is that some of these old hymns of the *Chants d'Espérance* are written by Westerners for Westerners. When we sing *"Blanc, plus blanc que neige"* (Whiter than snow), or *"Comme*

---

[331] Glenn Schwartz, When Charity Destroys Dignity: Overcoming Unhealthy Dependency in the Christian Movement (Bloomington: Authorhouse, 2007), 169.

un cerf altéré brame" (As the deer pants for the water) it's not relatable to the Haitians who have never seen snow nor a deer. Although most Western churches don't sing those hymns anymore, the Haitian churches hang on to them. Those lyrics are far from being part of the Haitian experience.

For most Haitians, song lyrics are their primary source of theology. As such, lyrics and rhythms that are indigenous should be incorporated into the Haitian religious experience. That would help make the gospel real to the average Haitian. Furthermore, using other cultural icons, such as Vodou's religious symbols, would also help the gospel be more real to Haitians who often feel like a divided house within themselves. How beautiful would it be to have the majestic Asòtò (Vodou drum) played alongside the keyboard in our churches? And wouldn't it be nice to have a set of *rara* instruments on the podium of the Tabernacle of Simon (Cayes) during the MEBSH annual convention?

In his article *Voodoo and Christianity: Compatibility or Irreconcilable Differences?*, J. A. Alexandre cautions that "There is a fine line between rejecting legitimate aspects of culture in the name of evangelism and adopting sinful elements of culture in the name of enculturation and tolerance."[332] While I'm not advocating for syncretism in the church, our musical instruments are not from the devil either.

There are a handful of churches that integrate local expressions in their theology. But the mainstream denominations accuse them of not being evangelical. According to Linda Crow with the Church

---

[332] J. A. Alexandre, Voodoo and Christianity: Compatibility or Irreconcilable Differences? Accessed 11/1/2020, https://www.equip.org/article/voodoo-christianity-compatibility-irreconcilable-differences/

of Nazarene, this particular denomination is successful in Haiti because the church is "truly Haitian". She notes that as far back as the late '60s, "The people have a freedom of worship which incorporates their culture into their songs, the order of the service, the entire working of the church. They have been allowed full freedom in expressing themselves."[333]

Some theologians think contextualization is dangerous. Some even argue that it leads to syncretism. But the current Chants d'Esperance, as it stands, is theologically flawed as most songs paint a distorted picture of God. We need to stop singing something like:

Isi ba mwen satisfè ak yon ti kay
Ak mezi byen Jezi vle ban mwen.
M konnen nan syèl la
Kote zanj yo ap chante
Mwen gen yon palè depi mwen sove[334]

I'm satisfied with just a cottage below
A little silver and a little gold
But in that city where the ransomed will shine
I want a gold one that's silver-lined

Or this one:

Papa mwen gen kay, avèk anpil tè,

---

[333] Crow, "Haiti, I love You", 38

[334] A couple years ago, a Haitian man was singing this song; I told him to give me his land because I don't care about a palace with the street paved with gold in heaven. He smiled, because he knows what he is singing about is not true for him. From No.38 Mélodies Joyeuses des Chants d'Esperance

Pla men li kenbe tout fòtin li fè,
Pyè presye, diaman, lajan avèk lò,
Tout bwat li yo plen, nan richès li pi fò.

Joupa oubyen kay, sa pa fè m anyen;
Anwo a, y ap bati yon palè pou mwen;
Pandan m ap tann li, m a chante chan sa a:
Tout glwa pou Bondye, mwen se pitit Wa a.

My Father is rich in houses and lands,
He holdeth the wealth of the world in His hands!
Of rubies and diamonds, of silver and gold,
His coffers are full, He has riches untold

A tent or a cottage, why should I care?
They're building a palace for me over there;
Though exiled from home, yet still may I sing:
All glory to God, I'm a child of the King

One of my hometown bands *Orchestre Meridional des Cayes*, in their lengthy Meringue piece *Pitie Pou Fanm* (Have Mercy for Women), recounted the creation story as it is written in the Bible. Every time I listen to the song, I can't help but wonder what's wrong with praising and worshiping God on a meringue-rabordage, troubadour, konpa, rara, or rasin air. Why shouldn't the powerful Asòtò drum of Vodou be used to praise God? Do you think God will be offended by our native rhythms and instruments?

It seems that the Haitian secular bands have a better image of the character of God than their Protestant counterparts do. One only needs to listen to Boukman Eksperyan's prayer *Bondye*

Manman Nou, Skah Shah's *Yaveh,*[335] Magnum Band's *Jehovah,* Frères Déjean's *La Prière,* and Accolade de New York's *La Foi,* to be convinced that the traditional culture worldview is closer to the biblical worldview than the Haitian Protestant expression.

Have you listened lately to Emeline Michel's lyrical prayer, *Ban'm la Jwa?* You can nit-pick her theology if you want to, but why wouldn't you sing that in your church? Is it because of its *rara* air? Do you think Emeline's beautiful voice was given to her by a *lwa?* Aren't all good gifts from God (James 1:17)? Since you are convinced that the *lwa* are *dyab,* can anything good come from the *dyab?* How people use their God-given gift is between them and God. When someone is under the influence of the devil, there is usually nothing good to show for it.

When Michel sings the lyrics below, is she praying to the *dyab?*:

Bondye pa ban mwen chay ou konnen m paka pote,
Beni m ak sa lajan paka achte.
Lafòs pou'm ret kanpe, pasyans pou'm jwenn sa ou sere pou mwen.
Tanpri Bondye, kore lafwa m, beni m ak kè poze.
Ban m la klèvwayans pou mwen kabre danje.
Tout sak gen pou rive, nan pla men w vin mwen trase.[336]

---

[335] Skah Shah is one of the greatest konpa bands of all time. Their 1978 vinyl record, which include *Yahve,* should be registered as a national heritage.

[336] Haitian singer and songwriter Emeline Michel is internationally known for her vibrant voice on Haitian traditional rhythms. *Banm la jwa* is from her album Rasin Kreyol, accessed 1/20/2020,
https://www.wikimizik.com/lyrics?song=1334&title=Ban%20M%20Lajwa&artist=Emeline%20Michel#.XiX4RchKiUl

Oh, God don't give me a burden I cannot bear,
Bless me with what money cannot buy.
Strength to stand still, patience to find what you have stored for me.
Please, God, hold still my faith, bless me with your peace.
Give me clairvoyance to avoid danger.
Whatever happens, my life is in the palm of your hand.

When you read and listen to the lyrics of Boukman Eksperyan's masterpieces *Tribilasyon* and *Sa'm Pèdi*, wouldn't you say they are better than some sermons you've heard lately? The question is how in the world a *rasin* group like Boukman Eksperyans preaches something so comforting? Are they singing about a *lwa* or our Lord Jesus? Could *Bondye* be actively working in their lives? Part of the lyrics is as follows:

Remèt mizè w bay moun ki renmen w lan
Sila ki te bay lavi l pou l te sove n
Fò n ka wè se nan li ke nou ka sove
Li kapab delivre w nan tout tribilasyon
Sa ki pi enpòtan se pou n kwè nan li
O gad'on lavi, mwen ta viv tout tan
E se nan li, nou ta viv nèt ale.[337]

Take your sorrow to the one who loves you
The one who gave his life to save us
Surely it is in him that we can be saved
He can save you from all tribulation
Most importantly, believe in Him
Oh what a life, I want to live forever

---

[337] "Tribilasyon", Boukman Eksperyans from their Album: Vodou Adjae, 1991, Produced by: Daniel Beaubrun, Lyrics by: Eddy François

And in him, we would live forever

Other than Emeline Michel who is, in my view, the embodiment of Haitian culture, there are not a lot of Haitian artists who bring tears to my eyes more than Yole Derose. She is not only known for her natural and breathtaking beauty; she is also a beloved Haitian singer with an angelique voice. Yole and her late husband Ansy were a crowd pleaser when I was growing up as a teenager. The message in their duo hit, *Si Bondye,* is as relevant today as it was 40 years ago. Part of the lyrics speak to us as if they were taken straight from the Bible:

Si Bondye ban-n lespri se poun'n kapab semble'l
Si Bondye ban'n coeur se poun'n kapab renmen
Si Bondye ban-n la pawol se poun'n kapab pale
Poun'n sa di tout san'n dwe di
Depi na'p di sa ki vre
Pou nou pale tout pawol san ke'n pa blesse peson'n
Si bondye ba nou yeux se pou nou kapab we
Si Bondye ban'n zorey se poun'n kapab tande
Si Bondye ban'n memwa se poun'n kapab songe
Tout san'n we tout san'n tande[338]

God gives us spirit so we can be like Him
God gives us a heart so we can love
God gives us words so we can speak
To say anything

---

[338] "Si Bondye", Ansy and Yole Derose, accessed 2/20/2020 https://www.wikimizik.com/lyrics?song=367&title=Si%20Bondye&artist=Ansy%20 &%20Yole%20Derose#.Xk7RO-hKiUk

To say what is true
To say anything without hurting others
God gives us eyes to see
God gives us ears to hear
God gives us memories to remember
What we see and what we hear

Unfortunately, for many Protestants, one's religious affiliation matters more than one's message. Consequently, Haitian artists whom they perceive as not being part of their religious sects are frowned upon. They would rather listen to "Christian" artists even if the message is wrong. I'm not asking you to sing Boukman Eksperyans at your church (actually I am), but when the fear of losing your salvation replaces your relationship with God, you're a zombie.

We indeed need to have discernment to live our lives in obedience to our Savior to show the visible Kingdom community. However, in doing so, we shouldn't flee from this world or hide away from our culture. Rather, we should live in the world but remember that our true citizenship is in the Kingdom.

Us and Them: A Call to Covenant Family

Aaron Rogers, the well-known American Football player, said this while reflecting on religion, "Religion can be a crutch, ... because it's set up binary, it's us and them, saved and unsaved, heaven and hell, it's enlightened and heathen, it's holy and righteous ... that makes a lot of people feel better about themselves."[339]

---

[339] "Aaron Rodgers Opens Up About Religion to Danica Patrick: 'I Don't Know How You Can Believe in a God'", Jason Duaine Hahn, accessed February 14, 2020

Unfortunately, this is what being a Christian means to a lot of people. I know of a pastor from the Baptist denomination of my hometown who would not go to his niece's wedding because she is Catholic. He didn't want to be seen socializing with unbelievers. There was another one who would not go to a family member's funeral because it would be celebrated at the local Catholic Church. It used to be the case that some denominations would not let their members marry a person from a different denomination. Those pharisaical attitudes need to stop. Jesus didn't care about his reputation. He simply did not sin. Again, religion is when you lose your common sense, and isolate yourself from your social responsibility in the name of God.

Throughout the NT, the church is portrayed as a family of brothers and sisters (Mat 12:50). In his book *Repenting of Religion*, Greg Boyd notes: "God is not first and foremost interested in acquiring a people who happen to believe all the right things and act in all the right ways. God's first concern, and His only concern, is to have a people who are united with him in love."[340]

From Religion to Following Jesus

There was a rich religious man who hurried over Jesus as Jesus was out on his way to Jerusalem. The man was concerned about his eternal life; so he wanted to make sure he was on the right path. He asked Jesus "What must I do to get eternal life?" This question is a classic definition of religion: getting eternal life is something you do by staying away from the seven deadly sins, following the rites and

---

https://www.yahoo.com/entertainment/aaron-rodgers-opens-religion-danica-200501823.html

[340] Boyd Gregory, *Repenting from Religion* (Grand rapids: Baker Books, 2004), 79

rituals, going to church and reading the Bible, participating in all religious activities, tithing, and making offerings. The rich, religious man did all that. But Jesus told him there is one more thing, "Go and sell all your possessions and give the money to the poor, and you will have treasure in heaven. Then come, follow me (Mark 10:21)." In other words, Jesus told him to leave his religion and follow him. The man went away sad because Jesus would not let him use his religion as a path to eternal life. Apparently, to follow Christ is not done just by being a good, law-abiding person, or by being religious. The rich ruler let religion get in his way of following Jesus.

Unfortunately, some people make following Christ equal to how much you know the Bible, having the right theology, and believing a particular set of doctrines, rituals, and traditions. Religion sees sharing the gospel as an event, but for the followers of Christ, it is a process. Jeremy Myers says it best,

> The gospel is about loving others like Jesus. It is about showing others what Jesus looks and acts like through our own lives and actions. It is about living here on earth according to the rules of heaven. It is about freedom from trying to live up to the standards of men, and instead showing the whole world a new way of life and liberty in Jesus Christ.[341]

Why are we limiting the Spirit of God to Protestantism? Can Jesus not heal a Vodouit, a non-believer, or a non-Christian? Are cases like the daughter of the Canaanite woman in Matthew 15:21-28 a one-time event?

---

[341] Myers, Jeremy. *Close Your Church for Good: Removing Religion to Reveal Jesus.* Redeeming Press. Kindle Edition. Location 7256.

Jesus did not call anyone to a new religion. All he said was follow me. Religion leads people to the church (building), whereas the follower of Christ points people to the kingdom of God.

I certainly agree with Bruxy Cavey who notes in his book *The End of Religion*, "The primary mission of Jesus was to tear down religion as the foundation of people's connection with God and to replace it with himself."[342]

Think about this. During his ministry, Jesus encountered many hostile situations. But all of them were with religious people.[343] Stop your religion, and be the church and the person you want to be. While the Haitian constitution grants the freedom of religion. I'm calling you to be free from religion.

From Institution to Community

Due to the rise of armed gangs and the level of violence in Port-Au-Prince and its suburbs, a lot of places of worship are either closed or relocated. The UEBH (Evangelical Baptist Union of Haiti) is one of the oldest Baptist missions in Haiti. Perched on top of a hilly green enclave in Bolosse near Martissant, their headquarters includes a magnificent church, a high school, and their flagship seminary. However, the Bolosse's neighborhood is one of the poorest and gang-infested areas of Port-au-Prince.

As the socio-economic and living conditions of its residents deteriorated, and as gangs started to use the UEBH space to terrorize the community, it became obvious that it was too dangerous for UEBH to do any activities in the area. Consequently, after 85 years,

---

[342] Cavey Bruxey, *The End of Religion* (Colorado Springs: NavPress, 2007), 23.
[343] Ibid

at the time of this writing, when UEBH closed the doors of its headquarters at the end of 2020, it was not a surprise for their neighbors.

While the government is to blame for failing to protect a cherished institution, the degradation of Haitian society is also to blame, and the church as an institution is a victim of its failure. Can you imagine the church of Corinth asking the Romans for protection? One of the problems of Haitian churches is their lack of integration into the lives of the people in their community.

UEBH sees itself as a national institution that should be protected, but it seems like it cares more about its properties than it does its members who live next door. Having a sumptuous church building in a poor neighborhood is as irrelevant as having a golden showerhead in your house with no running water. And what good is your Christian school if your next-door neighbor cannot afford the tuition?

Like any other big mission organization, UEBH has failed to carry out its mandate. Instead of majoring in neighborology, they run away from the gangs, the prostitutes, the destitute, and the people who cannot afford to move with them. Jeremy Myers was right when he pointed out, "Most churches have surprisingly little contact with their closest neighbors. If your church closed, the neighbors might wonder what happened, but there would likely be little noticeable difference in their lives."[344]

Isn't it telling that Vodou is more of a community-based religion than Haitian Christianity? In Haitian Vodou, community happens

---

[344] Myers Jeremy. Close Your Church for Good: Removing Religion to Reveal Jesus. Redeeming Press. Kindle Edition.

in the lakou. As Beaubrun Mimerose (Manzè) describes it, the lakou is "a place of multidimensional life where several families or, rather, an extended family shares all aspects of life (spiritual, economic, cultural)."[345] Some of the most famous lakou in Haiti are *Lakou Souvenans, Lakou Soukri,* and *Lakou Badjo.* I don't know any church in Haiti that has the same characteristics as a *lakou.*

Although Haitians are a communal people by nature, it is increasingly obvious that Haitians are losing their identity and a sense of community. The rapid rise of technology including the propagation of news through social media, the rise of violence in our neighborhoods, the lack of respect for elders, and rising cases of sexual abuse of women and minors have all contributed to the moral deterioration of the Haitian people.

In the midst of all of this, the Protestant churches in Haiti are going backward. Instead of being a community, their adherents are merely headcounts. They are unconcerned by the plight of the poor. They want big attractional churches, so they build cathedrals like the Catholics, by milking the poorest of the poor out of every penny.

As Winston Churchill once said, "We shape our buildings, thereafter they shape us." In this quote, Churchill is saying what we value and who we are are a reflection of the buildings we build. In Haiti church building is a source of pride and power for the religious leaders and the laity. The bigger the building, the more powerful the leaders are. Success then is how big is my building and how

---

[345] Beaubrun Mimerose, P. (2010) Nan Dòmi: An Initiate's Journey into Haitian Vodou, Translated by D.J. Walker (San Francisco: City Lights Books, 2013), 34.

many members it has. As one pastor in Port-au-Prince puts it, "We are especially proud of our attractive church building."[346]

How do you reconcile that the biggest churches in Haiti are in the poorest neighborhoods where most people won't even venture during the day? For example, the Second Baptist Church of Port-au-Prince is a megachurch in a gang-infested area in the Bel Air and St Martin neighborhood.

When a church is run like an institution, there is a hierarchy. An organizational chart is created just like a business enterprise. Peers are treated as subordinates, and leaders compare and contrast your church to others.

Additionally, worship and preaching time are programmed, and members are expected to be faithful in their attendance and financial contributions. Instead of displaying a calvary-like love toward others, there are power struggles and fights for positions.

Eventually, as an institution, the church needs rules, regulations, human, and financial resources. Instead of being a community of believers where every member participates as an organic expression of the body of Christ, the church is now being run like a business where the pastor is the CEO. When the church is an institution, churches with less than 50 people are called "stations". Instead of seeing these churches as models of covenant communities, local missions consider them irrelevant until they acquire more members.

Conversely, when the church is a community, the people are the church. In a community-driven church, you are moved from

---

[346] Linda Crow, "Victory Over Voodoo", 61

being a spectator at a Sunday event to a full-fledged participant in an act of fellowship. The rules and regulations, if any, are set by the community instead of a board of deacons, and there is no need for a lead pastor because everybody is either a pastor (servant), an apostle, an evangelist, a teacher, or a prophet (Eph. 4:11-12). Everyone has at least one of those God-given gifts for the work of ministry.

In a community-driven church, tithes and offerings are not treated like taxes, instead, they are used as gifts for the needs of the community. In a community-driven church, resources are shared for the common good, and members are engaged in mutual aid by identifying their problems and coming up with solutions.

Through community covenant, partners can all be effective ministers to each other and live in mutual submission and accountability to one another. Community is where people can actively engage in mutual ministry by discovering, discerning, and developing their ministry gifts and skills, and by actively serving each other. There can certainly be leaders and elders where it's appropriate, but in this context, leadership is not a position of power, but a gift-sharing position.

In that regard, every member is treated equally regardless of gender, class, profession, education, disability, health, or economic status. In a community-driven church, life is shared. The result is a sense of belonging displayed through commitment and involvement.

It's a fact that the poorest Haitian Protestants have contributed more of their limited resources to the church than the well-to-dos. Not only do they put proportionally more money on the offering plate, but they are also the first to volunteer their time for church activities, including events where manual labor such as yard work, construction projects, and cleaning are concerned. What if instead of raising funds from the poor to build cathedrals, the church would alleviate poverty among themselves by helping a disadvantaged kid with school tuition, volunteering to tutor and mentor the younger generation, and financing a community member's business initiative? If a church doesn't take care of its members, it likely won't see the needs of the community around it. God is not impressed by your massive building, nor is He glorified by your stained glass windows and sumptuous altars. All He asks for is that "through love, serve one another" (Galatians 5:13). Would your church commit itself to reflect God's character by loving and caring for its people?

Us and Them: A Call to Dialogue

In an era of religious pluralism, many scholars and church leaders in the past have called for interreligious dialogue. To cite a few, the Catholic priest Joseph Augustin who first introduced the *tambour* (drums) in the Catholic church, Laennec Hurbon, Jean Fils-Aime, Fr. Micial Nerestant, Fritz Fontus, Celucien Joseph, Fr. Smarth William, and Fr. Kawas Francois.

I hope, through this book, we can keep the conversation going.

The Catholic church has turned over a new leaf from its past practices. Not only are they more lenient to living in harmony with Vodou and Protestantism, but also with the Second Vatican Council, they shifted from "no salvation outside the church" to numerous interreligious dialogue initiatives. Pope Benedict XVI called the need for interreligious dialogue a sacred duty:

In our troubled world, so frequently marked by poverty, violence, and exploitation, dialogue between cultures and religions must more and more be seen as a sacred duty incumbent upon all those who are committed to building a world worthy of man," he said. "The ability to accept and respect one another, and to speak the truth in love, is essential for overcoming differences, preventing misunderstandings, and avoiding needless confrontations. [...] A sincere dialogue needs both openness and a firm sense of identity on both sides, in order for each to be enriched by the gifts of the other.[347]

Pope Francis has been actively calling for interreligious dialogue. In his speech at the Interreligious and Ecumenical Gathering at the Bandaranaike Memorial International Conference Hall, in Colombo, he said:

Dialogue is essential if we are to know, understand, and respect one another. But, as experience has shown, for such dialogue and encounter to be effective, it must be grounded in a full and forthright presentation of our respective convictions. Certainly, such dialogue will accentuate how varied our beliefs, traditions, and practices are. But if we are honest in presenting our convictions, we will be able to see more clearly what we hold in common. New avenues will be opened for mutual esteem, cooperation, and indeed friendship.[348]

---

[347] See, "Pope Calls Dialogue a Sacred Duty" Benedict XVI in
https://zenit.org/articles/pope-calls-dialogue-a-sacred-duty/
[348]http://w2.vatican.va/content/francesco/en/speeches/2015/january/documents/pap
a-francesco_20150113_srilanka-filippine-incontro-interreligioso.html

While one might find the urge to defend their religion, interreligious dialogue is not a debate because it's not about defending your faith and your religious affiliation, and you don't have to compromise your faith and your belief system to be tolerant.

As Laurentin Magessa points out, "Tolerance implies that you acknowledge the other as other in his or her comprehension and expression of values."[349] Also one should refrain from attempting to evangelize and criticize. It should be about a community of people being open to learning and sharing their values respectfully. It's about being open to truth in religious traditions other than your own.

Religious dialogue is harder when the major denominations of the Protestant church in Haiti won't even talk to each other. Isn't it surprising that Vodou is the most tolerant and the most peaceful among the three major religions in Haiti? Mésina Paulémon was right to wish,

> *Que toutes les confessions religieuses d'Haïti se mettent ensemble, non pour organiser le sabotage du vodou! Car le vodou doit s'épurer et montrer que ce n'est pas lui mais la magie et la sorcellerie qui véhiculent la malfaisance. Il est anti sorcier et par son tambour, ses rythmes, ses danses, il est capable de soutenir une spiritualité ouvrant sur la liberté.*[350]

(Let all Haiti's religious denominations come together not to organize the sabotage of vodou! For vodou must purify itself and show that it is not vodou, but magic and sorcery that are

---

[349] Laurentin Magesa. African religion in the Dialogue Debate: From Intolerance to Coexistence (Zurich: Lit Verlag GMBH &Co. KG Vien, 2010), 75

[350] For more see Mésina Paulémon, "*Vodou et Evangélisation*", 226

the vehicles of evil. Vodou is anti-sorcery, and through its drumming, rhythms, and dances, it is capable of sustaining a spirituality that opens onto the future to support a spirituality that leads to freedom.)

Ending Religion: A Call for Revolution

The idea of "Ending Religion" and calling for a revolution may appear to be provocative, given the profound influence religion has had throughout Haitian history and on individual lives. In *The Shaking of the Foundations*, Paul Tillich reasons that: "We call Jesus the Christ not because He brought a new religion, but because He is the end of religion, above religion and irreligion, above Christianity and non-Christianity."[351] In essence, Jesus died to put an end to religion.

According to the Protestant worldview, getting rid of Vodou and having faith in God would solve Haiti's problems. I can only imagine a Haiti free from the shackles of religion, so I suggest that getting rid of religion would set Haiti free.

This is a call for the empowerment of individuals to think critically and live authentically, free from imposed religious constraints. This is a call for Haitians to reclaim their spiritual and cultural heritage without external interference or stigma.

Rethinking Evangelization

Although the scholarship on the modern missionary movement is abundant, new theories and practices have produced the same

---

[351] Paul Tillich, *The shaking of the Foundations* (New York: Charles Scribner's Sons, 1948), 102

result in Haiti. If the message received is wrong, then it is likely that what will be passed along to others will also be wrong. As George Bernard Shaw says, "What you fellows don't understand is that you must get a man through his religion and not through yours."[352]

Haitian evangelicals have learned to stay away from the people they are trying to win for Christ because they are *lemond* (of this world). Their favorite method of evangelization is behind the pulpit, and some prowl the streets, as early as 4:00 A.M., with a megaphone hoping the sinner will repent and join in their club. As Myers argues,

> Leadership never works when we only preach at people from afar. Leadership never works when we threaten people to change their ways "or else." True leadership does not consist only of telling people to be godly by following us and our example. It is not wrong to give people an example to follow (as Paul did, 1 Cor 4:16; 11:1), but no one will listen if our only message is that people need to believe like us, dress like us, act like us, and talk like us before they can be accepted by us.[353]

Jesus befriends and hangs out with people. He had no problem conversing with prostitutes, tax collectors, and the low-lifes of the Jewish society of his time. Certainly, your religion must not keep you from reaching out to the people at the *gadyè* (cock fighting arena), talking to a prostitute, participating in social activities in your

---

[352] George Bernard Shaw, cited in Laurenti Magesa, African Religion in the Dialogue Debate: From Intolerance to Coexistence (Berlin: Lit Verlag Dr.W. Hopf, 2010) 27

[353] Myers, Jeremy. Close Your Church for Good: Removing Religion to Reveal Jesus. Redeeming Press. Kindle Edition.

neighborhood, or sharing a meal with a ougan. Jesus would, and he did.

In the same way, we must not be scared to have a theological conversation with the educated elite. Paul didn't (see Acts 17).

When Paul was in Athens, he was disturbed as he noticed the number of altars, idols, and objects of worship dedicated to the Greek gods. As he met with the educated elite for a debate, and having complimented them for their religiosity, Paul told them about a particular altar he saw in town with an inscription, "To the unknown god." Instead of smearing the Athenians as devil worshippers and idolaters, Paul observed their culture and beliefs, and when the opportunity arose, he found a common ground to tell them about the unknown God.

One of the mistakes missionaries make in Haiti is to think that all Vodouists, especially the *ougans* and *manbos* are uneducated and lower-class peasants. Some Vodou priests and priestesses are indeed uneducated, but there are also some highly educated *ougans* and *manbos* with master's and doctoral degrees.

Lumping all Haitians together is an evangelization method that will not work. Using top-down evangelizing techniques by failing to take into account the respondent's worldview is doomed to fail. When we evangelize to a Haitian by saying "the Bible says," it may not mean anything to that person. Or when we say "Jesus loves you and he died for you," we need to remember that Jesus is not a big part of the Vodouist worldview. What if we use Paul's approach? What if we find a common ground?

You can have the best catchphrase such as *"Haiti pour Christ, Christ pour Haiti",* but insofar as salvation is defined as a one-time kneeling and saying the sinner's prayer, you will always have "split-level Christianity" among your converts. Furthermore, salvation is always presented to Haitians as a change of behavior: you stop and quit your old ways (Vodou, smoking, drinking) before you are accepted. But salvation is a process: come then you'll be changed.

Being saved is a way of life. If the church wants to see people converted, it should start seriously focusing on loving people. Going after converts with simply the threat of hell is pure religious coercion.

A compulsion for church growth and new converts should not be the driving force for evangelization. When numbers are the result, churches and missionaries are tempted to inflate numbers by organizing haphazard crusades, campaigns, and revivals. As Alister McGrath argues in his book *Evangelicalism and the Future of Christianity*, "We need to take the trouble to relate the message to its audience. The gospel presentation must be receptor-oriented—we need to be sensitive to the hurts, needs, and concerns of individuals."[354]

In his book *Repenting of Religion*, Greg Boyd notes: "God is not first and foremost interested in acquiring a people who happen to believe all the right things and act in all the right ways. God's first concern, and his only concern, is to have a people who are united with him in love."[355]

Rethinking the Role of Missionaries

---

[354] McGrath, Alister. *Evangelicalism and the Future of Christianity* (Downers Grove: InterVarsity Press, 1995), 103

[355] Boyd Gregory, *Repenting from Religion* (Grand rapids: Baker Books, 2004), 79

I cannot deny that some missionaries have positively influenced and changed the religious and social landscape of Haiti during their time there. For example, the controversial missionary L. Ton Evans who at one point advocated for U.S. troops on Haitian soil, was more a diplomat than a missionary. However, in his lobbying effort, he was molested, beaten, and jailed by the U.S. Marines during the occupation. Although at that time he did not understand the Haitian culture, he was a fervent defender of the Haitians who were being brutalized and murdered by the U.S. army.[356]

S.E. Churchstone Lord was a missionary with the African Methodist Episcopal Church. Like Evans, he was like a whistleblower who reported back to the NAACP the racist treatment of the Haitians during the early years of the occupation.

Mark B. Bird believed that education was the key to the future of Haiti. Harold and Yvah Heneise were pillars of the *Grand Nord.* The Turnbulls were known throughout Haiti for various reasons.

At MEBSH, several missionaries had spent decades of their lives in the southern countryside of Haiti. To cite a few, Florent Toirac labored tirelessly in reaching people in the southern region without great concern for his safety. Curtis Holmes was an African American missionary from Detroit, Michigan, who, in the 1970s, lived in Camp-Perrin to immerse himself in Haitian culture.

I cannot ignore the passion of David Hartt at *Radio Lumière*, Edwin Walker at IBL, and Dudley Nelson at *Hôpital Lumière.* There were also Louis Markwood known mostly for his daily

---

[356] Olsen, Scott H. "*Reverend L. Ton Evans and the United States Occupation of Haiti.*" *Caribbean Studies* 26, no. 1/2 (1993): 23-48. Accessed February 13, 2020. www.jstor.org/stable/25613207.

devotional at *Radio Lumière*, Johannes and Luise Schürer at IBL and *Centre Lumière* respectively, Don Nelson and Bernice Johnson at the *Centre de Santé Lumière*, Herb and Shirley Shoemaker were in various roles at MEBSH, especially at Reciprocal Ministries, Don Adams spent several years in the *Nippes* region, and Lamar and Pat Myers were known for their music and Bible teaching ministry.

A lot has changed in Haiti since the early wave of the Western missionary movement. The old lie, still being promoted by some missionaries and mission agencies that Haitians are dumb, lazy, slow learners, and unteachable has been debunked long ago. Haitians from all social strata have advanced degrees in multiple fields. It's been an open secret for centuries that Haitians are smart people.

So why are sending agencies, such as WT and AC HarvestCall, constantly asking for new missionaries? What is their motive? Are missionaries still needed in Haiti? If so, in what capacity? Why is the status quo still okay? Can we get rid of the word missionary, at least in Haiti?

The Westernization and the zombification of Haitian society is all but complete. Zombie churches are all over the place. That's one of the reasons the new missionaries do not even bother to learn Creole, immerse themselves in Haitian culture, or share the gospel by life and word.

Instead, they focus on leading and managing their humanitarian organizations. The fact that their primary form of fellowship is with other missionaries is clear evidence that there is no life shared with the people they are supposed to serve. If following Jesus is, in part, to be engaged in building relationships with other people, the Western missionary movement in Haiti fails miserably.

Although there are plenty of studies that show the old missionary methods are not effective, the old movement is still carried on in Haiti as if it were new. Although the new missionaries and their sending agencies have read books by popular missiologists and scholars such as Charles Kraft, Robert Priest, Craig Ott, David Bosh, Paul Hiebert, Glenn Schwartz, David Hesselgrave, Robert Lupton, Brian Howell, Robert Reese, and others, yet the paternalistic attitude of the new missionary movement and the "white savior complex" have not changed. New ideas, but old behaviors.

The greatest error of the Western missionary movement in Haiti is their failure to learn from the missteps of the past. For example, the Apostolic Christian HarvestCall agency claimed in their January 2018 bulletin that "direct financial aid of $40,000 per month is needed to support operations at *Hopital Lumière* in southern Haiti. Financial support is also needed to cover the living expenses of the HarvestCall missionary families now living on campus at *Hopital Lumière.*

Is there a plan if the missionaries are recalled? What will happen if the donation stops? Are there any exit strategies? Why are job openings such as Hospital Administrator, Director of Nursing, Information Technology Support, Auto and Diesel Mechanic, Social Media, Finance and Accounting, and Bible teachers advertised on their website, not filled by Haitians? There are plenty of talented young Haitian professionals around. The money spent to support a missionary family for one of these positions would cover the salary of at least four local professionals.

Sadly, some mission agencies are run like their secular counterparts where foreign nationals are always in leadership positions. Their goal, it seems, is to keep their charity recipients in constant need and their U.S. stakeholders feeling good about doing "God's mission".

For some mission agencies, sustainability is having a steady flow of new missionaries and funding so that they can keep the insanity going like a rat on a treadmill. In a December 2020 email sent out to their supporters, HarvestCall put an urgent plea for new missionaries to step up in key missionary roles in Haiti:

> Even though Haitians have stepped up to assume many key roles in the operation – particularly medical roles — HarvestCall staff are still needed for oversight...The sobering reality is that if there are no candidates for these positions before January 31, 2021, we will no longer be able to fulfill our contractual obligations to effectively operate the hospital. At that time, the Hospital Lumiere Governing Board will begin searching for another organization to take over.[357]

Still, HarvestCall trusts God to come through in time of need:

> We believe that God is fully in control and we will trust him. Our prayer is this – "God we know you can send missionaries, we believe you will send missionaries, and God, if you do not send missionaries we will continue to trust you!" We do not

---

[357] For more see the December 2020 HarvestCall's supporter's email "Hospital Lumiere at a critical juncture – can we continue to operate?",

know the Lord's plan, but we want you to be aware and pray with us through the weighty decisions ahead.[358]

While I also trust and believe God can send workers out into the field, I wonder if HarvestCall will listen if God tells them to start training Haitians to fulfill these roles. Will they listen if God tells them that a missionary is not always needed in a leadership position? And will they still trust God if He tells them that the Nursing Director and the Administrator they are looking for are 20 miles away in Les Cayes, not in Indiana or Illinois?

If history teaches us anything, HarvestCall should learn from the painful and ugly breakup of WT and MEBSH. After over fifty years of codependency, WT told MEBSH that they were leaving, and the local leaders felt like a jilted lover, begging for compassion and refusing to take no for an answer.

Meanwhile, the Haitian staff at the hospital feel helpless since they have been conditioned to think they can't do anything without the *blan*'s[359] help. That's why when the *blan* and the financial support stop, the local institution collapses. This is the story of Hospital Lumière for the last thirty years. I know for a fact that the *Hopital Lumière* is one of the most important hospitals in southern Haiti, but you cannot attract well-qualified Haitian doctors and nurses with a meager salary while their American counterparts are compensated to the U.S. industry's standards.

---

[358] Ibid

[359] A blan is usually a white person, but it can also be anybody who is not Haitian regardless of the color of his/her skin.

Although WT gave up full leadership control of MEBSH in 1987, the damage was already done. MEBSH, which still legally owns the hospital, is not involved at all. They signed it away to other *blan* who have the money to run it.

So what would it take for *Hopital Lumière* to fully function and be managed by Haitians? It will require leadership and vision. Sadly, these are exactly the qualities lacking at MEBSH, which never recovered from its dependency syndrome to being an independent indigenous church.

Consequently, after more than eighty-six years, MEBSH is still a foreign institution managed by indigenous leaders.

"How about the partnership side", you ask. As Dan Shoemaker of Reciprocal Ministries International at MEBSH admits, "'Partnership' has become something as a buzzword in mission right now."[360] From my own experience, there is no such thing as a partnership between the local church in Haiti, the missionaries, and their sending agencies. On paper and their websites, maybe. But on the field, it's a different story. There is nothing reciprocal in their reciprocal ministries. It's rather a utilitarian relationship where the poor are being used for mission agencies' self-serving purposes.

Additionally, most field missionaries are social workers who lead NGOs and parachurch groups, therefore they don't see the need to report to the local church. In most cases, the local mission doesn't even know when a missionary comes and leaves. Occasionally one would see them going up and down the roads with their trucks and motorcycles, but nobody knows who they are, and what they do.

---

[360] Cited in Janel K. Bakker, "Sister Churches", 44

In the rare case where a missionary labors side by side and under the leadership of a local church is so insignificant that it's not worth mentioning. It's against the norm. For most agencies, partnership is replaced by sponsorship – that is, finding a direct or indirect way to give and for local people to receive. If the missionary cannot be a true co-laborer, we will still do the same thing over and over and expect a better Haiti.

In his article, *Short-term Missions for Long-term Partnership*, Daniel Richett argues that "The imperatives of partnership are a common identity in worldview and values, a shared vision, a mutually supportive and respectful relationship, a pattern of open two-way communication, a focus on achievements, and willingness to learn and change."[361]

Some U.S.-based parachurch organizations use the local church as a legal entity so that their organizations can function in the country without any government oversight. They do this by putting the logo of the local church on their trucks and SUVs, but it's only for their protection and security. By keeping the same *modus operandi*, the Western missionary movement further the dependency and "dead aid" and promoted at the same time the "*apre Bondye se blan*" erroneous belief.

Missionaries and mission agencies need instead to promote self-reliance among independent and mission-established churches. In her article, *The Cure for Dependency: Teach Your Churches to Give*, Donna R. Downes argues that missionaries and mission agencies must commit to making a difference in the cure of

---

[361] Daniel, Rickett. "Short-term Missions for Long-term Partnership", accessed 2/22/20, http://www.danielrickett.com/wp-content/uploads/2011/04/Short-term-Mission-for-Long-term-Partnership.pdf

dependency. Otherwise, she says, "We are condemning ourselves to a type of ethnocentric and paternalistic ministry that will result in fostering ministries that are forever dependent on Western resources-a situation that some mission leaders, sad to say, are willing to accept and tolerate because it means a continuance of their own positions and power."[362]

Sadly, Haitian churches see the missionary as someone they can depend on to come through when financial support is needed. They like having the *blan* to visit their churches because there will be a big crowd and the offering for that Sunday will be fatter than usual. Unfortunately for the local churches, the new missionaries know how to play the game, as they have been trained not to fall for the perceived needs of the local church. I am always amused when I hear field missionaries tell their short-termers, "Don't give money or anything valuable to the locals, it creates dependency." The irony is that the field missionary, by being there in the first place, creates dependency. When will missionaries stop doing what is wrong? Having good intentions does not make it right. If you're in Haiti as a missionary managing one of the thousands of NGOs or you are a humanitarian aid worker, you should seriously consider whether you are part of the old Western patriarchal and colonial system. I'm not asking you to disengage, but if you can't be a partner with God in loving the Haitians, and if you cannot show them the true beauty of the cross by loving them unconditionally, are you needed? If you love the people of Haiti, you should start packing.

---

[362] "The Cure for Dependency: Teach Your Churches to Give", Donna Downes, accessed 2/26/20 in https://missionexus.org/the-cure-for-dependency-teach-your-churches-to-give/

Getting off Dependency

I argued in a previous chapter, that the dependency of some individual aid recipients, Haitian churches, and local institutions on foreign aid is like a cancer with no cure in sight. As Robert Lupton in *Toxic Charity* puts it bluntly, "For disadvantaged people to flourish into their full God-given potential, they must leave behind dependencies that impede their growth."[363]

For Lupton, "Relationships built on need do not reduce the need. Rather, they require more and more need to continue."[364] Have you ever wondered why a feeding organization has been cooking rice and beans for "hungry" kids in Haiti for more than thirty years, with rice and beans imported from Miami? Or why water is still scarce in parts of Haiti where an organization claims to have installed 805 water wells?

Dependency is not related only to monetary aid, but also to technical expertise as well. A *blan* is always needed for this type of surgery at the hospital, for this construction technique, for digging water wells, or for a Greek course at the Bible school. The problem is not a lack of Haitian expertise, but the thinking that says the *blan* can do it for free. It must change.

Not only is there nothing free in this world, but people need to realize that somebody has to support the *blan* to be in Haiti. While most Haitians get by with less than $200 a month, the average support for a single missionary in Haiti is about $6000 a month, and you can double that for a family of four. Consequently, the *blan* has

---

[363] Lupton, Robert D. Toxic Charity: How Churches and Charities Hurt Those They Help (and How to Reverse It). New York, NY: HarperOne, 2011. p102
[364] Lupton, "Toxic Charity", p61.

every reason to keep the local people in need. His or her livelihood depends on the people's dependence on charity.

Poul Engberg-Pedersen argues, "Aid is a mindset problem, more than a financial constraint."[365] It's not something that cooperation can cure. After all, who earns the right to tell the stories? Have you ever read field stories from the recipient's perspective? Who put words on the lip of the recipient? Who is doing the surveys? Who takes the pictures of a happy kid with a lollipop or a "poor" Haitian woman minding her own business? Who edits and translates the letters from your sponsored child? Who writes the newsletters and updates on what God is doing in Haiti?

Perspective matters, but whose perspective? The powerful, the provider, the mission agency, the missionary, and the field director? As Robert Reese suggests, "Both Western and non-Western Christians need to evaluate how they see each other: as rich versus poor, powerful versus weak, white versus black, superior versus inferior, or as fellow pilgrims in Christ?"[366]

To get off dependency and dead aid, a major paradigm shift needs to occur among the national church, the *blan*, the local people, and the local institutions. Here are a few ideas:

1. ***Learn how to say no:*** First the local institutions and church organizations need to learn how to say no to foreign aid. I know it's going to be hard to cut the umbilical cord of aid. But at your age, if you're only getting milk from your mom,

---

[365] Poul Engberg-Pedersen. "Moving out of Aid Dependency: Money, Mindsets and Politics. Or: We are all aid dependent!", accessed 2/23/20, https://www.un.org/en/ga/second/62/pepedersen.pdf

[366] Reese, "Roots and Remedies of the Dependency Syndrome in World Missions," 148

you're dying. It's time to grow up. Second, fund providers need to stop the toxic handouts. Stop financing poverty. In 2018 Haitians in the diaspora sent $3.2 billion[367] to their friends and family in Haiti. For the first three months of 2021, the monthly average of money transferred was $260 million.[368] What a waste! Most of these aid recipients are able people who sit on their butts as they wait for the next transfer. I used to send money too, but I'm getting smarter. The *blan* also needs to learn how to say no. As long as the money is coming from the *blan* or any other foreign entities, aid recipients will never see the need to be self-sustaining. The blan needs to stop the paternalistic attitude of "our way is the best and only way."

2. ***Sevre blan an*** (wean off the white aid) At some point you will need to progressively tell the *blan* it's time to go for you to swim on your own. Use local resources to build your church. Why wait years for some men to come from Indiana, USA, to make benches for your church? Are there not any Haitian carpenters in your area? Is there not any lumber?

3. ***Treat pastoring a church as a gift not as a job***: Not a lot of pastors in Haiti have big wealthy churches where they can draw a living wage from. This reality puts the pastor in a precarious situation where he makes questionable ethical decisions. Large mission organizations such as MEBSH

---

[367] This indicator is according to both the World Bank and Trading Economics. For more see https://tradingeconomics.com/haiti/remittances

[368] See "*Perte sèche de 4 milliards de gourdes chaque mois pour les bénéficiaires de transfert, révèle Fritz Alphonse Jean*", accessed 3/17/2021, https://lenouvelliste.com/article/227372/perte-seche-de-4-milliards-de-gourdes-chaque-mois-pour-les-beneficiaires-de-transfert-revele-fritz-alphonse-jean

should support their pastors or encourage them to be bi-vocational ministers and self-supporting. If your church can't be self-sustaining, you're doing religion, and you may as well close the church. Get off the demands of religion, and be a community-driven church. Know yourself. Just because you attended a Bible school, that's not enough of a reason to be a pastor. Why do you want to pastor a church anyway in that system? Is it for prestige? Is being ordained worth the headache?

4. ***Take ownership of your choices***: Stop giving your kids away to sham orphanages and *restavèk*. You have choices; stop having babies if you cannot take care of them. Stop saying *se pa fòt mwen* (it's not my fault), and *mwen sou kont Bondye* (I'm in God's hands). Be responsible for your actions by taking ownership of your decisions, good or bad. Certainly, as a community, we should still come around those who are unfortunate through no fault on theirs. But practice smart giving. Another Haitian proverb says, "Se bon kè krapo ki fè l san tet," meaning: Don't let people take advantage of your kindness.

5. ***Be a Tentmaker***: As the Haitian band Skah Shah sings in their magnificent piece, *Pour Demain*: *"Aprann nenpòt sal ye, la bon pou ou demen."* Go to school, and learn a trade. Find a job, or be your own boss. "Pito w travay pase w mande," (better to work than to beg) says the Haitian proverb. Find something you're good at, and do it better than anyone else. Be the best mechanic, the best accountant, the best baker, the best electrician, the best engineer, the best

nurse, the best plumber, and so on. You will always have food on your table.

6. ***Stop useless projects***: Every theory about poverty and development has been tested and tried in Haiti. The country is an international experiment lab. Every NGO says their approach is different and it's about the community. Yet, money keeps pouring in without sustainable results. Stop bringing from overseas resources that are available locally. Let the projects be community-initiated and funded. If it's not coming from the community, it's not worth it. Do income-generating projects. Put values in local assets.

7. ***Invest in people***: Stop building big churches you cannot afford. Set aside your tithes and offerings to support the less fortunate with their education. Start small income-generating projects using the church resources. Encourage and support your community by buying locally. Invest in the poor by helping them to be self-reliable. In some cases, do group lending instead of straight giveaways.

I know every set of circumstances is different. Other experienced missiologists and economists have many other suggestions. I'm not advocating that we stop giving aid to someone in need, what I'm saying is that there is a difference between being dependent and being poor. We can certainly agree that for families, local institutions, and churches to be self-sustainable, foreign aid needs to stop.

A Theology of Liberation: Let My People Go

While this book takes, on the one hand, a critical approach to religion in Haiti, on the other hand, it's a call to action. If Haiti needs a theology of liberation, it is from religion. Freedom from religion is about ensuring that individuals can live their lives without undue influence or coercion from religious leaders, religious zealots, and parachurch organizations.

A theology of liberation is about promoting a pluralistic society where diverse viewpoints are protected and where others' rights to their own beliefs and practices are respected. If you desire to see "Haiti for Christ and Christ for Haiti", then you need to free yourself by letting others go from the yoke of religion. Being free from the cages of religious systems will be the death of religion in Haiti.

Conclusion

By now you probably concluded that I've lost it. No, I'm good. I know I opened a can of worms. While some of you will see this book as an attack on your faith, others will take it as a wake-up call. Still, if I come across as negative, rude, and arrogant, it's because I'm trying to set you on fire for a revolution.

My critics from the conservative denominations in Haiti, the diaspora, and some leaders of religious institutions will probably say that living in the U.S. has turned me into a liberal hack. Again, no. I'm only more open to questioning my beliefs and hearing new perspectives. Some leaders of MEBSH told me, "*Si se pat MEBSH, mwen pa t ap kote m ye a, se paske papa m te pastè nan MEBSH ki fè m sa m ye a.*" (If it was not for MEBSH, I would not be where I'm today, and I would not be who I am if my dad was not a pastor at MEBSH).

This is a stupid theory that isn't even worth debunking. MEBSH did not pay for my education. My parents did, and they were smart because they put a high value on education. Moreover, I have friends who are not part of MEBSH or even Protestants, and they are very successful in life. While I'm grateful for God's grace, that is not a reason to turn a blind eye to religious oppression. While this book is not a referendum on MEBSH, I have to keep them honest.

I know other people are more qualified than I am, to write on this subject. However, I write as a Haitian who has witnessed and experienced some of the issues raised in the book. In addition, the majority of my research is based on first-person accounts, and I have spent several years in Haiti and abroad interviewing people with a variety of views and backgrounds.

Furthermore, I was born and raised in a conservative Baptist religious environment, and I have worked for NGOs and with missionaries in Haiti for several years. My dad's churches have had sister churches, and the local mission organization (MEBSH) he was a part of is still dealing with the dependency syndrome.

As an American, I've had the privilege of being educated in U.S. universities and seminaries. In a sense, the Western perspective has also shaped my thoughts and actions. Not to mention that I've been on STM trips, and I've perpetuated dependency on multiple occasions. I'm as guilty as anyone else.

My friend, Kevin Callaghan, always advises one to be mindful of the two ditches in every argument. "*Tout kòd gen de bout*" [Every rope has two ends] claims a Haitian proverb. But we can certainly agree that religion in the Haitian experience has done more harm than good. Most surveys report that Haiti is a Christian country. In fact, Haiti has probably dethroned Jamaica for having more churches per square mile than any other country in the Caribbean. So why is Haiti labeled as the poorest country in the Western Hemisphere?

Religion?

Since Haiti is 95% Christian, is Christianity one of the reasons Haiti is known as a pariah state, a bird's nest of corruption, a dump, and an international experimental lab? As numerous studies[369]

---

[369] For more, see Tom J. Rees' study published in the Journal of Religion and Society, Vol 11 (2009). Rees analyses data from over 50 countries to find the link between poverty gap and religious belief. See also a 2010 Gallup survey of over 100

show, societies with the worst social inequalities, health disparities, and corruption, are more religious.

In other words, if you want to keep Haiti poor, bring in more religion. As Tom Reese argues, "Religion is a complicated, multifaceted beast."[370]

The last twenty years have been tough on the Haitian people and the country. The violent acts that are being perpetrated daily by gangs and those in power as well as the level of violence seen in the constant uprisings are the norm nowadays. They are done by people who consider themselves Christians and religious. It was not too long ago that Haitians were known to be a caring, loving, and generous people. External influences and religious oppression have done a great job of eroding that and the Haitian traditional family life and values. Gone are the gentleness, the resiliency, and the optimism that Haitians were known for. What happened to our hospitality? Why are our *lakou* destroyed? What happened to our communal identity?

While it's true that Haitians are very religious, it is safe to say that both Christianity and Vodou have failed Haiti. After several years of defending his religion and Baptist faith, Jules Casséus finally admits that Christianity is a complete disaster in Haiti.[371] Would you agree that more religion is not going to stop Haiti's moral decay? As

countries on the correlation of religion and poverty.
https://news.gallup.com/poll/142727/religiosity-highest-world-poorest-nations.aspx
[370] Tomas James Rees, "*Why some countries are more religious than others*"in Epiphenom, accessed 12/12/2020,
https://www.patheos.com/blogs/epiphenom/2009/07/why-some-countries-are-more-religious.html
[371] Jules Casséus, Haïti What Kind of Church…What kind of Freedom? Ivah Heneise, Trans (Limbé Séminaire Théologique Baptiste d'Haïti: 1994), 71

it was during the colonial period, Christianity failed and is still failing to bring about the freedom of the cross and to advance the kingdom of God.

In effect, Christianity has remained a stranger in the Haitian religious experience. Hence, religion has never been and never will be the answer to Haiti's woes. I believe we can have a Haiti where life can be lived in its fullness. For this hope to come to pass, we need to untangle ourselves from the web of lies we have internalized, and we need to check the religious stories we've told ourselves and change the narratives. We need to go back to the ancient boundary stone that our ancestors had set up. We do that the Jesus' way by loving others sacrificially and by connecting in an inclusive community. Isn't it time for a religious revolution?

You may also assume that I have a beef with organized religion and the missionary movement. You're partially right. While I'm against any religious system that keeps people in bondage, while I am against the paternalistic attitude of some missionaries, and while I'm against religious organizations that hold Haitians captive with social programs, I'm all in favor of a church made up of all followers of Jesus who are known for their outlandish love. This Church is not a mission compound, building, institution, or ideology, but it's all of us, followers of Jesus.

Following Jesus is a way of life. He left a blueprint for us to follow (1 Pet 2:21). During his ministry Jesus acted out the way of the kingdom as He hung out with the outcasts, fringe dwellers, and the lowlifes of his time. He talked to prostitutes, accepted worship from people with questionable character, and partied with tax collectors and other people who were considered scumbags.

In doing so, Jesus was tearing down walls by revolting against the classism, greed, sexism, and self-centeredness of his time. He ultimately showed us the way to the cross by going to the cross. Jesus was about restoring broken relationships and liberating those who were captives. As followers of Christ, we are supposed to imitate him. For this reason, how we live our lives matters. Jeremy Myers rightly points out, "The gospel is not just concerned with what happens after we die; it is even more concerned with what happens while we live."[372]

Thus, my invitation is for you to drop your religion and view God differently. He is pure genuine love. It's a scandalous love all the way to the cross. While we may change, while we may have our ups and downs, and while we may be prone to mistakes, our behavior does not determine how God relates to us. If you think God loves certain people more than others, you are ripe for a rude awakening. You are going to be disappointed to know that he loves the local *ougan* as much as He loves your beloved pastor. His grace and mercy are for all. We are all sinners in need of his grace.

While we should all strive to be like Him, the reality is that we are at different stages in our walk. As Frank Viola rightly argues in his book *Revise Us Again*, we are all a "rough draft" getting constantly edited by the Holy Spirit. We need to trust that God is active in everyone's life. Yes, including the *manbos* and the *ougans*. Can God be already at work in all areas of the Haitian people's lives, such as the *peristil*, the institutional church, the government, the gangs, the school system, the market, the *rara*, and the *gadyè*? Can the Vodouist feel the gentle nudge of the Holy Spirit? Can the

---

[372] Jeremy Myers, *Close Your Church for Good: Removing Religion to Reveal Jesus* (Redeeming Press: Kindle Edition) Location 4784.

Vodouist follow Christ without being a Christian? You better believe it.

Therefore, let the Spirit work in everyone's heart as He sees fit.

While some of you are more open to questioning the religious system you're a part of, more needs to be done. So, let me ask you this again: Are you worn out from religion? Does your religion keep you from loving and serving others? Are religious rituals taking a toll on your resources? Are you a slave to religious activities? Are you living in fear of making the *lwa* angry? Do you feel coerced to tithe, do *manje lwa*, or give offerings? Are you manipulating the spirits to enrich yourself and gain social standing? Are you tired of religious traditions, rituals, and taboos? Are you preaching Christianity instead of Christ? Do you believe that God takes notes of every sin for future punishment? Does your religious leader act like a middleman between you and *Bondye*? Does your religious affiliation make you feel superior to others?

To be honest, most of you would answer yes to all of these questions, and I'm also sure you're saying that I am making sense. Would you like to liberate yourselves from the grip of religion? If you answer yes to one or more of the above questions, don't just agree with me. I need you and others like you to start an anti-religious campaign, a revolution. What Haiti needs right now is a bunch of religious *"rejete"*. Religious powers used to coerce previous generations to say *"Satan je renonce"*, but our new slogan should be *"Religion je renonce"*. It's time for you to be done with religion and be part of the Church *(ekklesia)*. Are you ready to be a revolutionary?

I appeal to all Haitian Vodouists, Catholics, and Protestants to dump your religion, even if it means closing your place of worship. Be free from religious performances to meaningful fellowship as the E*kklesia*. As Jeremy Myers puts it, "Since it is for freedom that Christ has set us free, let us live fully free lives; lives free of judgment, anger, malice, despair, hate and all such things that destroy this world and destroy our lives."[373]

If you want to be a religious person, pick up your cross[374] and follow Jesus. Be in the religion of loving and serving others even if it leads to death. The death of Jesus reveals that we are free from our slavery to death so that we can live a life of obedience to the will of God which is the exact opposite of any religious system.

So, if you're a Haitian Christian (Catholic or Protestant), you probably know that you have the indwelling power of God in you. Therefore, walk and live in the freedom of the Holy Spirit (Rom. 7:6; Gal.5:13). Can you still be a Christian and a follower of Christ? Sure, but why do you still want to be a Christian? I would suggest that you stop following a system for a life of freedom, a covenant relationship in Christ. It's one thing to be a Christian, but it's something entirely different to be a follower of Christ.

You should seriously reconsider why you believe what you believe, why you blindly follow the rituals and traditions of your denomination, and what it means to be a follower of Christ. You

---

[373] Myers, "Close Your Church for Good", Kindle Location 9693.

[374] "Pick up your cross" is usually associated with a theology of resignation among Haitian believers. They mistakenly believe that the difficulties of life are their cross, as they complain "se kwa pa m".

should only be known for God's outrageous love flowing through and out of you (John 13:35).

If you're a Vodouist, you already know that *Bondye, Granmèt la,* who is above all *lwa*, cares about you, and "The God who made the world and everything in it, this Master of sky and land, doesn't live in custom-made *peristil* or need the human race to run errands for him, as if He couldn't take care of himself (Acts 17: 24-25)." You should know that *Bondye* is not too distant to care about you. He is passionately in love with you. No *vèvè* is needed to reach Him.

He is right here. The same God that Boukman prayed to in 1791 is the same God who sent his son Jesus to put an end to all sacrifices. *Les Mystères* have been revealed in the Son. There is a new priest in town, and He has a new way of doing things. Jesus is the Supreme and the last "*Ati*"[375], and "as the priest, Christ made a single sacrifice for sins, and that was it!... It was a perfect sacrifice by a perfect person to perfect some very imperfect people (Heb. 10:12-14)."

Because the *manje lwa* are not effective in accomplishing their purpose, *Bondye* has done away with them. All *sèvis* and offerings have been taken care of on the cross. How? "By that single offering, he did everything that needed to be done for everyone who takes part in the purifying process...Once sins are taken care of for good, there's no longer any need to offer sacrifices for them" (Heb 10:15). You can stop drawing *vèvè* and making other rituals to call on the Spirit or spirits. You have direct access to *Bondye Gran Mèt la* by the Holy Spirit. *Nan Ginen* or the Kingdom of God is here and now.

---

[375] Highest priest in Haitian Vodou.

As Father Roland Pierre so aptly put it in his Editorial for *Sèl*: "The kingdom of God is not to be found in the sky. It's in our midst."[376]

However, if you still want to be a *chwal* (horse) of the spirits, and if you're longing to be mounted by a *lwa*, the ultimate horseman is the Holy Spirit. Once He possesses you, you're mounted for life. "What should I do?" you ask.

Following Christ is not a change of religion as some Christians have suggested (*ou rantre nan pwotestan*); it's the act of dying to self by surrendering your life to Jesus and to being his follower. No special ceremony and no special prayers are needed to be mounted by the Spirit of God and to be under the lordship of Christ. When Jesus tells you "follow me", just acknowledge that by saying "Here I'm Lord, I want to be your follower".

Then as a follower of Christ, let the Spirit scrap all the things from your lifestyle that are not consistent with your new life in Christ, and live in the newness and the freedom of the Spirit (Rom 7:6). It will take time, but don't worry. Following Christ is a continuous and long process (2 Cor 4:16, 2 Cor 3:18, Rom 12:2). It's not based on what you do, but it's God making you one spirit with Him (1 Cor 6:17). So what are you waiting for?

> Now that we know what we have—Jesus, this great High Priest with ready access to God—let's not let it slip through our fingers. We don't have a priest who is out of touch with our reality. He's been through weakness and testing, experienced it all—all but the sin. So let's walk right up to him and get what

---

[376] "Editorial", Roland Pierre, Sèl No2. Moua-D Jin 1972, access 3/17/2024 Digital Library of the Caribbean, https://dloc.com/AA00089969/00002/images/0

he is so ready to give. Take the mercy, accept the help (Hebrews 4: 14-16).

After all that has been said, if you still want to cling to your religion, it's your prerogative. But know that your religion is useless if you don't love. In the end, love wins because everything will be under the lordship of Christ. Therefore, love God not by becoming more religious, but by becoming like Him every day. Love others not by trying to convert them to your religion, but by treating them with kindness, forgiveness, honor, compassion, dignity, and respect. Love yourself by renewing your mind daily and treating yourself with care, dignity, and respect in your thoughts and actions. Love creation by honoring, enjoying, and stewarding the earth. Live a cross-centered life. Love sacrificially.

À bas religion, vive la révolution!

Appendix A

The three main religions in Haiti have more in common than differences.

Vodou	Catholicism	Protestantism
Rites & Ceremonies		
Vodou ceremony	Mass	Church service
Water Baptism/ Initiation	Water Baptism/Initiation	Water baptism/ Initiation
Infant Baptism Rite of passage	Infant Baptism / Confirmation (Initiation)	Infant Dedication Infant baptism
Manje lwa/ Eucharist	Eucharist	Communion/Lord's Supper
Initiation	Confirmation	Indoctrination/Anointing
Special Ceremonies		
Thanksgiving services	Thanksgiving services	Thanksgiving services
Dedication of Peristil/Altar	Dedication of a Church/Altar	Dedication of a Church

	Penance	Fasting
Rite of Anointing	Rite of Anointing	Rite of Anointing
Exorcism	Exorcism	Exorcism
Order of Service		
Invocation/Call of the Spirit or Spirits	Invocation/Call of the Spirit	Invocation/Call of the Spirit
Singing/Dancing	Worship/Singing	Worship Singing/ Dancing
	Scripture reading	Scripture reading
Prayer	Prayer	Prayer
	Sermon	Sermon
Spirit possession/Tongue/Trance	Pentecostal catholicism	Spirit possession/Tongue/Trance

Selected Bibliography

Abbott Elizabeth, *Haiti: The Duvaliers and their Legacy* (New York: Touchstone, 1988)

Anderson Mildred, *Beyond All This: Thirty years with the mountain people of Haiti* (Light Messages, 2010)

Aubin Eugène, *En Haïti; planteurs d'autrefois, nègres d'aujourd'hui* (Paris: A. Colin, 1910), Kindle Edition.

Bacon Jean, *Le Christ Noir en Terre Vaudou* (Quebec: Publications MNH, Inc.), 1999.

Bakker Janel K., *Sister Churches: American Congregations and Their Partners Abroad* (New York: Oxford University Press), 2014.

Beaubrun Mimerose, P. (2010) *Nan Dòmi: An Initiate's Journey into Haitian Vodou*, Trans. by D. J. Walker (San Francisco: City Lights Books, 2013)

Bediako Kwame, *Jesus and the Gospel in Africa.* (Maryknoll: Orbis Books, 2004.)

Bellegarde Dantès, *Haïti et ses Problèmes* (Montréal: Éditions B. Valiquette [1941?]).

Bisnauth Dale, *History of Religions in the Caribbean* (Trenton: Africa World Press, 1996).

Borthwick Paul, *Western Christians in Global Mission: What's the Role of the North American Church* (Downers Grove: InterVarsity Press, 2012).

Boyd Gregory A. *The Myth of a Christian Nation* (Grand Rapids: Zondervan, 2005).

_____*Repenting from Religion* (Grand Rapids: Baker Books, 2004).

Brown Karen McCarthy (*Mama Lola: A Vodou Priestess in Brooklyn* (Berkeley: University of California Press, 1991).

Casséus Jules, *Nous les Baptistes* (Port-au-Prince: La Presse Évangélique, 1985)

Cavey Bruxy, *The End of Religion* (Colorado Springs: NavPress, 2007).

Cinéas J. B., *L'Héritage Sacré.* (Port-au-Prince: Editions Henri Deschamps, 1945).

Conley Joseph L. *Drumbeats that Changed the World: A History of the Regions Beyond Missionary Union and the West Indies Mission, 1873–1999* (Pasadena: William Carey Library, 2000).

Corey Benjamin, L. *Unafraid: Moving Beyond Fear-based Faith* (New York: HarperCollins Publishers, 2017).

Cooke Graham. God Revealed: Your Image of Him Changes Everything (Grand Rapids: Chosen, 2003,2005)

Courlander Harold, *The Piece of Fire* (New York: Harcourt, Brace & World, Inc., 1964).

Crow Linda, *Victory Over Voodoo* (Kansas City: Nazarene Publishing House, 1975).

_____*Haiti, I Love You* (Kansas City: Nazarene Publishing House, 1970).

C.L.R. James. *The Black Jacobins* (New York: Random House, Inc, 1963).

Deren Maya, *Divine Horsemen: The Living Gods of Haiti* (Kingston: McPherson & Company, 2004)

Desmangles G. Leslie. *The Faces of the Gods* (Chapel Hill: The University of North Carolina Press, 1992).

Ellis A. B. *The Ewe-speaking Peoples of the Slave Coast of West Africa: Their Religion, Manners, Customs, Laws, Languages, &c.* (Chicago: Benin Press, 1965).

Fils-Aimé Jean, *Et si les Loas N'Etaient pas des Diables? Une Enquête à la Lumière des Religions Comparées* (Québec: Les Éditions Dabar, 2008).

George Sherron Kay, *Called as Partners in Christ's Service: The Practice of God's Mission* (Louisville: Geneva Press, 2004)

Greene Anne, *The Catholic Church in Haiti: Political and Social Change* (East Lansing: Michigan State University Press, 1993)

Hardin Michael. *The Jesus Driven Life: Reconnecting Humanity with Jesus.* Lancaster: JDL Press, 2010,

Hiebert Paul G., *Anthropological Insights for Missionaries* (Grand Rapids: Baker Book House, 1985)

Hiebert Paul G., Shaw, R. Daniel, and Tite Tie'nou, *Understanding Folk Religions: A Christian Response to Popular Beliefs and Practices* (Grand Rapids: Baker Books, 1999)

Heneise Yvah. *By The Light of My Kerosene Lamp* (Valley Forge: International Ministries, 1982)

Hesselgrave David J., *Communicating Christ Cross-Culturally, 2ⁿᵈ ed.* (Grand Rapids: Zondervan Publishing House, 1991).

Hood Robert. *Must God Remain Greek?: Afro Cultures and God-Talk* (Minneapolis: Fortress Press, 1990)

Howell Brian M., *Short-Term Mission: An Ethnography of Christian Travel Narrative and Experience* (Downers Grove: IPV Academic, 2012)

Hurbon Laënnec, *Le Phénomène Religieux dans la Caraïbe* (Paris: Karthala, 2000)

_____ *Dieu dans le Vaudou Haïtien* (Port-au-Prince: Editions Henri Deschamps, 1987).

_____*Voodoo: search for the Spirit* (New York: Harry N. Abrams, Inc., 1999)

_____ *Le barbare imaginaire* (Paris: Les Éditions du Cerf, 1988)

Hurston N. Zora, *Tell my Horse* (New York: Harper Perennial, 1990)

Casas Bartolomé de las, *A Brief Account of the Destruction of the Indies Or, a faithful NARRATIVE OF THE Horrid and Unexampled Massacres, Butcheries, and all manner of Cruelties, ... the time of its first Discovery by them.* Kindle Edition.

Janvier Louis-Joseph, *La République d'Haïti et ses Visiteurs (1840-1882): Un Peuple Noir Devant les Peuples Blancs* (Paris: Marpon et Flammarion, Libraires et Editeurs, 1883.

James C. L.R., *The Black Jacobins* (New York: Vintage Books, 1963).

Jeune Joel R., *I Sneezed in My Casket!: For God Cannot Lie* (Self-published, Xlibris, 2012)

Joint Gasner, *Libération du vaudou dans la dynamique d'inculturation en Haïti* (Roma: Pontificia Università Gregoriana, 1999).

Johnson Bernice, *She Did What She Could: The missionary journal of Bernice Johnson* (Graham: Andrews Memorial Baptist Church, 2002)

Johnson David and Jeff VanVonderen, *The Subtle Power of Spiritual Abuse* (Minneapolis: Bethany House Publishers, 1991)

Johnson Jean, *We Are Not the Hero: a Missionary's Guide to Sharing Christ, Not a Culture of Dependency* (Sisters: Deep River Books, 2012)

Kane J. Herbert, *The Christian World Mission: Today and Tomorrow* (Grand Rapids: Baker Book House, 1981)

Kawas François, *Vaudou et Catholicisme en Haïti à l'aube du XXIe Siècle* (Port-Au-Prince: Imprimerie Deschamps, 2011).

_____ *L'Etat et L'Eglise Catholique en Haïti au XIXe et XXe Siècles* (1860-1980) (Paris: L'Harmattan, 2009).

Kiyungu D. Mafuta, *Double Appartenance des Chrétiens Africains? Inculturation et pluralité religieuse* (Paris: L'Harmattan, 2010).

Laguerre Michel S., *Voodoo Heritage* (Beverly Hills: Sage Publications, Inc, 1980)

Lavallé Bernard, *Au Nom des Indiens* (Paris: Editions Payot & Rivages, 2014)

Lingenfelter Sherwood G. and Mayers Marvin K., *Ministering Cross-Culturally: An incarnational Model for Personal Relationships* (Grand Rapids: Baker Book House, 1986)

Lupton Robert D. *Toxic Charity: How Churches and Charities Hurt Those They Help (and How to Reverse It)* (New York: HarperOne, 2011)

Magesa Laurentin, *African religion in the Dialogue Debate: From Intolerance to Coexistence* (Zurich: Lit Verlag GMBH & Co. KG Vien, 2010)

Mahn-Lot Marianne. *Christophe Colomb* (Paris: Editions du Seuil, 1960)

Manigat Max, *Mots Créoles du Nord d'Haïti* (Coconut Creek: Educa Vision Inc, 2007)

McGee B. Gary, Miracles, Mission, and American Pentecostalism (New York: Orbis Books, 2010)

McGrath Alister, *Evangelicalism and the Future of Christianity* (Downers Grove: InterVarsity Press, 1995)

Métraux Alfred. *Voodoo in Haiti* (New York: Schocken Books, 1972)

Montilus Guerin, *Dompim: The Spirituality of African People* (Nashville: Winston-Derek Publishers, Inc., 1989)

Mulrain Georges MacDonald. *Theology in Folk Culture: The Theological Significance of Haitian Folk Religion*. Frankfurt amMain: Verlag Peter Lang, 1984)

Murrell Nathaniel S. *Afro-Caribbean Religions: An Introduction to Their Historical, Cultural, and Sacred Traditions* (Philadelphia: Temple University Press, 2010)

Myers Bryant L., *Walking With The Poor: Principles and Practices of Transformational Development* (Revised and Expanded Edition), (Orbis Books. Kindle Edition)

Myers Jeremy, *Close Your Church for Good: Removing Religion to Reveal Jesus*. Redeeming Press. Kindle Edition.

_____, *Dying to Religion and Empire: Giving up Our Religious Rites and Legal Rights (Close Your Church for Good Book 3)* Redeeming Press. Kindle Edition.

Napoléon Lusson. *La Mission Evangélique Baptiste du Sud d'Haiti (MEBSH): Un Octogénaire dans le Bicentenaire du Protestantisme en Haïti* (Port-au-Prince: Imprimerie Media-Texte, 2016)

Neil Stephen A. *History of Christian Mission (Rev. for the 2nd ed. The Pelican History of the Church)* (New York: Penguin Books, 1986).

Nelson G. Dudley, *As the Cock Crows: Reflections of a Medical Missionary to Haiti* (Franklin: Providence House Publishers, 1997)

Nida Eugene A. *Message and Mission* (South Pasadena: William Carey Library, 1960)

Olivier Fritz, *The Relevance of Christian Education for Lay Pastors in Haiti: A New Vision* (North Charleston: Booksurge, 2007).

Ott Craig, Strauss Stephen J., and Tennent Timothy C., *Encountering Theology of Mission: Biblical Foundations, Historical Developments, and Contemporary Issues* (Grand Rapids: Baker Academic, 2010

Paquin Lyonel, *The Haitians: Class and Color Politics* (Brooklyn: Multi-Type, 1983)

Petit-Monsieur Lamartine, *Vers un Nouvel Écho d'Haiti* (Xlibris Corporation, 2011)

Pressoir Catts, *Le Protestantisme Haïtien Vol.1* (Port-au-Prince: Imprimerie de la Société Biblique et des Livres Religieux d'Haïti, 1945)

Price-Mars Jean, *Ainsi Parla l'Oncle: Essais d'ethnographie* (New York: Parapsychology Foundation Inc., 1928. Nouvelle édition, 1954)

Ramsey Kate, *The Spirits and the Law: Vodou and Power in Haiti.* University of Chicago Press. Kindle Edition

Reese Robert, *Roots and Remedies of the Dependency Syndrome in World Missions* (Littleton: William Carey Library, 2010)

Rigaud Milo, *Secrets of Voodoo* (San Francisco: City Lights Books, 1985).

Riou Roger, *The Island of My Life: from petty crime to priestly mission* (New York, Delacorte Press: 1975)

Robert Paul. *Catholicisme Et Vou*dou. Sondeos; No. 82. (Cuernavaca: Centro Intercultural De Documentación, 1971).

Romain Charles-Poisset, *Le Protestantisme dans la Société Haïtienne* (Port-au-Prince:

Imprimerie Henri Deschamps, 1986)

Saint-Amand Edris, *Bon Dieu Rit* (Paris: Domat, 1952.)

Schwartz Glenn, *When Charity Destroys Dignity: Overcoming Unhealthy Dependency in the Christian Movement* (Bloomington: Authorhouse, 2007)

Smarth William, *Histoire de l'Église catholique d'Haïti 1492-2003: Des Points de Repères (Vol II)* (Port-au-Prince: Les Éditions CIFOR, 2015).

Sir Spencer St. John's, *Hayti or the Black Republic* (New York: Schribner and Welford, 1889).

Scheu Patricia, *Serving the Spirits*

Smith Craig, *Whitemans's Gospel* (Winnipeg: Indian Life Books, 1997)

Spell Kathleen, *Haiti Dairy: Compiled from the Letters of Paul Orjala* (Kansas City: Bacon Hill Press, 1953)

Stoddard Theodore L., ed. *Religion and Politics in Haiti*, ICR Studies 1 (Washington, D. C.: Institute for Cross-Cultural Research, 1966).

Tillich Paul, *The Shaking of the Foundations* (New York: Charles Scribner's Sons, 1948)

Thoby-Marcelin Phillippe and Marcelin Pierre, The Pencil of God, trans. Leonard Thomas (Cambridge: The Riverside Press, 1951)

Toirac Florent D., *A Pioneer Missionary in the Twentieth Century* (Winona Lake: Florent D. Toirac, 1986).

Tucker Ruth A., *From Jerusalem to Irian Jaya* (Grand Rapids: Zondervan, 2004)

Verger Jean-Claude de, *Vodou Et Catholicisme En Haïti, Ou, Étude De Sociologie Culturelle Et Religieuse.* (Saint-Léonard, Québec: Éditions Métuca, 1999).

Verschueren J. *La République d'Haiti. Tome 1: Panorama d'Haïti. Le pays et la mission (*Editions Scaldis / P. Lethielleux, Éditeur, Wetteren (Belgique) - Paris: 1948)

Viola Frank, *Insurgence: Reclaiming the Gospel of the Kingdom* (Grand Rapids: BakerBooks, 2018)

Walker S. Edwin III, *Astonishing Grace* (Bloomington: WestBow Press, 2015).

Wilentz Amy, *The Rainy Season: Haiti Since Duvalier* (New York: Simon and Schuster, 1989)

www.ingramcontent.com/pod-product-compliance
Lightning Source LLC
Chambersburg PA
CBHW030911120626
46554CB00001B/99